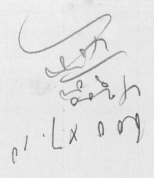

Martin Droeshout sculpsit London.

To the Reader.

This *Figure*, that thou here seest put,
    It was for gentle *Shakespeare* cut;
Wherein the *Graver* had a strife
    With *Nature*, to out-doe the *Life* :
O, could he but have drawn his *Wit*
    As well in *Brasse*, as he has hit
His *Face* ; the *Print* would then surpasse
    All, that was ever writ in *Brasse.*
But since he cannot, *Reader,* look
    Not on his *Picture,* but his *Book.*

                B. J.

SHAKESPEARE AND THE RIVAL POET

*Displaying Shakespeare as a Satirist and Proving
the Identity of the Patron and the
Rival of the Sonnets*

BY
ARTHUR ACHESON

*With a Reprint of Sundry Poetical Pieces by
George Chapman
Bearing on the Subject*

JOHN LANE: THE BODLEY HEAD
LONDON AND NEW YORK
M CM III

PREFACE.

The research of text-students of the works of Shakespeare, undertaken with the object of unveiling the mystery which envelops the poet's life and personality, has added little or nothing of actual proof to the bare outlines which hearsay, tradition, and the spare records of his time have given us. It has, however, resulted in evolving several plausible conjectures, which, if followed and carried to the point of proof, would lend some form and semblance of his personality to these outlines, and materially assist in visualizing for us the actual man. In this class of conjectural knowledge I would place the following questions:

The question of the personal theory of the Sonnets with its attendant questions of order and chronology, and the identity of the three or four figures, the "Patron," "The Rival Poet," "The Dark Lady," and "The Mr. W. H." of the Dedication.

I would also mention in this class the question of the chronology of the plays, for though we have fairly accurate data regarding a few of them, and fairly plausible inferences for nearly the whole of them, we cannot give an actual date for the first production of any one of them.

Lastly in this class, and attendant upon the Sonnet theories, I would mention the question of the intention of the poem called "Willobie His Avisa," regarding Shakespeare and his connections. If any one or two of these things were actually proved, a new keynote to research would be struck, but at present these are all still matters of opinion and dispute. The probability that they would always remain so, has tempted some pseudo-Shakesperians into wild and extravagant inventions, and some honest critics into strange fantasies regarding them. The lengths to which these types of critics have been carried have so reacted upon many others, of a more careful and scientific mind, that they, fearful of being accused of extravagance, have withdrawn behind the barriers of settled fact, and fearfully venture fearful opinions of all that lies beyond their defenses; or else, with the reactionary and stultifying tendency of aging conservatism, sink back upon the conclusions of the older master critics, looking askance, if deigning to look at all, at whatever differs from them. The study of which this book is the result was undertaken altogether for my own pleasure, and in an honest endeavor to get, if possible, some new light upon these debated questions. I had, primarily, no idea or intention of writing upon the subject, but was drawn thereto by a strong conviction of the truth and critical value, as well as a plain cognizance of the originality of most of the theory and proof herein set forth. I have endeavored to tell what I have found as clearly and concisely as possible, and

believe I have in some instances converted conjecture into proof.

For the convenience of the reader, I have appended a reprint of certain poems of George Chapman's connected with my argument.

It would be difficult for me to tell to whom or
to what sources I am indebted for help in this
search, as my reading has been desultory and scat-
tered. Professor Minto's conjecture regarding
Chapman certainly cannot pass unmentioned; it is
undoubtedly the key to my findings. I desire also
to acknowledge a very courteous response from
the able editor of the excellent Temple Edition, Mr.
Israel Gollancz, to an inquiry I made of him regarding a dark point in my work.

ARTHUR ACHESON.

CHICAGO, *April 7, 1902.*

al Chambran say
John Florio was
Holofernes.

CONTENTS.

" And though thou had'st small Latin, and less Greek,
From thence to honour thee I would not seek
For names ; but call forth thundering Æschylus,
Euripides, and Sophocles to us,
Pacuvius, Accius, him of Cordova, dead,
To life again, to hear thy buskin tread
And shake a stage : or, when thy socks were on,
Leave thee alone, for the comparison
Of all that insolent Greece, or haughty Rome,
Sent forth, *or since did from their ashes come.*"

—BEN JONSON. 1623.

SHAKESPEARE AND THE RIVAL POET.

CHAPTER I.

INTRODUCTORY.

DURING the past hundred years many attempts
have been made at writing a life of Shakespeare.
Patient research has brought to light much interesting material and many important facts which
have greatly enlarged the limited knowledge of the
poet's doings which was extant when Steevens
wrote: " All that is known with any degree of cer-
tainty regarding Shakespeare, is—that he was born
at Stratford-upon-Avon,—married, and had children there,—went to London, where he commenced
actor, and wrote poems and plays,—returned to
Stratford, made his will, died, and was buried."
The facts which have been added have, however,
merely increased the evidence of these plain outlines, without casting much new light upon that
which would best enable us to understand his works
and the spirit in which he wrote, that is—his actual
personality.

We do not grasp the full value of any literary
work till we are enabled, by the knowledge which
we have of the writer's personality, to put ourselves

to some extent in his place. It is to this desire to understand thoroughly and enter into the spirit of a writer's work, and not to mere morbid curiosity, that we may impute the public demand for biographical details of popular authors.

In the works of most writers the subjectivity of their material and style reveals their point of view and shows us their actual ideas. The highest canons of dramatic art, however, demand absolute objectivity of treatment. An author's personality, introduced and plainly recognized by an audience in a drama, destroys the perspective and kills the illusion as surely as would the introduction of a Queen Anne cottage in the scenery of a Roman play.

Shakespeare, fully conscious of the demands of his art, has so effectually hidden his own personality and feelings in his work that it has come to be generally believed that they are not to be found there. Because his art is so exquisite shall we deem him an artificer who chisels puppets, instead of an artist who molds his heart and soul into form and figure? Because he does not wail like Heine and tell us that "Out of my own great woes I make my little songs," may we not by searching find him out? I am convinced that we may, and that while the investigation of moldy records and parish registers has given us some idea of how he bought and sold property, sued his debtors, etc., the real man, the poet and philosopher, lover and hater, friend and foe, may be discerned only by a critical and sympathetic study of his own works. His dramas are so artistically objective, and his in-

Qu: Who was the "Passionate Pilgrim"?

dividuality so carefully hidden, that this would be
an almost impossible task were it not for the great
autobiographical value of the Sonnets, and the side
lights which the story they contain throws upon
his other works.

In the Sonnets Shakespeare becomes entirely
subjective; they were not meant for publication,
and, looked at in a true light, are two series of poetic epistles: one to his friend, and one to his mistress.

The earliest mention we have of the Sonnets is
in the year 1598, in Meres' " Palladis Tamia," where
they are called, " his sugred sonnets amongst his
private friends." There can be little doubt but that
Meres refers to the Sonnets which we know, or, at
least, to some portion of them.

In 1599 two of the Sonnets, Nos. 138 and 144,
appeared in a somewhat garbled form, in a collection of poems by various hands,—but all attributed
to Shakespeare,—published by Wm. Jaggard, under the title of " The Passionate Pilgrim."

We have no other record of any of the Sonnets
till 1609, when the whole collection, as we know
them, and a poem entitled " A Lover's Complaint,"
were published by Thomas Thorpe with the follow-
ing title-page: " Shake-speares | sonnets. | Never
before Imprinted. | At London | By G. Eld for
T. T. and are | to be solde by William Aspley. |
1609. | " This edition was ushered to the world by
Thorpe with the following dedication: " To the
onlie Begetter of these insuing sonnets Mr. W. H.
all happinesse and that eternitie promised by our

ever-living poet wisheth the well-wishing adventurer in setting forth. T. T." No other edition of the Sonnets appeared until the year 1640, when they were published, along with other poems purporting to be by Shakespeare, under the heading: " Poems: written by Wil. Shakespeare. Gent. Printed at London by Tho. Cotes, and are to be solde by John Benson, dwelling at St. Dunstan's Churchyard. 1640." Several of the Sonnets in Thorpe's collection are omitted from this edition, and those that appear are prefixed with titles of the publisher's own invention. Whatever personal touches there may be in the Sonnets were quite lost sight of by this date. Thorpe, in his dedication, plainly recognizes their personal nature when he wishes " Mr. W. H. " " that eternitie promised by our ever-living poet," yet it is very probable that Thorpe was quite in the dark as to their full history, and believed the medium through whom he received them to be their true begetter. It may be that he was purposely deceived, and allowed to use the term " Mr. W. H." in order to hide their private nature and to shield the real begetter from the public eye.

I shall prove later on that William Herbert, Earl of Pembroke, was not the patron addressed in these Sonnets, and shall, I believe, give very convincing evidence that Henry Wriothesley, Earl of Southampton, was that figure, yet I do not think it at all improbable that Pembroke was the " Mr. W. H." addressed by Thorpe, nor unlikely that the Sonnets were published through his influence and with his cognizance. It is reasonable to assume that the favor of Pembroke and his brother Montgomery, mentioned by Hemminge and Condel in the folio dedication as having been shown to Shakespeare, had commenced before the year 1609, and it is also quite possible that this favor was the result of Southampton's influence with these noblemen. We know that Southampton and Pembroke were friends, or at least very intimate acquaintances; we also know that they both, at some period, gave their countenance and patronage to Shakespeare; that he and his poems should then be a topic of common interest with them is most likely, and also, that Southampton should bring these Sonnets in manuscript to the notice of Pembroke; they having all, or nearly all, been written previous to his advent at Court in 1598, as I shall prove.

Between Spring 1593 and Autumn 1594

Played before Court Xmas 1594

Shakespeare was already famous, and openly acknowledged as a literary star of no small magnitude by this year. Between the end of 1598 and 1601, Southampton, then out of favor with the Court, owing to his marriage with Elizabeth Vernon in defiance of the Queen's wishes, was, through his friendship with the Earl of Essex, drawn into the political vortex which ended in the death of Essex and his own imprisonment in the latter year, he remaining in prison until March, 1603. By this time the Sonnets in manuscript had, no doubt, ceased to be read, and it may be that Pembroke had never seen them till they were brought to his notice by Southampton, in or about the year 1609. Pembroke, recognizing their worth, may have brought about their publication, and in this way have become their begetter. I offer this merely as a plausible suggestion. In the light of the evidence which I shall hereafter adduce as to the identity of Southampton as the patron, this theory as to the " Mr. W. H." of Thorpe's dedication is much more reasonable than that set forth by Mr. Sidney Lee in his " Life of Shakespeare," where he endeavors to prove a claim for a certain printer and publisher named William Hall.

If William Hall was the procurer of these Sonnets, as suggested by Mr. Lee, why should he donate them to a rival publisher? for so Mr. Lee leads us to infer: if he had sold them, Thorpe would not have felt himself under any obligation to flatter him with a dedication. Thomas Thorpe undoubtedly uses the word " begetter " in the sense of inspirer; no quibbling will do away with this fact. The words, " To the onlie begetter of the insuing sonnets, Mr. W. H. all happinesse, and that eternitie promised by our ever-living poet," plainly show that Thomas Thorpe fully believed " Mr. W. H. " to be the inspirer of the Sonnets and also the person who in certain of them is promised eternity; he certainly would not look upon the publisher's hack, William Hall, in this light.

Neither publishers nor writers, at that date, made free with the names and titles of noblemen to usher their wares to the world, without having first secured that right, or being fully assured, by a previous experience, of their liberty to do so.

One year later than the date of the publication

of the Sonnets, we find that Thorpe dedicated Healey's translation of St. Augustine's " Citie of God " to the Earl of Pembroke, in language which strongly suggests a previous similar connection with that nobleman.

It has been suggested that a publisher would not dare to take the liberty of addressing a titled nobleman as " Mr."; and I have no doubt that Thorpe would much more willingly have published the Sonnets with a flourish of titles, but was probably prevented from doing so by Pembroke himself, for the reasons I have already suggested. The fact that Thorpe issued the Sonnets with a dedication is fair proof that he had not come by them dishonestly.

Mr. Lee assumes that Thorpe was a piratical publisher of no standing, but the fact that he published matter by Ben Jonson and Chapman, who were both very careful of their literary wares, and fully realized their value, proves that he was a fairly reputable publisher.

Mr. Lee goes rather out of his way to abuse the Elizabethan publishers' profession. There were, no doubt, dishonest publishers in those days, but the lack of definite copyright laws at that date makes it difficult to judge what was dishonesty. Publishers then, no doubt, compared quite as favorably as in this day with men in other channels of trade; but we do not find them, either then or now, presenting each other with valuable copyrights gratis, nor writing fulsome dedications to one another.

In working out my theory I have left Thorpe and his dedication out of the question, and searched in the Sonnets themselves for light; I have discussed it here, principally, to show that Thorpe in 1609 recognized their personal tone. This personal idea was quite lost sight of by the year 1640, when Benson published them, and was not revived until about a hundred years after their first issue. During that period they were read, when read at all, as impersonal literature.

Thorpe was a pirate. He only occupied a shop The Tigers head in St Pauls Churchyard for a short time in 1608 and issued 3 publications from there. He probably procured Johnsons Masques of Blackness and Beauty and Chapmans "Byron" All members of the Stationers Co except Thorpe (as far as is known) developed into printers or booksellers. He was a rogue. He was buried an alms room in the hospital of Ewelme Oxfordshire 3/12/1635.

Thomas Thorpe was possibly in fear for his Catholic past. Was he the brother of Robert Thorpe executed in York 1591? He was in Rheims with him

CHAPTER II.

THE PERSONAL THEORY.

For about two hundred years now critics and students have given more or less thought and research to the Sonnets as personal documents, hoping to find therein some light on the poet's personality and life.

Early in the eighteenth century attention was called to their personal tone, by Gildon, who conjectured that they were all written by Shakespeare to his mistress. Dr. Sewall, in 1728, reached the same conclusion. Their examination of the Sonnets, however, must have been of a most cursory nature. In 1781 Malone first suggested that the Sonnets were written to two persons, a patron and a mistress; dividing them as they are usually divided by critics at this day; from 1 to 126 to the patron, and the remaining twenty-eight to the mistress. Since that period various critics have delved into them, seeking the hidden story; all sorts of theories have been propounded; some with a slight show of foundation, and some with none.

The "Mr. W. H." of Thorpe's dedication has been a fruitful source of conjecture, and has led many students away on a wild-goose chase, and from far richer grounds of research.

Nothing in the Sonnets or plays will ever positively reveal this enigma; outside evidence may; this is quite a different thing, however, from proving the identity of the patron. It is very evident that Thorpe was quite in the dark on that point, and that he believed the " Mr. W. H." to whom he dedicated them to be the patron indicated. Shakespeare certainly had no hand in their publication; several of the Sonnets are plainly incorrect in places; one Sonnet—No. 145—is undoubtedly the work of another hand, and the canzonette, as L'Envoi to the first series, is mistaken for a sonnet, and is marked as incomplete, with brackets for the supposedly missing lines. These blemishes show that Shakespeare was not consulted as to their arrangement for publication; besides which, we have his own plain statement, in the Sonnets themselves, that they were not written for sale.

Censored!

After Malone's suggestion for the division of the Sonnets into two series, the next conjecture of any value was made by Dr. Drake, in 1817, when he proposed Henry Wriothesley, Earl of Southampton, as the patron, offering no other proof, however, than the palpable fact that " Venus and Adonis," and " Lucrece," were dedicated to that nobleman. He would not believe that the Sonnets 127 to 154 were addressed to a real woman, and supposes that they were written, as were many other sonnets of that day, to an imaginary mistress. Dr. Drake has had many followers in this theory; in his recent book Mr. Sidney Lee voiced the same ideas.

In 1818 a Mr. Bright conceived the idea that William Herbert, Earl of Pembroke, was the patron

Proof that Shake-speare did contribute the Sonnets is shown by the 153 Son as derived from Watson's 100th Sonnet of Passionate Centurie

addressed in the Sonnets, taking the " W. H." of Thorpe's dedication for his grounds, coupled with the fact that Shakespeare's fellow actors, Hemminge and Condel, in 1623, dedicated the first folio to this nobleman. Mr. Bright, while nursing his idea in the hope of finding further light, was forestalled in the public announcement of it by Dr. Boaden in 1832. Since that date students of the Sonnets have been divided into two camps, viz.: Southamptonites and Pembrokites. There are some few free lances who attach themselves to neither side; believing that the Sonnets are mere poetical exercises, composed at different times, in an assumed character, by the poet for the amusement of his friends. Much interesting work has been done by the champions of both the former theories. The most voluminous writer on the side of Southampton was Mr. Gerald Massey (1864): on the side of Pembroke, Mr. Thomas Tyler is at this date the undoubted leader. Mr. Sidney Lee has recently espoused the Southamptonite cause, but has not adduced any new nor definite proof in support of the theory. Mr. Lee, in his excellent and painstaking book, makes the mistake, common with many critics who have written on the Sonnets, of neglecting the Sonnets themselves, and adducing all his proof from outside sources. The " dark lady " and her influence he dismisses as a trivial incident, which, while possibly an actual fact in Shakespeare's life, was of so small moment, and such short duration, that it cannot have affected the tenor of his work.

This is shown by the use of the line "Love kyndling fire" which occurs in the 153rd line of H & L. See John 21 verses 7 to 11

The story or stories of the Sonnets, as they rest to-day, are built altogether upon inference and conjecture. Both conjecture and inference are of course valuable, if they work from settled data or known fact, but, so far, little actual fact or conclusive data have been adduced.

The interesting story which Mr. Tyler builds around the Pembroke theory seemed to me most conclusive; the only things which appeared to render it doubtful were the mistiness of his chronology for the Sonnets and the imputation of ingratitude towards Southampton, with which it inferentially charges Shakespeare. I can much more readily believe a story of even grosser sensuality than that revealed in the " dark lady " Sonnets, on the part of Shakespeare, than believe him capable of the ingratitude to his early patron with which the Pembroke theory necessarily charges him, and which, it also would show us, that he himself in the Sonnets has the baseness to extenuate. To Mr. Tyler's excellent book, however, I owe my interest in the Sonnets, and must admit that, for a long time after reading it, I was a confirmed Pembrokite. Of all the arguments used by Mr. Tyler, the one that most interested me was that suggested by Professor Minto in his " Characteristics of the English Poets " (1885), identifying George Chapman as the " rival poet." This, while merely inference, was of a stronger and more plausible nature than any other theory regarding that figure, and seemed to me to offer a good basis for further investigation.

For the last ten years I have, in a haphazard way, and at odd moments, pursued this theory, seldom being without a copy of the Sonnets in my pocket; reading them in my moments of leisure, searching for evidence of their history, till I have come to have them by heart, though never having made any set effort to memorize them. I have also, during these years, read most of Chapman's poems very thoroughly, with the same object in view, though not, I may say, with the same pleasure; and in the case of Chapman also, I have unconsciously memorized many passages. This habit, or trick of memory, has stood me in good stead, in revealing to me parallels which otherwise might have passed unnoticed. It was not long till I made one or two discoveries, which, to my mind, demolished the basis of the Pembroke theory. To this, then, I gave no more thought, and pursued my investigations irrespective of the claims of Southamptonite or Pembrokite.

The Pembroke theory is based upon the suggestion that the Sonnets to the patron were all written in and after the year 1598; consequently, if conclusive evidence be adduced of their earlier production, the theory straightway falls to the ground.

I have not wrought with the idea of supporting the contention of either the Southamptonites or Pembrokites. Having steeped my mind in the Sonnets, I was forced to a belief in their personal nature and their autobiographical value, and set myself the task of giving, if possible, a definite date for their production; feeling assured that this would be the best manner in which to settle the personality of the patron and friend to whom they were addressed. The opportunities for outside research which I possess being limited, any new light I might find I must look for in the Sonnets themselves, and finding any indications there to guide me, follow where they pointed. In this way I have been led to make a study of those plays in which the style and versification, as well as the passionate and poetical treatment of the theme of love, indicated the period of the Sonnets, as containing the same elements. By this method I have made some further discoveries which will greatly strengthen the basis for a more extended research and a deeper study of Shakespeare's plays, as touching on his own individuality.

I shall show conclusively that Professor Minto's conjecture as to Chapman's identity as the " rival poet " is absolutely true. From the same data I shall prove the truth of the contention of the Southamptonites; I shall throw an altogether new light on " Love's Labour's Lost," and " Troilus and Cressida," and give a definite date for their production and their revision; I shall show the truth of very interesting internal evidence in the Sonnets, which has hitherto been quite misunderstood or altogether unnoticed, and shall set a fairly definite date for their production.

I should like to continue my investigations further, before publishing any of the results I have attained, but my findings are so palpable to anyone who, having the key, follows out the theory, that I am fearful that someone else may light upon it, and put me in the position of Mr. Bright with Dr. Boaden, for all have the key, which is the happy suggestion of Professor Minto that I have already mentioned.

I thought I saw in Shakespeare's references to the "rival poet" something stronger than mere fear of a rival, and searching the Sonnets, have found other references than that suggested by Professor Minto, which not only more plainly indicate Chapman, but are also of a more satirical character.

Being thus thoroughly convinced that Chapman was the poet indicated and attacked, I thought it probable that some indications of the reason for the rivalry, or for Shakespeare's enmity, might be found in Chapman's own poems; I believe that I shall fully establish this fact. If, then, I can positively prove the identity of the rival, and that the rivalry was not a passing phase, but enduring and bitter, the bitterness and duration of the rivalry will plainly prove the fact of the continued and valuable friendship and patronage so fought for; if the patron and rival are seen to have been living actualities, the dark mistress necessarily cannot be an imaginary being, as not only the Sonnets written to her, but also the Sonnets written to the patron, prove that, for a short period at least, she also entered into his life.

I shall show very plainly that Shakespeare carries his friendship for Southampton and his rivalry against Chapman into certain of his plays. If a platonic masculine friendship and a poetic rivalry lead him to this extent, it is even more probable that the passionate love for a woman of such a highly strung, poetic, and sensitive nature as Shakespeare's should still more strongly influence his dramatic work.

I have not identified the " dark lady," but do not on that account agree with a recent writer, and many other critics of a like mind, that " it was the exacting conventions of the sonneteering contagion, and not his personal experience, that impelled Shakespeare to give the ' dark lady ' of his Sonnets a poetic being."

If there is one figure more real than the others in the Sonnets, it is the " dark lady "; the rival poet is a phantom, and the patron a myth, in comparison with this black-eyed daughter of Eve. This writer further says: " there is no greater, and no less ground, for seeking in Shakespeare's personal environment the original of the ' dark lady ' in the Sonnets, than for seeking there the original of the Queen of Egypt." To me it seems extremely probable that not only Cleopatra, but also Rosaline and Cressida, are poetic idealizations of this willful, sensuous, and sprightly young woman.

Many commentators reject the personal theory of the Sonnets as a whole, yet accept as personal some individual Sonnets that fit their theories and tastes. Either they are, as a whole, mere exercises of poetic imagination, or they are, as Wordsworth, with a poet's keen insight, recognized, " this key " with which " Shakespeare unlocked his heart."

Many critics have accepted and followed the personal theory of the Sonnets till they have run foul of this shocking person, the "dark lady," when, finding that further acquiescence in the theory would topple our unconventional Elizabethan actor-poet from the Bowdlerized pedestal upon which their staid Victorian imagination had placed him, they have abandoned the quest. Mr. Knight and Mr. Massey are notable instances of this class. Mr. Massey did some valuable work in elucidating Dr. Drake's theory as to Southampton's connection with the poet, but in order to preserve Shakespeare intact upon his pedestal, he imagines a most extraordinary tale, without the merest shadow of proof, and in several places takes unwarrantable liberties with the text of the Sonnets, to fit them to his theory. In quoting Mr. Knight as an advocate against the personal theory, he says: " Mr. Knight has found the perplexities of the personal theory so insurmountable that he has not followed in the steps of those who have jauntily overleaped the difficulties that meet us everywhere, and which ought, until fairly conquered, to have surrounded and protected the poet's personal character as with a chevaux-de-frise. He has wisely hesitated, rather than rashly joined in making a wanton charge of gross immorality and egregious folly against Shakespeare." So careful is he of the lay figure into which his imagination has transformed that being of bounding, exultant blood, who wrote:

" From woman's eyes this doctrine I derive.
    They sparkle still the true Promethean fire,

LLL: IV - 3

See also Southwell's St. Peter's Complaint LVI - LX

They are the arts, the books, the academies,
That show, contain, and nourish all the world ":

that remorseful, and deep-seeing spirit that wrote
the Sonnets:

" Poor soul, the centre of my sinful earth,"
        etc. (146),

and

" The expense of spirit in a waste of shame,"
        etc. (129).

Without fear for Shakespeare, I can wish the
matter of the " dark lady " probed to the end; feeling confident that, when all is known, Shakespeare
will be none the less Shakespeare; Mr. Browning
to the contrary, notwithstanding.

I believe, from what I find in the Sonnets, that
our poet's connection with this woman commenced
at almost the same period as his acquaintance with
Southampton, in about 1593, and that it was continued until about the beginning of 1598. I
believe, also, that he genuinely loved her,
and fired with the passion and intensity of his
love, produced in those years the marvelous rhap-
sodies of love in " Romeo and Juliet," " Love's Labor's Lost," and other of his love plays, which have
so charmed the world, and still charm it, and shall
continue to do so while the language lives.

If ever a man lived who sounded the human heart

to its depths, and gauged its heights, that man was Shakespeare, and such knowledge as he had, and shows us of life, may not be attained by hearsay, nor at second hand.

We know somewhat of the manner in which he produced his plays; research has shown us in many instances their sources, at least the sources of their plots; we know how he took the bare skeletons of history, the shreds and patches of romance and tradition, the "loose feathers of fame," and on them built the splendid structure of his plays, seldom altering the outlines of the plots, yet, withal, so transfiguring them with the light of his genius that in his hands they became new creations. So, we may fairly assume, he, to some extent, took incidents of his daily life, and the characteristics of the men and women with whom he came in contact, and clothing them with the radiance of his fancy, incorporated them in his plays.

That this is very true, in at least two plays, I believe I can prove by the light of the Sonnets. That the Sonnets are personal documents, that in them Shakespeare spoke his real feelings to real people, is a conclusion which I think all will reach who will follow my argument, and who will make a study of the Sonnets with their minds cleared of cant. The personality which we find there revealed may, it is true, lose somewhat of the Olympian, but dim, proportions which we have been used to give the poet; but it will take on a humanity and a nearness which will vastly enhance both him and his work in our eyes.

As our greatest men recede into history, while their proportions enlarge in our mental vision, their characteristic lineaments are lost in the glow of the halos with which our regard endows them. This tendency is as old as the race: in remote times, by this process our ancestors made them gods; in these days we are more like to make them wooden gods.

While I contend that the Sonnets are largely autobiographical, and that they reveal a real friend and patron, as well as a real rival, and mistress, yet I fully recognize the fact that the language is that of poetry and may not always be taken at its face value. Many of them, no doubt, are topical, and some of them can be shown by their form and expression to be reflections of more trivial sonnets by other writers, who openly disavowed reality for their goddesses and mistresses, but this, instead of detracting from their personal value, as argued by Mr. Lee and others, rather adds strength to it when we consider the nature and object of the references and reflections noted. Let us take one instance where such a reflection seems very strong: Henry Constable and Bernard Griffin, in the following sonnets, were, no doubt, somewhat influenced in their imagery and ideas by Chapman's "Amorous Zodiac," which preceded their verses in date of production. Constable writes as follows:

"OF HIS MISTRESS UPON OCCASION OF HER WALKING IN A GARDEN.

" My lady's presence makes the roses red,
    Because to see her lips they blush for shame:

The lily's leaves, for envy, pale became,
And her white hands in them this envy bred.
The marigold abroad her leaves doth spread,
Because the Sun's and her power is the same;
The violet of purple colour came,
Dyed with the blood she makes my heart to shed.
In brief, all flowers from her this virtue take:
From her sweet breath their sweet smells do pro-
ceed,
The living heat which her eye-beams do make
Warmeth the ground and quickeneth the seed.
The rain wherewith she watereth these flowers
Falls from mine eyes, which she dissolves in
showers."

And again, Bernard Griffin writes to his mistress
in the following strain:

"My lady's hair is threads of beaten gold,
Her front the purest crystal eye hath seen,
Her eye the brightest star of heaven holds,
Her cheeks red roses such as seld have been,
Her pretty lips of red vermilion dye,
Her hands of ivory the purest white,
Her blush Aurora, or the morning sky,
Her breast displays two silver fountains bright,
The sphere her voice, her grace, the Graces three,
Her body is the saint that I adore,
Her smiles and favors sweet as honey bee,
Her feet fair Thetis praiseth ever more,
But, oh, the worst and last is yet behind
For of a griffin she doth bear the mind."

Shakespeare, with one or both of these sonnets very evidently in his mind, writes of his mistress:

Mistress

" My mistress' eyes are nothing like the sun;
Coral is far more red than her lips' red:
If snows be white, why then her breasts are dun;
If hairs be wires, black wires grow on her head.
I have seen roses damask'd red and white,
But no such roses see I in her cheeks;
And in some perfumes is there more delight
Than in the breath that from my mistress reeks.
I love to hear her speak, yet well I know
That music hath a far more pleasing sound:
I grant I never saw a goddess go,
My mistress, when she walks, treads on the ground:
　And yet, by heaven, I think my love as rare
　As any she belied with false compare."

Here we find Shakespeare, far from being governed by the " exacting conventions of the sonneteering contagion " and giving an imaginary " dark lady " " a poetic being," flying directly in the face of conventions, and painting with most strongly realistic strokes a very flesh-and-blood being. In this, as in several other instances in the Sonnets, Shakespeare refers to or parodies other sonneteers, who write to imaginary mistresses, or else write extravagantly to and almost deify real ones; not reflecting nor indorsing their extravagances, but directly opposing and mocking them with his reality.

While what has been called " the sonneteering

contagion," lasting in England from about 1590 to 1598, in all probability influenced Shakespeare to the use of this form of verse, and while he necessarily is somewhat influenced by the form and expressions used by other writers whose poems he read, these facts do not detract from the value of his Sonnets as personal documents, as it is only in form and expression that he is influenced.

To anyone who, having read Shakespeare's Sonnets, fails to find the intimate and personal note, I would say, read them again, and again, and again if necessary; it is there. Shakespeare wrote his Sonnets as private epistles to his patron and to his mistress, who circulated them amongst their friends, but that they were not written for publication or for sale, we have his own plain avowal in the 21st Sonnet:

" I will not praise *that purpose not to sell.*"

That this is the correct meaning of this line I will prove in a later chapter.

CHAPTER III.

THE order which Thorpe used in his issue of the
Sonnets, in 1609, is still generally recognized as
correct by Shakespearean critics. I may, therefore,
be deemed presumptuous in assailing that which
has been so long accepted without question; however, after many years of interested and analytic
study of the Sonnets, I am forced to take issue
against the infallibility of Thorpe's arrangement.
The regard in which this arrangement has been
held has arisen largely from the fact that Thorpe
issued the Sonnets during the poet's life, and, therefore, possibly with his cognizance or under his su-
pervision. I am fully convinced, and believe I can
give fairly conclusive proof, that Shakespeare had
no hand in their arrangement or publication.

Someone has said that, if one Sonnet can be
shown to be out of its place and away from its context, the whole value of Thorpe's order is at once
destroyed.

I shall adduce several very plain instances where
this is the case, and yet I admit a very great sequential value for his arrangement. In order to
properly estimate this value, it is necessary to understand the conditions under which Thorpe produced his edition.

I believe I shall clearly show that many of the Sonnets were written previous to 1595, and that the period of the production of the whole series ante- dates 1601. As the Sonnets were not published till 1609, they were, then, held in manuscript for from ten to fifteen years. We know that the Son- nets were produced at different times during a period of at least three years.

In the 108th Shakespeare says:

" What's in the brain that ink may character,
  Which hath not figured to thee my true spirit?
  What's new to speak, what new to register,
  That may express my love, or thy dear merit?
  Nothing, sweet boy; but yet, like prayers divine,
  I must each day say o'er the very same;
  Counting no old thing old, thou mine, I thine,
  Even as when first I hallowed thy fair name."

This plainly proves that Sonnets were written in the earlier, as well as the later periods of the friend- ship revealed in the Sonnets.

Sonnet 104 says:

" To me, fair friend, you never can be old,
  For as you were when first your eye I eyed,
  Such seems your beauty still.   Three winters cold
  Have from the forests shook three summers' pride,
  Three beauteous springs to yellow autumns turn'd
  In process of the seasons have I seen,
  Three April perfumes in three hot Junes burn'd,
  Since first I saw you fresh, which yet are green."

This extract shows that the sonnet-writing had at the date of its production lasted for three years. We may then assume that the manuscripts from which Thorpe worked were detached books or sequences, and not one large manuscript containing the whole of the Sonnets as we know them. Though they were written as private epistles to the poet's patron, and mistress, they were evidently shown by their recipients to their friends, and passed amongst them to be read. In 1598 Meres mentions Shakespeare's "Sugred sonnets amongst his private friends," and I believe I shall show that Chapman had read some of them in manuscript many years before their eventual publication. We see, then, that the Sonnets were passed among Southampton's friends as they were written.

If we can get any idea of the number of the groups or sequences, we will begin to understand Thorpe's difficulties in chronologically arranging the whole series: to get any such idea, we must necessarily go to Thorpe's edition. We will, therefore, begin at the beginning and seek for palpable sequences.

We see very clearly that the first seventeen Sonnets are closely connected and plainly of the same group; the 18th and 19th Sonnets, while differing somewhat in subject, are also very evidently connected with the first group, but neither the 20th, 21st, 22d, 23d, 24th, or 25th are in any way related, either in sense or figure; the 26th Sonnet, however, is very similar in tone, and is plainly the last Sonnet of a sequence. In nearly all of the later Sonnets

we find a most distinct avowal of the poet's love
for his friend, and also a plain record of that friend's
avowal of love for the poet; we find hopes, fears,
and even jealousy, and the clearest proofs of a very
intimate friendship and close personal relations. In
the first group we find none of this; friendship is
not once mentioned, the poet's love for the patron
is alluded to, but in a most conventional manner,
and only two or three times in the whole sequence.

There can be little doubt, then, that these were
the earliest Sonnets of the whole series. We find
only nineteen Sonnets which show continuity: now
sequences were not written of this number; twenty,
however, was a very common number for sonnet-sequences at that period; this, then, was very evidently such a sequence: where is the missing Sonnet? Certainly not either 20 or 21; I shall prove
this couple to be detached and topical, having no
connection whatever with the first sequence, nor
even with any succeeding Sonnets which come any-
where near them. These two Sonnets were written as an attack upon Chapman and a poem which
he published in 1595, called "The Amorous Zodiac"; this will be proved in a later chapter. A
very casual reading will show that neither the 22d
nor 23d Sonnet is connected with the first group,
and also that they have no connection with each
other; they evidently belong elsewhere. The 24th
Sonnet is not connected with this group; its proper
context will be found in Sonnets 46 and 47. I shall
give these three Sonnets at length, to prove their
connection.

SONNET 24.

" Mine eye hath played the painter and hath stell'd
  Thy beauty's form in table of my heart;
  My body is the frame wherein 'tis held,
  And perspective it is best painter's art.
  For through the painter must you see his skill.
  To find where your true image pictured lies;
  Which in my bosom's shop is hanging still,
  That hath his windows glazed with thine eyes.
  Now see what good turns eyes for eyes have done:
  Mine eyes have drawn thy shape, and thine for me
  Are windows to my breast, where-through the sun
  Delights to peep, to gaze therein on thee;
    Yet eyes this cunning want to grace their art,
    They draw but what they see, know not the
      heart."

SONNET 46.

" Mine eye and heart are at a mortal war,
  How to divide the conquest of thy sight;
  Mine eye my heart thy picture's sight would bar.
  My heart mine eye the freedom of that right.
  My heart doth plead that thou in him dost lie,
  A closet never pierced with crystal eyes,
  But the defendant doth that plea deny,
  And says in him thy fair appearance lies.
  To 'cide this title is impanneled
  A quest of thoughts, all tenants to the heart;
  And by their verdict is determined
  The clear eye's moiety and the dear heart's part:

As thus: mine eye's due is thine outward part
And my heart's right thine inward love of
heart."

SONNET 47.

" Betwixt mine eye and heart a league is took,
And each doth good turns now unto the other:
When that mine eye is famish'd for a look,
Or heart in love with sighs himself does smother,
With my love's picture then my heart doth feast
And to the painted banquet bids my heart;
Another time mine eye is my heart's guest
And in his thoughts of love doth share a part:
So, either by the picture or my love,
Thyself away art present still with me;
For thou not farther than my thoughts canst
move,
And I am still with them and they with thee;
  Or, if they sleep, thy picture in my sight
  Awakes my heart to heart's and eyes' delight."

The sequence of ideas and the connection of these
Sonnets, one with another, are too palpable for
comment.

The 25th Sonnet is very plainly not connected,
in either subject or figure, with the first sequence;
the concluding lines,

" Then happy I, that love and am beloved
Where I may not remove nor be removed,"

show a much more advanced stage in the poet's

friendship with Southampton than that indicated in the first sequence; the true context for this Sonnet will be found in the 29th Sonnet, which, however, should precede it:

SONNET 29.

"When in disgrace with fortune and men's eyes,
I all alone beweep my outcast state,
And trouble deaf heaven with my bootless cries,
And look upon myself, and curse my fate,
Wishing me like to one more rich in hope,
Featured like him, like him with friends possess'd,
Desiring this man's art and that man's scope,
With what I most enjoy contented least;
Yet in these thoughts myself almost despising,
Haply I think on thee, and then my state,
Like to the lark at break of day arising
From sullen earth, sings hymns at heaven's gate;
   For thy sweet love remember'd such wealth
      brings
   That then I scorn to change my state with
      kings."

SONNET 25.

"Let those who are in favour with their stars
Of public honour and proud titles boast,
Whilst I, whom fortune of such triumph bars,
Unlook'd for joy in that I honour most.
Great princes' favourites their fair leaves spread
But as the marigold at the sun's eye,
And in themselves their pride lies buried,

For at a frown they in their glory die.
The painful warrior famoused for fight,
After a thousand victories once foil'd,
Is from the book of honour razed quite,
And all the rest forgot for which he toil'd:
  Then happy I, that love and am beloved
  Where I may not remove nor be removed."

If the two Sonnets here quoted be critically compared with their present contexts, it will be seen
very clearly that they are out of place.

The 26th Sonnet is very palpably the end of the
first sonnet-sequence and should be numbered 20.
It has no connection with any other Sonnet or Sonnets in the whole series: it undoubtedly belongs to
the earliest stage of the poet's connection with the
nobleman; in it he fearfully avows his love, and no
love is indicated as being given by Southampton, or
even hoped for by the poet. It was very evidently
sent to Southampton accompanying some other matter, as we find in the lines:

" To thee I send this written ambassage,
  To witness duty, not to show my wit:
  Duty so great, which wit so poor as mine
  May make seem bare, in wanting words to show it,
  But that I hope some good conceit of thine
  In thy soul's thought, all naked, will bestow it."

By the words " this written ambassage " Shakespeare certainly does not mean this single Sonnet,

but very evidently alludes to the group of which this Sonnet is the end.

Here, then, we have one sequence of twenty Sonnets intact. This sequence, however, has little personal value; it is a dissertation upon the advantages of matrimony and a fulsome panegyric upon the physical beauty of this young nobleman. These Sonnets were written at an early stage of the poet's connection with Southampton, not in the spirit of the later Sonnets, as a friend to a friend, and touching upon intimate personal things, but as a poetical exercise, such as any poet might write to any patron. This is the only twenty-sonnet sequence in the whole series; nearly all the remaining Sonnets were written in small groups, as letters in verse, touching upon matters personal to the two friends. The number of Sonnets in these epistles differ; very often they were written in couples, sometimes in threes, and occasionally in fours. In one case I think I find a sequence of ten Sonnets, and to this sequence I would attach the canzonette, No. 126, as L'Envoi.

These small groups or sequences, however, are not always intact: as in the case of the first twenty-sonnet sequence, the last or the first Sonnet of a group is often detached, and to be found far removed from its proper context, and mixed in with other Sonnets to which it has no possible relation. I think I have rendered this very plain in the instance of the 26th Sonnet and its obvious connection with the first group, also in the case of the 24th Sonnet, when compared with its context in the

46th and 47th; and again in the 25th and 29th Sonnets.

I shall now point out a few other instances where such disarrangement is so palpable that a mere comparison will convince the reader; and at the same time I shall indicate several of the small groups of two, three, and four Sonnets, which plainly show that they are whole in themselves and not connected with any long sequence.

We have disposed of the Sonnets up to 26, and shall continue from that point.

Sonnets 27 and 28 are a very plainly connected couple; they have nothing whatever to do with 26 or 29, as I have previously shown: I do not find in the whole series any other Sonnets connected with this pair, and believe that they together make one of the before-mentioned poetical epistles.

Sonnets 30 and 31 are also a separate and distinct pair, treating of one particular subject, or revealing a particular mood of the poet's mind; this couple is also a letter written during absence. I am inclined to believe that these two Sonnets were written from Stratford in 1596, and that they reflect the pathetic gloom of the poet's mind caused by his son Hamnet's death at that date.

Sonnet 32, though treating of death, as do the two preceding Sonnets, and placed in its present connection by Thorpe, probably on that account, has no connection whatever in sense or style with the two preceding Sonnets, as a comparison will plainly show. The proper connection for this Sonnet will be found in Sonnet 81; this latter Sonnet,

when critically compared with its present contexts,
Sonnets 80 and 82, will be seen to be out of place:
both 80 and 82 treat very plainly of the rival poet;
Sonnet 80 ends with a figure in which the poet,
comparing himself to a worthless boat, and his rival
to a ship of "tall building and of goodly pride,"
says:

" Then if he thrive and I be cast away,
    The worst was this, my love was my decay."

Here we find no possible reference to the subject
of death, and there can be little doubt but that it
was the word "decay," at the end of this Sonnet,
which misled Thorpe into placing the 81st Sonnet
in its present connection. I shall quote both the
32d and the 81st Sonnets to show their very plain
connection:

SONNET 32.

" If thou survive my well-contented day,
    When that churl Death my bones with dust shall
        cover,
    And shalt by fortune once more re-survey
    These poor rude lines of thy deceased lover;
    Compare them with the bettering of the time,
    And though they be outstripp'd by every pen,
    Reserve them for my love, not for their rhyme,
    Exceeded by the height of happier men.
    O, then vouchsafe me but this loving thought:
    ' Had my friend's Muse grown with this growing
        age,

A dearer birth than this his love had brought,
To march in ranks of better equipage:
    But since he died, and poets better prove,
    Theirs for their style I'll read, his for his love.'"

SONNET 81.

" Or I shall live your epitaph to make,
Or you survive when I in earth am rotten;
From hence your memory death cannot take.
Although in me each part will be forgotten.
Your name from hence immortal life shall have,
Though I, once gone, to all the world must die:
The earth can yield me but a common grave,
When thou entombed in men's eyes shall lie.
Your monument shall be my gentle verse,
Which eyes not yet created shall o'er-read;
And tongues to be your being shall rehearse,
When all the breathers of this world are dead;
    You still shall live—such virtue hath my pen—
    Where breath most breathes, even in the mouths
        of men."

Sonnets 33, 34, and 35 are most distinctly of the
same sequence. This group forms the poet's first
epistle to his friend upon the subject of the " dark
lady "; they were, most probably, written from
Stratford in 1596, as were, no doubt, all of the
Sonnets touching upon this subject. We find four
distinct letters: two to Southampton, and two to the
" dark lady." In both the series to the patron and

the series to the mistress these groups are separated
by Sonnets touching on quite different matters; it
is extremely improbable that Shakespeare wrote
these intervening Sonnets at that time, or that any
Sonnets bearing on other subjects were written between these two epistles. In the series to the patron we find 33, 34, and 35 as one epistle, and 40,
41, and 42 as a second; both referring to Southampton's indiscretions. In the series to the " dark lady "
we find two couples treating on the same subject;
and both divided by several Sonnets; as in the case
in the patron series—Sonnets 133 and 134 for the
first epistle, and 143 and 144 for the second. In
neither series have these groups any connection
with their immediate contexts, consequently they
are not parts of larger sequences. Had Thorpe
found these Sonnets in detached sheets, there can
be little doubt but that he would have placed them
all together in each series, as they very plainly treat
of one and the same subject. The fact that we find
them separated, and divided in both series into two
groups, lends very strong color to my contention
regarding all the Sonnets following the first sequence—that they were written at different times,
in small groups and as poetical letters. It is quite
unlikely that either Southampton or the " dark
lady," in passing Shakespeare's Sonnets on to their
friends, would let these particular groups out of
their hands. I have already shown where other
small sequences are broken and divided; here, however, are four small groups quite intact. Thorpe
very evidently found these groups quite unimpaired;

they, no doubt, owing to their private nature, having been less handled than the other sequences.

I do not at present intend to attempt to indicate the sequential misplacement of Sonnets nor the chronological disorder of sequences through the whole series; I wish merely to prove my contention that the Sonnets were written in small detached groups, of twos, threes, fours, etc., and to show that many of them are away from their proper groups. I desire also to prove that whole sequences are chronologically misplaced. These facts have, I believe, been here sufficiently proved; however, I shall adduce two more very plain instances. If Sonnet 56 be compared with Sonnet 55, it will be clearly seen to be the beginning of a new sequence and 55 the ending of some other group. When we compare 56 with 57, no connection whatever is to be found between them. Sonnet 56 reveals a reunion after separation and ends with a figure, in which the poet likens his absence to the winter. The proper connection for this Sonnet will be found in No. 97, which not only continues the simile with which the 56th Sonnet ends, but shows the same reunion, and speaks of the same absence; these ideas and figures continue on into the 98th and 99th Sonnets, making a very distinct group of four. I shall quote these Sonnets to prove this very obvious sequence:

SONNET 56.

" Sweet love, renew thy force; be it not said
    Thy edge should blunter be than appetite,

Which but to-day by feeding is allay'd,
To-morrow sharpen'd in his former might:
So, love, be thou; although to-day thou fill
Thy hungry eyes even till they wink with fulness,
To-morrow see again, and do not kill
The spirit of love with a perpetual dulness.
Let this sad interim like the ocean be
Which parts the shore, where two contracted new
Come daily to the banks, that, when they see
Return of love, more blest may be the view;
   Or call it winter, which, being full of care,
   Makes summer's welcome thrice more wish'd,
      more rare."

SONNET 97.

" How like a winter hath my absence been
From thee, the pleasure of the fleeting year!
What freezings have I felt, what dark days seen!
What old December's bareness every where!
And yet this time removed was summer's time;
The teeming autumn, big with rich increase,
Bearing the wanton burthen of the prime,
Like widowed wombs after their lord's decease:
Yet this abundant issue seemed to me
But hope of orphans and unfather'd fruit;
For summer and his pleasures wait on thee
And, thou away, the very birds are mute;
   Or, if they sing, 'tis with so dull a cheer
   That leaves look pale, dreading the winter's
      near."

SONNET 98.

" From you have I been absent in the spring,
  When proud-pied April, dress'd in all his trim,
  Hath put a spirit of youth in every thing,
  That heavy Saturn laugh'd and leap'd with him.
  Yet nor the lays of birds, nor the sweet smell
  Of different flowers in odour and in hue,
  Could make me any summer's story tell,
  Or from their proud lap pluck them where they
      grew:
  Nor did I wonder at the lily's white,
  Nor praise the deep vermilion in the rose;
  They were but sweet, but figures of delight,
  Drawn after you, you pattern of all those.
    Yet seem'd it winter still, and, you away,
    As with your shadow I with these did play."

SONNET 99.

" The forward violet thus did I chide:
  Sweet thief, whence didst thou steal thy sweet
      that smells,
  If not from my love's breath? The purple pride
  Which on thy soft cheek for complexion dwells
  In my love's veins thou hast too grossly dyed.
  The lily I condemned for thy hand,
  And buds of marjoram had stol'n thy hair;
  The roses fearfully on thorns did stand,
  One blushing shame, another white despair;
  A third, nor red nor white, had stol'n of both,
  And to his robbery had annex'd thy breath;
  But for his theft, in pride of all his growth

A vengeful canker eat him up to death.
　More flowers I noted, yet I none could see
　But sweet or color it had stol'n from thee."

Here is a case in which we find a Sonnet away
from its proper context, as well as a sequence out
of its chronological order. Thorpe placed these
Sonnets as Nos. 97, 98, and 99, not from any relation which he supposed they had to the Sonnets
immediately preceding them, but from a connection
which he imagined they had with the Sonnets from
100 onwards. If the 100th Sonnet and those that
immediately follow be analyzed, they will be seen
to indicate, not an absence of the poet's, but of
Southampton's, and also to show strong evidence of
a recent estrangement. Sonnets 56, 97, 98, and
99, however, display only an absence, and that an
absence of the poet's in the country; the figures and
similes therein used plainly reveal Shakespeare's
renewed acquaintance with rural life. I am convinced that this sequence belongs to a period much
earlier than the Sonnets preceding or succeeding it,
and think that they were the first Sonnets written
after the poet's return from Stratford, upon the occasion of his visit in 1596.

Sonnets 78 to 86, though probably nearly all of
the same period, do not form a connected sequence,
though, with one exception, they all refer to the
rival poet. The exception I notice is Sonnet 81,
which I have hitherto shown should be coupled with
the 32d Sonnet.

Group 87 to 96, I am inclined to believe, is a

sequence; they all refer to the growing coldness of the friend and patron. The later Sonnets of this sequence, 93, 94, 95, and 96, have a tone of admonition not to be found in any other group or single Sonnet in the whole series; the canzonette, No. 126, however, displays the same admonitory tone, and, I am inclined to believe, belongs as L'Envoi to this ten-sonnet sequence: it certainly has no bearing upon its present context.

Thus I have shown that Shakespeare, in the earliest stage of his acquaintance with Southampton, addressed him in a more or less formal sequence of twenty Sonnets; when the acquaintance had ripened into friendship, he wrote letters in the form of small sonnet-sequences; later on, a coldness having arisen, caused no doubt by Chapman's encroachments with his Homeric translations, sometime in 1597, when Southampton for a time seems to have been inclined to accept that poet's dedications, Shakespeare expostulates with his friend in the Sonnets running from 78 to 86, and finally bids him farewell in a sequence of ten Sonnets, 86 to 96, with the canzonette 126 as L'Envoi. His return to the use of a long sequence shows formality, caused no doubt by the strained relations between the poet and his friend. A period of silence now intervenes of somewhat lengthened duration. In 1598, upon Southampton's return from the Continent, the friendship is renewed, and Shakespeare welcomes the return of love in several of the Sonnets, from 100 onwards.

This group, from 100 to 125, were, I believe,

nearly all written in 1598, though some of the later
Sonnets may belong to 1599; one or two of them, I
am quite convinced, are out of place in this series,
and belong to a much earlier period; for instance,
Sonnet 103, while apparently of the same nature and
dealing with the same subjects as Sonnets 100,
101, and 102, when critically read will be found
to be quite distinct from this group: the true
place for this Sonnet is probably between 76
and 77.

The 105th Sonnet is also evidently out of its
place, though I do not at present see its proper context.

With these exceptions I believe that all the Sonnets between 100 and 125 were written after the
reunion between the poet and his friend. I am inclined to the opinion that Sonnets 66, 67, and 68
belong also to this series, and that they refer to
Southampton's imprisonment late in 1598, after his
marriage to Elizabeth Vernon in defiance of the
Queen's commands.

In a later chapter I shall prove that Sonnets 69
and 70 are of the same period as Sonnets 20 and
21, and that they refer to Chapman and a poem of
his, in which he attacks Shakespeare. Even without this proof which I shall adduce, as to the early
date of these two Sonnets, they themselves plainly
show that they were produced anterior to the date
of the incidents revealed in Sonnets 33, 34, and 35,
and 40, 41, and 42. The following lines in Sonnet 70 have always puzzled critics, seeing that this
Sonnet is placed by Thorpe as of a later date than

those mentioned above which show Southampton's admitted sensuality:

" And thou present'st a pure unstained prime.
 Thou hast passed by the ambush of young days,
 Either not assailed, or victor being charged."

When this Sonnet is fully proved to be of an earlier date, the apparent contradiction is resolved.

Though exception may be taken to some of the inferences which I have here drawn, I think it will be admitted that I have proved that many single Sonnets are away from their connections, and groups of sonnets out of their chronological order in Thorpe's arrangement; several of the instances of disorder which I have adduced are so very obvious that they will not be questioned.

In the light of the foregoing arguments, we begin to get some idea of the difficulties under which Thorpe labored in making his edition.

With the exception of the first large sequence of twenty Sonnets, the whole series were written in small groups, and bound together in some crude way; probably either stitched or gummed, in what Shakespeare calls " books "; in two of the Sonnets he uses this term. In the 23d Sonnet:

" O let my books be then the eloquence
 And dumb presagers of my speaking breast,"

and in the 77th Sonnet:

" And of this book this learning may'st thou taste."

When Shakespeare's rather large and ungainly caligraphy is borne in mind, we may infer that in these books or sequences, each sheet contained a single Sonnet; being read for a period of from ten to fifteen years in this form, it is reasonable to suppose that, in passing from hand to hand, the manuscript would become more or less worn, and that the first or the last sheet of a book might often have been detached from its context, and in some instances, especially in the case of the older manuscripts, whole sequences may have become disorganized. The continuity, then, which Thorpe gives us in the large groups at the beginning, and in many of the smaller groups, he undoubtedly found in the manuscripts, but, in placing the loosened leaves and dispersed sequences, he had to use his own judgment and was wrong in many instances.

In placing the groups, we may infer that he went altogether upon his own judgment; and he has certainly displayed a fairly good idea of the continuity and personal nature of the poems. It took no very great perspicacity to recognize, in the first sequence, the earliest of the Sonnets, and in placing the last series, beginning with the 100th and ending with the 125th Sonnet, the references in several of these Sonnets to a three-years' friendship, as well as the allusion to the peace of Vervins in the 107th Sonnet, guided him in giving them their present position.

Thorpe seems also to have recognized the fact that the series referring to the " rival poet," and to the temporary coolness of the patron, immediately preceded the rather prolonged period of silence and estrangement shown in some of the later Sonnets to have elapsed. There can be no doubt, however, that between the 19th Sonnet and the canzonette, No. 126, he has misplaced many single Sonnets and also many sequences.

The Sonnets in what is known as the "dark lady" series, were also, I believe, written in small detached groups, and sometimes even singly. The 129th Sonnet, upon the sexual passion, is very evidently a separate exercise, as is also Sonnet 146, this latter being very probably suggested by one of Sir Philip Sidney's upon the same subject, as follows:

"Leave me, O love, that reachest but to dust,
And thou, my mind, aspire to higher things;
Grow rich in that which never taketh rust:
What ever fades but fading pleasure brings.
Draw in thy beams, and humble all thy might
To that sweet yoke where lasting freedoms be,
Which breaks the clouds and opens forth the light
That doth both shine and give us sight to see.
Oh, take fast hold! let that light be thy guide
In this small course which birth draws out to
	death,
And think how evil becometh him to slide
Who seeketh heaven, and comes of heavenly
	breath;
Then farewell, world, thy uttermost I see:
Eternal Love, maintain thy life in me."

SONNET 146.

" Poor soul, the centre of my sinful earth,
  Starved by these rebel powers that thee array,
  Why dost thou pine within and suffer dearth,
  Painting thy outward walls so costly gay?
  Why so large cost, having so short a lease,
  Dost thou upon thy fading mansion spend?
  Shall worms, inheritors of this excess,
  Eat up thy charge? is this thy body's end?
  Then, soul, live thou upon thy servant's loss,
  And let that pine to aggravate thy store;
  Buy terms divine in selling hours of dross;
  Within be fed, without be rich no more:
     So shalt thou feed on Death, that feeds on men,
     And Death once dead, there's no more dying
        then."

Sonnet 141 was very evidently written with
" Ovid's Banquet of Sense " in mind.

This poem was published in 1595, and as I shall
show that Sonnets 20 and 21, and 69 and 70 also
refer to poems of Chapman's published at the same
time, we may infer that the 141st Sonnet to the
" dark lady " is of the same period as the Sonnets
above mentioned.

The 143d Sonnet seems to be a reflection of some
verses in the poem of " The Two Italian Gentlemen." As the play, " The Two Gentlemen of Verona," is usually supposed to be founded upon the
story in that poem, we may assume that this Sonnet is of the same period as that play. The drama-

tization of that subject very probably occurred to Shakespeare because of its resemblance to his own and his friend's actual experience. It has often been remarked that the ending of this play seems strained and unnatural, and quite out of accord with Shakespeare's art; where he makes Valentine voluntarily surrender Sylvia to Proteus, who, however, shamed by his friend's magnanimity, refuses the sacrifice and returns to his old love. Here we find the incidents of the Sonnets fully repeated.

I shall show that Shakespeare, in two other plays, undoubtedly introduces his own personal feelings, and in one of them quite departs from accepted convention in order to do so. I am very strongly of the opinion that this is the case with "The Two Gentlemen of Verona," and that it was written in 1596 while Shakespeare was at Stratford, and at the same time that the two epistles in Sonnets 33, 34, and 35, and 40, 41, and 42, were written to the patron, and the corresponding epistles in the "dark lady" series to the mistress. I shall quote the 143d Sonnet and one verse from "The Two Italian Gentlemen," to show the resemblance:

SONNET 143.

"Lo, as a careful housewife runs to catch
One of her feather'd creatures broke away,
Sets down her babe, and makes all swift dispatch
In pursuit of the thing she would have stay;
Whilst her neglected child holds her in chase,
Cries to catch her whose busy care is bent

To follow that which flies before her face,
Not prizing her poor infant's discontent:
So runn'st thou after that which flies from thee,
Whilst I thy babe chase thee afar behind;
But if thou catch thy hope, turn back to me,
And play the mother's part, kiss me, be kind:
   So will I pray that thou mayst have thy ' Will,'
   If thou turn back and my loud crying still."

A verse from " The Two Italian Gentlemen ":

  " Lo! here the common fault of love,
    To follow her that flies,
   And fly from her that makes her wail
    With loud lamenting cries."

The punning " Will " Sonnets which have been
so often read as indicating the patron as well as the
poet, under the name of " Will," if properly analyzed, clearly prove the falsity of this reading. No
other wills than the poet's name and the woman's
individual " will " are indicated.

The 153d and 154th Sonnets, while probably connected with this series, are very evidently mere poetic exercises and have no particular personal value.

The 145th Sonnet is undoubtedly by some other
hand. Shakespeare certainly did not write it, nor
did anyone to whom the title of poet might be applied: it is possibly a flight of Southampton's own
muse.

The Sonnets to the " dark lady " were produced
at the same period as those to the patron, though

very probably in a more intermittent manner. I am very strongly of the opinion, however, that only a portion of the Sonnets to the " dark lady " have survived, and that many even of the series to the patron have been lost.

At some future date I hope to attempt a rearrangement of the whole series. It will be a comparatively easy matter to replace single Sonnets in their true contexts, but the chronological placing of misplaced groups may be done only inferentially. The theory which I am here evolving, and which will develop more clearly in the next and later chapters, will, however, throw much new light on this problem.

CHAPTER IV.

THE PATRON, AND THE RIVAL POET OF THE SONNETS.

WE have no record that any other noblemen than
Pembroke, his brother Montgomery, and Southampton, ever gave what might be called " patronage " to Shakespeare. The dedications to " Venus
and Adonis " and " Lucrece " plainly prove that
Southampton showed him such favor in the years
1593 and 1594.

From a passage in Hemminge and Condell's dedication of the first folio of Shakespeare's plays, " To
the most noble and incomparable paire of brethren,
William, Earle of Pembroke and Philip, Earle of
Montgomery," we may infer that these noblemen,
at some period, gave their countenance to our poet.
The passage to which I refer reads:

" But since your lordships have beene pleas'd to
thinke these trifles some-thing, heeretofore; and
have prosequted both them, and their Author
living, with so much favour: we hope, that (they
out-living him, and he not having the fate, common with some, to be exequutor to his own writings) you will use the like indulgence toward them,
you have done unto their parent."

At the age of eighteen, and in the year 1598, Pembroke first came to Court.

As I shall give fairly conclusive proof that the first seventeen Sonnets, wherein the poet urges his young friend and patron to marry, were written previous to 1595, it may be taken for granted that a youth of fourteen was not addressd. If any of the Sonnets can be proved to have been written very near the same time as " Lucrece," Southampton must necessarily be considered the patron and friend addressed in these Sonnets, when the dedication to " Lucrece " is born in mind.

The dedication to " Lucrece " reads : " The love I dedicate to your Lordship is without end, whereof this pamphlet without beginning is a superfluous moiety. The warrant I have of your honourable disposition, not the worth of my untutored lines, makes it assured of your acceptance. What I have done is yours, what I have to do is yours, being part in all I have devoted yours ; were my worth greater my duty would show greater, meantime as it is, it is bound to your lordship, to whom I wish long life still lengthened with all happiness.

> " Your lordship's in all duty,
> " WILLIAM SHAKESPEARE."

This dedication was prefixed to " Lucrece " and published with it in 1594. In the light of the words, " What I have done is yours, what I have to do is yours, being part in all I have devoted yours," and, if we would credit Shakespeare with even a shred of sincerity, we must admit that the early Sonnets, if they can be proven to have been produced in 1594 or 1595, must also have been addressed to Southampton. If, then, it be admitted that Sonnets written in these years are addressed to Southampton, the later Sonnets of the patron series, 100 to 125, must necessarily be addressed to the same person when we consider their internal evidence. For instance:

SONNET 102.

" Our love was new, and then but in the spring,
    When I was wont to greet it with my lays," etc.

SONNET 103.

" For to no other pass my verses tend
    Than of your graces and your gifts to tell."

SONNET 104.

" To me, fair friend, you never can be old,
    For as you were when first your eye I eyed.
    Such seems your beauty still. Three winters
        cold
    Have from the forests shook three summers' pride,
    Three beauteous springs to yellow autumn turn'd
    In process of the seasons have I seen,
    Three April perfumes in three hot Junes burn'd
    Since first I saw you fresh, which yet are
        green," etc.

SONNET 105.

" Let not my love be call'd idolatry,
  Nor my beloved as an idol show,
  Since all alike my songs and praises be
  To one, of one, still such and ever so," etc.

SONNET 108.

" What's in the brain that ink may character
  Which hath not figured to thee my true spirit?
  What's new to speak, what new to register,
  That may express my love, or thy dear merit?
  Nothing, sweet boy; but yet, like prayers divine,
  Counting no old thing old, thou mine, I thine.
  Even as when first I hallowed thy fair name,"
      etc.

These extracts prove very clearly that the Sonnets
from which they are taken were written to the same
person to whom the earlier Sonnets were addressed.

In order to approximate the dates for the production of the Sonnets, and admitting that Southampton was the patron addressed, it is necessary to
consider the earlier dedications of " Venus and
Adonis " and " Lucrece " to this nobleman.

In 1593 the first fruits of Shakespeare's pen were
given to the world. No atom of proof exists to
show that, previous to the publication of " Venus
and Adonis," Shakespeare had done any serious
literary work. He was known as an actor, and it
is true, as an actor who had taken upon himself to
revamp the literary work of others, thereby calling

down upon his head, in 1592, the spleen of Robert Greene; but that he had no established fame as a writer, though considerable reputation as an actor, both Greene's attack and Greene's publisher's apology go to show.

Robert Greene died in September, 1592. The last thing he wrote, "A Groat's-worth of Wit Bought with a Million of Repentance," which he addressed to certain fellow-writers for the stage, contained what has been recognized as a spiteful attack upon Shakespeare. Greene warns his fellows to "beware of puppets that speak from our mouths and of antics garnisht with our colours," and speaks of "a certain upstart crow beautified with our feathers, that with his 'tygers hart wrapt in a players hide' supposes he is as well able to bumbast out a blank verse as the rest of you, and being an absolute Johannes factotum, is, in his own conceit, the only Shake-scene in a countrie," etc. The words "tygers hart wrapt in a players hide" parody a line from "Henry VI.," "Oh Tiger's heart wrapt in a woman's hide," and the words "Shake-scene" is evidently intended as a play upon the name of Shakespeare and an indication of his profession. Some time later Greene's publisher, Henry Chettle, published an apology for Greene's attack, in a preface to his book, "Kinde Hartes Dream." He writes: "I am as sory as if the originall fault had beene my fault, because myself hath seene his demeanour no lesse civill than he excellent in the qualitie he professes, besides divers of worship have reported his uprightnes of dealing, which argues his honesty, and his facetious grace in writing that approves his art."

While both this attack and this apology prove that Shakespeare, at that period, had tried his hand at the drama, it also proves that he had, as yet, no established place as a dramatist, but was recognized as "excellent in the qualitie he professes," that is, the actor's profession. Greene's umbrage was taken largely at the fact that one of Shakespeare's profession should attempt to encroach upon the dramatist's domain.

There are good grounds for believing that Shakespeare, at this period, had tried his hand in improving some old historical plays. In the three plays treating of the reign of Henry VI. his touch is plainly to be seen, but criticism has long ago settled that in these works he only amended and revised; therefore, when he, in his dedication to " Venus and Adonis," plainly avows that poem to be " the first heir of my invention," I am inclined to take him at his word. The Sonnets were certainly not written previously, as both these words and the general tone of the dedication prove; in fact, the distant and respectful air of this dedication precludes any previous intimacy and perhaps even acquaintance between Shakespeare and Southampton. Next year, in 1594, " Lucrece " was published, and dedicated to the same nobleman in a more assured tone, proving that the dedication of the previous poem had been accepted in a friendly spirit by the patron, and also plainly showing that the poet had in some manner been rewarded for his labor; but even this dedication does not show a very intimate acquaintance; the words of the dedication "the warrant I have of your honourable disposition," while conveying a suggestion of benefits received, have yet only the manner of a poet to a patron: it is but reasonable to assume, however, that a more intimate acquaintance soon followed the second dedication. It is to this period, then, that I assign the first sonnet-sequence. This is the season in their friendship spoken of in one of the later Sonnets as

"When first your eye I eyed."

This first sonnet-sequence was evidently finished towards the end of 1593, or early in 1594. In these Sonnets we find the poet urging his young patron to marry: these admonitions, however, break off suddenly in the 17th Sonnet, and in the 18th and 19th Sonnets the poet promises the immortality which his pen shall achieve; a strain which runs thereafter through the whole of the remainder of the series to the patron. When we recall the fact that, late in 1594, Southampton became enamored of Elizabeth Vernon, whom he married four years later, the reason for the cessation of the theme of the first seventeen Sonnets becomes apparent. The date which I assign for the first sonnet-sequence (1593 to 1594), coupled with the internal evidence we find in some of the later Sonnets,—where a three-years' term is given for the friendship,— brings the beginning of the latest series, from 100

to 125, to the end of 1597 or the early part of 1598.
The intermediate series, Nos. 20 to 99, must, therefore, have been written between the spring of 1594
and the end of 1597. The last series, from 100 to
125, however, show that there has been a period of
silence and perhaps estrangement between Shakespeare and his friend: the lines in the 100th Sonnet,

" Where art thou, Muse, that thou forget'st so long
    To speak of that which gives thee all thy might? "

And,

" Rise, resty Muse, my love's sweet face survey
    If time have any wrinkle graven there,"

seem to indicate that the period of silence has been
rather longer than between any of the previous
groups of Sonnets. I would place the duration of
this silence at from nine to twelve months, and believe the Sonnets written last, preceding this
silence, to be the series from 86 to 96, in which he
refers to the growing coldness of his friend. The
canzonette, No. 126, was appended as L'Envoi, in
all likelihood, to this series, as I have previously
suggested.

The " rival poet " is the central figure in the
series from the 78th to 86th Sonnet, and from the
86th to 96th there is evidence of a growing coldness, caused, no doubt, by Chapman's supposed success with Shakespeare's patron. In Sonnet 86 appears the indication which, Professor Minto conjectured, pointed at Chapman as the rival. I shall

take this matter up and discuss it fully in another chapter.

In assigning this chronology to the Sonnets, I was for a while nonplused by the 107th. Mr. Gerald Massey's suggestion, that this was Shakespeare's gratulation upon the liberation of Southampton in 1603, after his three-years' imprisonment under Elizabeth, fitted so well into the apparent meaning of the words that for some time I accepted it as true, yet all my data and inferences pointed so clearly to the years 1593-1594 to 1599, for the period of the Sonnets, that I could not imagine Shakespeare, after several years' disuse of this form of verse, returning to it to write one gratulatory Sonnet.

Upon examining this Sonnet and its context closely, I am quite convinced that Mr. Massey's conjecture is wrong. When properly analyzed the 107th Sonnet will be seen to be a part of a sequence and closely connected in sense and imagery with 104, 106, and 108: the 104th Sonnet ends with these lines:

" Ah, yet doth beauty, like a dial hand,
  Steal from his figure, and no pace perceived;
  So your sweet hue, which methinks still doth
          stand,
  Hath motion, and mine eye may be deceived:
      For fear of which, hear this, thou age unbred;
      Ere you were born was beauty's summer dead."

Sonnet 106 commences with the lines:

" When in the chronicle of wasted time
I see descriptions of the fairest wights,
And beauty making beautiful old rhyme
In praise of ladies dead and lovely knights,
Then in the blazon of sweet beauty's best,
Of hand, of foot, of lip, of eye, of brow,
I see their antique pen would have express'd
Even such a beauty as your master now.
So all their praises are but prophecies
Of this our time, all you prefiguring."

Sonnet 107 begins, " Not mine own *fears.*"
Compare with Sonnet 104, " *For fear* of which,"
etc.

Sonnet 107 continues:

> " *Nor the prophetic soul*
> *Of the wide world dreaming on things to come.*"

Compare this with Sonnet 106:

" So all their praises are *but prophecies*
Of this our time, all you prefiguring."

Sonnet 107 continues:

" Can yet the lease of my true love control,
Supposed as forfeit to a confined doom."

Compare with 104:

> " Hear this, thou age
> unbred;
> *Ere you were born was beauty's summer dead.*"

This comparison clearly proves that Sonnet 107 is not an aftergrowth, but an integral part of this sequence. The remaining lines of this Sonnet—

" The mortal moon hath her eclipse endured,
  And the sad augurs mock their own presage;
  Incertainties now crown themselves assured,
  And peace proclaims olives of endless age.
  Now with the drops of this most balmy time
  My love looks fresh, and Death to me subscribes,
  Since, spite of him, I'll live in this poor rhyme,
  While he insults o'er dull and speechless tribes:
    And thou in this shalt find thy monument,
    When tyrants' crests and tombs of brass are
      spent "—

very evidently refer, as suggested by Mr. Thomas Tyler, to the Peace of Vervins, which definitely put an end to the designs of Spain against England and Elizabeth, which had threatened for many years.

If the line,

" The mortal moon hath her eclipse endured,"

be accepted as referring to Queen Elizabeth, it takes on strong significance from the fact that a dangerous conspiracy against the life of Elizabeth was nipped in the bud just at this time: two men, Edward Squire and Richard Walpole, being executed after a full confession of the plot.

That the dates which I have suggested for the Sonnets have very strong circumstantial evidence, I believe all students of the Sonnets will agree, but

I shall now produce some new facts which will more definitely prove the truth of my contention.

In the 20th and 21st Sonnets I have found a clew which not only leads to a full identification of Chapman as the " rival poet," but gives us also a settled date for those two Sonnets which enables us to work out dates for the production of the whole of the remainder of the series, and incidentally, for several of the plays.

I believe I may state positively that these Sonnets were written in 1595,—they certainly could not have been written before that date,—and that they were not written later, other satirical strokes made by Shakespeare against Chapman—which I shall show—fully prove.

A very casual reading of these two Sonnets will show that they are connected one with the other. There are few of the Sonnets which have puzzled critics more than these; the most far-fetched explanations have been given for them, and extraordinary theories built upon them. Tyrwhitt suggested that the elusive " Mr. W. H.," of Thorpe's dedication, was a Mr. Wm. Hughes, taking the seventh line of the 20th Sonnet,

"A man in hew, all 'hews' in his controlling,"

as his key. From the fact that the word " hues " is spelled " Hews " in Thorpe's edition and that it is put in italics and inclosed between inverted commas, we may, in the light of the proof that Southampton is addressed infer two things: one,

Hew, a stroke of an axe

that Shakespeare intended this as an anagram for the initials of Southampton's name and title, Henry Wriothesley, Earl of Southampton, and the other, that Thorpe, however he came by them, worked from Shakespeare's original manuscripts. The making of anagrams was a common practice with the writers of that period; even Chapman indulges in it, as the following forced and stupid transposition of the name and title of the Earl of Salisbury proves.

" Robert Cecyl, Earle of Salisburye.
Curb foes; thy care, is all our erly be."

This Sonnet also mystified Coleridge, who believed that the whole series of Sonnets from 1 to 154 were addressed by the poet to his mistress, and supposed that the term " master-mistress " in the second line, and the references to a man contained in the seventh line, were introduced as a blind, to hide this supposed fact. Professor Dowden suggested that in the 21st Sonnet Shakespeare satirizes the extravagant conceits of such sonneteers as Daniels, Barnes, Constable, and Griffin. Mr. Wyndham is the only critic who has recognized the fact that Shakespeare in this Sonnet clearly indicates one, and not a number of poets. The concluding couplet of this Sonnet,

" Let them say more that like of hearsay well;
I will not praise that purpose not to sell,"

has proved a stumbling block to all commentators,

misleading one careful and conservative critic, who
supposes that the poet protests that he will not sell
his friend.

Let us now consider this Sonnet critically:

> "So is it not with me as with that <u>Muse</u>
> Stirr'd by a <u>painted beau</u>ty to his verse,
> Who heaven itself for ornament doth use
> And every fair with his fair doth rehearse,
> Making a couplement of proud compare,
> With sun and moon, with earth and sea's rich
>   gems,
> With April's first-born flowers and all things rare
> That heaven's air in this huge rondure hems."

[handwritten marginal notes: Spenser / Queen E. / play on fair & fairy / See The Faerie Queen 1st bk. / The Shepheards Calender April – Specially dedicated to Queen E.]

The words, "that Muse," very distinctly indicate one poet, and not a number of poets. This
"Muse," being "stirr'd by a painted beauty to his
verse," uses "heaven itself for ornament" and compares his mistress with the glories he beholds there;
couples her with the "sun and moon, with earth
and sea's rich gems"; with April's flowers and all
the rarities of the displayed universe. Shakespeare
then protests against such inordinate comparison
in the following lines:

> "O let me, true in love, but truly write,
> And then believe me, my love is as fair
> As any mother's child, though not so bright
> As those gold candles fix'd in heaven's air."

What does Shakespeare here mean by the expression "those gold candles fix'd in heaven's air"?

The only heavenly lights previously alluded to in the Sonnet are the sun and moon; he certainly would not refer to these bodies as "candles." He then very evidently indicates something mentioned by the "Muse" whom he attacks.

In the concluding couplet,

"Let them say more that like of hearsay well;
I will not praise that purpose not to sell,"

he indicates the fact that this poet has attempted to lay some bases for hearsay, that is, reputation or fame; and he protests that he will not make such claims for his own verse, as it is not written for sale.

It is little wonder that critics have failed to see the true sense of these last two lines, for, without knowing the object indicated or attacked, they are inscrutable.

Some years ago I came to the conclusion that Shakespeare in this Sonnet attacked some one poem and poet; and the minute descriptive details of the poem, which he gives us in the Sonnet, inclined me to hope that that poet might be identified. I accordingly began a systematic reading of Elizabethan verse, to, if possible, find the poem so plainly described. Being struck by the plausibility of Professor Minto's suggestion regarding Chapman, it occurred to me that that poet might also be referred to in this Sonnet. I had scarcely commenced a reading of Chapman's miscellaneous poems when I found, not only what I sought, but even stronger and more interesting evidence connecting that poet with Shakespeare.

A poem published by Chapman in 1595, called "*The Amorous Zodiac,*" *is unquestionably the poem indicated by Shakespeare in the 21st Sonnet.* In that poem Chapman, addressing his mistress, or, as is much more likely, his imaginary mistress, in thirty verses compares and couples her beauties with the signs of the Zodiac, as representing the months of the year; endowing her with all the graces of the seasons and the glories of the heavens.

If the first eight or ten verses of this poem be compared with the first eight lines of the 21st Sonnet, my contention will be fully justified, but should anyone still doubt, when the last four lines of the Sonnet are compared with L'Envoi of the poem, all doubts will cease. To make the Sonnet match the poem, it is not necessary to pick and choose verses or lines; the sequence of ideas between the poem and the critique runs plainly, from beginning to end.

I shall quote enough of this poem to prove the truth of my argument.

"THE AMOROUS ZODIAC.

I.

" I never see the sun but suddenly
　My soul is moved with spite and jealousy
　Of his high bliss, in his sweet course discern'd:
　And am displeased to see so many signs,
　As the bright sky unworthily divines,
　Enjoy an honour they have never earn'd.

II.

" To think heaven decks with such a beauteous
  show,
  A harp, a ship, a serpent, or a crow ;
  And such a crew of creatures of no prices,
  But to excite in us th' unshamefaced flames,
  With which, long since, Jove wrong'd so many
  dames,
  Reviving in his rule their names and vices.

III.

" Dear mistress, whom the gods bred here below,
  T' express their wondrous power, and let us
  know
  That before thee they nought did perfect make ;
  Why may not I—as in those signs, the sun—
  Shine in thy beauties, and as roundly run,
  To frame, like him, an endless Zodiac.

IV.

" With thee I'll furnish both the year and sky,
  Running in thee my course of destiny :
  And thou shalt be the rest of all my moving,
  But of thy numberless and perfect graces,
  To give my moons their full in twelve months'
  spaces,
  I choose but twelve in guerdon of my loving.

V.

" Keeping even way through every excellence,
  I'll make in all an equal residence
  Of a new Zodiac ; a new Phœbus guising.

When, without altering the course of nature,
I'll make the seasons good, and every creature
Shall henceforth reckon day, from my first rising.

VI.

" To open then the spring-time's golden gate,
And flower my race with ardour temperate,
I'll enter by thy head and have for house
In my first month, this heaven Ram-curled tress,
Of which Love as his charm-chains doth address,
A sign fit for a spring so beauteous.

VII.

"Lodged in that fleece of hair, yellow and curl'd,
I'll take high pleasure to enlight the world,
And fetter me in gold, thy crisps implies
Earth, at this spring, spongy and languorsome
With envy of our joys in love become,
Shall swarm with flowers, and air with painted
    flies.

VIII.

" Thy smooth embow'd brow, where all grace I see,
My second month, and second house shall be;
Which brow with her clear beauties shall delight
The Earth, yet sad, and overture confer
To herbs, buds, flowers and verdure-gracing Ver,
Rendering her more than summer exquisite.

IX.

" All this fresh April, this sweet month of Venus.
I will admire this brow so bounteous;
This brow, brave court of love and virtue builded;

This brow, where chastity holds garrison;
This brow, that blushless none can look upon,
This brow, with every grace and honour gilded,"
      etc., etc.

These verses compared with the following lines
from the Sonnet plainly reveal the parallel:

" So it is not with me as with that Muse
Stirr'd by a painted beauty to his verse,
Who heaven itself for ornament doth use
And every fair with his fair doth rehearse,
Making a couplement of proud compare.
With sun and moon, with earth and seas' rich
      gems,
With April's first-born flowers, and all things rare
That heaven's air in this huge rondure hems."

Chapman ends his poem with two verses as
L'Envoi, as follows:

L'ENVOI.

XXIX.

" Dear mistress, if poor wishes heaven would hear,
I would not choose the empire of the water;
The empire of the air, nor of the earth,
But endlessly my course of life confining,
In this fair Zodiac for ever shining.
And with thy beauties make me endless mirth.

XXX.

" But, gracious love, if jealous heaven deny
My life this truly blest variety,

Yet will I thee through all the world disperse;
If not in heaven, *amongst those braving fires,*
Yet here thy beauties, which the world admires,
Bright as those flames shall glister in my verse."

If these two verses be compared with the following six lines from the 21st Sonnet the whole parallel
will be seen to be complete:

" O, let me, true in love, but truly write,
And then believe me, my love is as fair
As any mother's child, *though not so bright
As those gold candles fix'd in heaven's air.*
Let them say more that like of hearsay well;
I will not praise that purpose not to sell."

This latter comparison, not only clearly shows
to what Shakespeare refers as " those gold candles
fix'd in heaven's air " but plainly reveals his stroke
at Chapman's vanity and self-praise, and also proves
what I have previously asserted—that Shakespeare
here avows that his Sonnets were not written for
sale.

The thrust which Shakespeare in this Sonnet
makes at Chapman's laudation of his own work,
and his mercenary motives, he repeats several
times both in " Love's Labor's Lost " and in
" Troilus and Cressida."

Though I find that Shakespeare in several other
Sonnets seems to indicate or parody other poets and
their poems, as in the sonnets of Constable and
Griffin already quoted, in none of them do I find the
unmistakable animus which is noticeable in nearly

all Sonnets, and in many passages in his plays, where he refers to Chapman. Why this hostility?

All students of the Sonnets will agree with me when I say that Shakespeare's personality, as we find it there revealed, is of much too magnanimous and gentle a spirit to gratuitously assail a fellow poet with such bitterness as we find in many passages indicating Chapman. This caustic tone displayed in some of the Sonnets, and even more strongly in the two plays I have mentioned, certainly bespeaks provocation. The mere fact that Chapman sought Southampton's patronage would not alone justify it, if at all: many other contemporary poets sunned themselves in the beams of this young Mæcenas' eye without adverse comment from Shakespeare. The poems of Barnes, Barnfield, and Nash addressed to Southampton prove this; we must, therefore, seek farther for the cause of this hostility; for that there was a decidedly bitter feeling between Chapman and Shakespeare from the very beginning of their recorded contemporary careers, and that each at various times, in prose and verse, sometimes very openly, and often covertly, attacked the other, I shall show so conclusively that I do not think any critic who follows my argument will dispute it.

The beginning of this enmity possibly antedates any plain record which we have of the work of either poet, but that the onus of it lay with Chapman I am prone to believe, from the mass of evidence which I find of this strange man's envious disposition and cantankerous temper. The latest thing which we have from his pen, written during his last illness and left incomplete at his death, is a virulent and vulgar attack upon his erstwhile friend and champion, Ben Jonson.

The overweening pride of learning and scholastic conceit with which Chapman was filled, and which marks and mars nearly all his original work, made him look with disdain upon aspirants for literary honors who were of less erudition. This disdain developed into stormy and rancorous abuse, when confronted by the success and popularity achieved by one of Shakespeare's comparatively limited scholastic attainments. His abuse reflects, not only upon what he is pleased to call Shakespeare's "ignorance and impiety," but also upon his supposed servility to patrons. A hundred years and over of painstaking research has failed to reveal that Shakespeare ever sought patronage, except in the case of Southampton, and then only in the earliest stage of his literary career: that he had some benefit, material and otherwise, of this patronage, we have good reason for believing, but that he made his own way in the world, by hard and consistent work, unflagging industry, and careful business methods, we have proof more than sufficient. Far otherwise with Chapman.

Mr. Swinburne, in his analytic and comprehensive introduction to Chapman's miscellaneous and dramatic works, says: "It has been remarked by editors and biographers, that between the years 1574 (at or about which date, according to Anthony Wood, he being well grounded in school learning was sent to the University) and 1594, when he published his first poem, we have no trace or hint to guide us, in conjecturing how his life was spent between the ages of fifteen and thirty-five. This latter age is the least he can have attained, by any computation, at the time when he put forth his 'Shadow of Night,' full of loud and angry complaints of neglect and slight, endured at the hands of an unthankful and besotted generation." Thus, in the year 1594, Chapman first comes into our ken, a rancorous and disgruntled man, and though, in the ensuing years, he accomplished great work in his Homeric translations, and also attained some meed of fame both as a dramatist and a poet, we find him to the last a very Timon in misanthropy. Not only in his prose and verse dedications does he rail against his rivals and curse his fate, but even in the poems for which the dedications are written he strays again and again from his subject to indulge in like abuse and railing. The history of English verse does not reveal in any other poet the self-consciousness manifested by Chapman in his poems; nor do we find in the work of any other poet or dramatist the absolute effacement of self exhibited by Chapman's great rival: were it not for the Sonnets, and the light which they throw upon some of his plays, his personality would be quite hidden.

Though we see that Chapman dedicates his earlier poems of 1594 and 1595 to men of learning and fellow-writers, and not to men of place and wealth, both the tone of these dedications, and internal evidence in these poems, prove that this was more from necessity than virtue. In " Ovid's Banquet of Sense," dedicated to his friend Matthew Royden, he breaks clean away from his subject to mourn his state, thus :

" In these dog-days how this contagion smothers
The purest blood with virtues diet fined,
Nothing their own, unless they be some other's
Spite of themselves, are in themselves confined,
And live so poor they are of all despised,
Their gifts held down with scorn should be di-
      vined,
And they like mummers mask, unknown, unprized :
A thousand marvels mourn in some such breast,
Would make a kind and worthy patron blest."

Even in his earliest published poem,—" The Shadow of Night " (1594),—which is also dedicated to Royden, he in many passages sounds the same doleful note. " A Coronet for his Mistress Philosophy " is nothing but lament for his friendless condition, and splenetic abuse of a more fortunate poet. There is scarcely an original poem by Chapman in which this mournful and abusive tone cannot be found. Even in his " Hymn to Christ upon the Cross " it reveals itself, and it is strange that he can abstain from it in his translations.

No contemporary poet so persistently supplicated patronage, yet none are so bitter and envious towards others who sought it and were successful. In later years we find him not too particular in his choice of patrons, so that they were men of position or wealth. He dedicated "Andromeda Liberata" most fulsomely to the notorious Carr, Earl of Somerset, and his still more notorious wife; in fact, it was written expressly for their nuptials and made Chapman the laughing-stock of the day. In the light of all this, I am inclined to take his strictures upon other poets who sought the patronage of the great with a grain of salt, and to impute his choler to plain envy of their success.

His early attacks upon Shakespeare, which I shall demonstrate later on, in all probability arose from this source, and possibly initiated the feud between them; his later attacks clearly reveal jealousy, not only of Shakespeare's literary reputation, but also of his increase in estate and wealth, and were no doubt intensified in virulence by the retaliatory measures adopted by our poet.

In Shakespeare's early rejoinders I notice rather an amused disdain than bitterness; in only one instance in his early retorts do I find bitterness, and this touch seems to refer to some smallness or treachery on the part of Chapman, which antedates the period at which our history of the enmity begins, or else it was introduced at a later date by Shakespeare, upon his revision of the play in which I find it. In "Love's Labor's Lost," in the gulling by Biron and his friends of the actors in the "Nine Worthies," the wit expended upon all the characters, except that which Holofernes personates, is of rather a playful and harmless nature; in the gibes directed at Holofernes, however, a most distinctly bitter and personal tone is discernible, and references are made that are entirely without point unless they refer to something not revealed in the play. That Chapman is pilloried in the character of Holofernes and that his ideas and theories are attacked and expressly mentioned in the play, I believe I can prove.

Chapman's "Amorous Zodiac," which Shakespeare attacks in the 21st Sonnet, was published in 1595 along with "Ovid's Banquet of Sense" and "A Coronet for his Mistress Philosophy." I shall in the next chapter prove that Shakespeare indicates and attacks these three poems, and shall also show that he attacks the theories evolved by Chapman in a poem published in the previous year, called "The Shadow of Night." In a still later chapter I shall show the reasons for Shakespeare's attacks, in the covert aspersions which Chapman casts at him in these poems and their dedications. I will show a renewal of this hostility a year or two later, when Chapman again seeks the favor of Southampton, to father the publication of his first Homeric translations, giving both Shakespeare's attacks and Chapman's rejoinders, and finally shall reveal a new outburst of this latent hostility on both sides, in the year 1609, and in this way not only cast a new light upon many of the Sonnets, "Love's Labor's Lost," and "Troilus and Cressida," but shall set a definite date for their production and forever place beyond cavil the value of the personal theory of the Sonnets.

CHAPTER V.

IT has been usual, with Shakespearean critics, to
assign a much earlier date for the production of
" Love's Labor's Lost" than that for which I
shall now contend.   Many writers place it in 1591,
and others have given it even an earlier date.

The earliest known publication of this play is the
quarto of 1598.   The earliest known references to
it are also in this year.   Meres mentions it with several other plays in his " Palladis Tamia," and an
obscure contemporary poet,—Robert Tofte,—alludes to it in one of his verses.   Tofte's reference,
however, is of such a nature as to lead us to infer
that it was not a new publication at the time he
wrote :

" Love's Labor's Lost I once did see, a Play
    Y-cleped so, so called to my pain.
Which I to hear to my small joy did stay,
Giving attendance on my froward Dame :
    My misgiving mind presaging to me ill,
    Yet was I drawn to see it 'gainst my will.

" Each actor played in cunning wise his part,
But chiefly those entrapped in Cupid's snare ;
Yet all was feigned, 'twas not from the heart,
They seemed to grieve, but yet they felt no care :

'Twas I that grief (indeed) did bear in breast,
The others did but make a show in jest." *

Many commentators are of the opinion that this
play is Shakespeare's earliest complete dramatic
effort; it is certainly, I believe, one of his earliest
comedies. I have already referred to the distinct
assertion which Shakespeare makes in the dedication to " Venus and Adonis," as to that poem being the " first heir " of his " invention." Critics
have usually passed over this plain avowal of the
poet's, alleging that he did not look upon his plays
in this light,—as children of his brain,—as they
were generally built upon plots which he borrowed.
I quite repudiate this view in reference to " Love's
Labor's Lost." Shakespeare undoubtedly amended
old plays by other hands previous to this, but no
proof exists to show that he wrote any complete
original poem or play, previous to the publication
of " Venus and Adonis." If Shakespeare had written " Love's Labor's Lost " before " Venus and
Adonis " he could not truthfully have made the
above-mentioned assertion, as this play is even more
distinctly an heir of his invention than that poem.
The groundwork of " Venus and Adonis," is borrowed from Ovid's " Metamorphoses," while in
Love's Labor's Lost " there is absolutely no plot or
plan to be so borrowed; it has no previously known
basis. Nothing that Shakespeare ever wrote is so
entirely his own as this play. Though he intro-

† " Alba; or, the Month's Mind of a Melancholy Lover," by
Robert Tofte, 1598.

duces a King Ferdinand of Navarre, and names that King's friends after well-known courtiers of Henry of Navarre, there is palpably no real history in the play, and the interest would be equally as great were purely imaginary names used. As a dramatic fiction, " Love's Labor's Lost " is

" Apart from space, withholding time."

It is purely a satirical comedy, in which the whole interest centers in the dialogue, repartee, and satire. The poetry of the play has all the distinguishing features of the early poems and sonnets; the same limpidity of diction and wealth of imagery.

I shall not rehearse the conjectures which are generally used to prove this play an early production, as the data which I shall adduce shall, I believe, place the date of its production beyond conjecture.

" Love's Labor's Lost " was certainly written later than both " Venus and Adonis " and " Lucrece," and also after the first twenty-sonnet sequence, and was very probably produced in 1595.

My reason for giving it this date is that I find it to be a distinct satire upon the theories and ideas set forth by Chapman in the two poems which he published in 1594, called " The Shadow of Night." I would be inclined to date the production of " Love's Labor's Lost " in 1594; after the publication of these poems of Chapman's, but that I find in the play references also to other poems which Chapman published in 1595. It is quite possible, however, that Shakespeare saw these latter poems of

Chapman's in manuscript previous to their publication, as there can be little doubt, from the tone of
the dedication to Matthew Royden, that Chapman
had previously sought other and greater names to
which to dedicate them, and had very probably
made an attempt upon Southampton's favor; in this
event, Shakespeare would probably have seen them
in manuscript; however, even could this be proved,
it would alter the date by only a few months.

It may be said by some who have read my arguments, and agree with the truth of the satire
set forth, that while there is full warrant for assigning the production of the play to a period later than
the poems satirized, there is no such warrant for
placing so definite a date. We know, however,
from Meres' and Tofte's references, that it was produced before 1598, and it shall be very clearly
proved here that it was written later than 1594 or
1595.

These poems of Chapman's which are satirized
were not of sufficient interest to the public for the
satire to be appreciated if produced any considerable time, say a year, after their issue. Shakespeare, no doubt, struck while the iron was hot,
while the reading world was still laboring through
the jumbled construction and cloudy rhetoric of
Chapman's earnest, but distorted and impenetrable
verses, and not yet quite decided whether a rapt and
inspired seer, or a befogged pedant, had appeared
in their midst.

This satire we must impute to the covert slings
and slurs which Chapman makes at Shakespeare in

these same poems. It is not now possible to elucidate all of the satirical points in the play that Shakespeare intended, but there can be little doubt that the playgoing public of that day recognized the full force of the satire, if we, after three hundred years, can find such strong evidence of it.

In "The Shadow of Night" Chapman, in several hundred lines of the most meandering and misty verse, relieved, it is true, by occasional fine lines, endeavors to tell the world some matter of apparently great moment; he incidentally bewails his own woes, and belabors and slangs his rival, as he invariably does in his original poems.

Mr. Swinburne says of this poem: "I sincerely think and hope that no poem with a tithe of its genuine power and merit, was ever written on such a plan or after such a fashion, as 'The Shadow of Night.'

"It is not merely the heavy and convulsive movement of its tangled and jarring sentences, that seem to wheeze and pant at every painful step, the incessant byplay of incongruous digressions and impenetrable allusions, that makes the first reading of this poem as tough and tedious a task for the mind as oakum-picking or stone-breaking can be for the body. Worse than all this is the want of any perceptible center towards which these tangled and raveled lines of thought may seem at last to converge. We see that the author has thought hard and felt deeply; we apprehend that he is charged as it were to the muzzle with some ardent matter of spiritual interest, of which he would fain deliver

He's lost his name

Ah, but once understood what a marvelous historical comment on the time!

himself in explosive eloquence; we perceive that he is angry, ambitious, vehement, and arrogant; no pretender, but a genuine seer, bemused and stifled by the oracular fumes which choke in its very utterance the message they inspire, and forever preclude the seer from becoming properly the prophet of their mysteries. He foams at the mouth with rage through all the flints and pebbles of hard language, which he spits forth, so to say, in the face of 'the prejudicate and peremptory reader' (his own words), whose ears he belabors with 'very bitter words,' not less turgid than were hurled by Pistol at the head of the 'recalcitrant and contumelious' Mistress Tearsheet: nor assuredly had the poet much right to expect that they would be received by the profane multitude with more reverence and humility than was the poetic fury of 'such a fustian rascal' by that 'honest, virtuous, civil gentlewoman.'"

Mr. Swinburne takes leave of this poem saying, that it "is incomprehensible to human apprehension" and that he leaves to others a solution to him insoluble. I do not pretend to have found that which so great a critic has abandoned,—the solution of this poem,—nor do I think it can be found. I apprehend in a general way that Chapman extols learning, philosophy, religion, etc., all of which he clothes with the garb of darkness and the night; that he attacks "the day and all its sweets," gayety, frivolity, lightness of heart, the love of woman, and very especially, what he calls "ignorance." It is rather curious to notice, in all Chapman's attacks

upon Shakespeare, how frequently he indicates him
by these words " ignorance and impiety ": it is also
noticeable that Shakespeare understands the stroke
as meant for him and with sardonic humor accepts
it to himself in some of the Sonnets where he no-
tices Chapman, as, for instance, in Sonnet 78:

" So oft have I invoked thee for my Muse
And found such fair assistance in my verse
As every alien pen hath got my use
And under thee their poesy disperse.
Thine eyes, that taught the dumb on high to sing
And heavy ignorance aloft to fly,
Have added feathers to the learned's wing,
And given grace a double majesty.
Yet be most proud of that which I compile,
Whose influence is thine and born of thee;
In other's work thou dost but mend the style,
And arts with thy sweet graces graced be;
   But thou art all my art, and dost advance
   As high as learning my rude ignorance."

In " Love's Labor's Lost " Shakespeare makes
Ferdinand, King of Navarre, and his lords, steep
their minds in the spirit of " The Shadow of
Night," and makes them swear to eschew, for three
years, all natural pleasures and the society of women, and give themselves up to study, fasting, and
philosophy: but in the character of Biron he introduces the " little rift within the lute "; for Biron,
though swearing as do the others to the vows imposed, mentally resolves to break them at the

first opportunity. Through the mouth of Biron, Shakespeare, I believe, speaks his own views in attacking the unnatural theories of " The School of Night " as set forth by Chapman.

In the pedantry and verbosity of Holofernes he caricatures Chapman's style, and in the person of Holofernes excoriates Chapman himself. He possibly ridicules the Euphuistic School in the character of Armado, and may also give us a caricature of a certain noted character, half wit and half fool, known as the " phantastical monarcho," who frequented London somewhere about this time. I shall confine myself, however, to those parts of the play in which I detect the satire upon Chapman and his theories.

Act I. scene 1 opens with the King addressing his fellow ascetics as follows:

> " *King.* Let fame, that all hunt after in their lives,
> Live register'd upon our brazen tombs,
> And then grace us in the disgrace of death:
> When, spite of cormorant devouring Time,
> The endeavour of this present breath may buy
> That honour which shall bate his scythe's keen edge,
> And make us heirs of all eternity.
> Therefore, brave conquerors,—for so you are
> That war against your own affections
> And the huge army of the world's desires,—
> Our late edict shall strongly stand in force:
> Navarre shall be the wonder of the world;

Our courte shall be a little Academe,
Still and contemplative in living art:
You three, Biron, Dumain, and Longaville,
Have sworn for three years' term to live with me
My fellow-scholars, and to keep those statutes
That are recorded in this schedule here:
Your oaths are pass'd; and now subscribe your
     names,
That his own hand may strike his honour down
That violates the smallest branch herein:
If you are arm'd to do as sworn to do,
Subscribe to your deep oaths, and keep it too.

   "*Long*. I am resolved; 'tis but a three years'
     fast:
The mind shall banquet, though the body pine:
Fat paunches have lean pates; and dainty bits
Make rich the ribs, but bankrupt quite the wits.

   "*Dum*. My loving lord, Dumain is mortified:
The grosser manner of these world's delights
He throws upon the gross world's baser slaves:
To love, to wealth, to pomp, I pine and die;
With all these living in philosophy.

   "*Biron*. I can but say their protestation over;
So much, dear liege, I have already sworn,
That is, to live and study here three years:
But there are other strict observances;
As not to see a woman in that term,
Which I hope well is not enrolled there;
And one day in a week to touch no food,
And but one meal on every day beside,
The which I hope is not enrolled there;
And then, to sleep but three hours in the night,

And not be seen to wink of all the day,—
When I was wont to think no harm all night,
And make a dark night too of half the day,—
Which I hope well is not enrolled there:
O, these are barren tasks, too hard to keep,
Not to see ladies, study, fast, not sleep!

    " *King.* Your oath is pass'd to pass away from
        these.

    " *Biron.* Let me say no, my liege, an if you
        please:
I only swore to study with your grace.
And stay here in your court for three years' space.

    " *Long.* You swore to that, Biron, and to the
        rest,

    " *Biron.* By yea and nay, sir, then I swore in jest,
What is the end of study? let me know.

    " *King.* Why, that to know, which else we
        should not know.

    " *Biron.* Things hid and barr'd, you mean, from
        common sense?

    " *King.* Ay, that is study's god-like recompense.

    " *Biron.* Come on then; I will swear to study so,
To know the thing I am forbid to know:
As thus,—to study where I well may dine,
When I to feast expressly am forbid;
Or study where to meet some mistress fine,
When mistresses from common sense are hid;
Or, having sworn too hard-a-keeping oath,
Study to break it, and not break my troth.
If study's gain be thus, and this be so.
Study knows that which yet it doth not know:
Swear me to this, and I will ne'er say no.

"*King.* These be the stops that hinder study quite,
And train our intellects to vain delight.
"*Biron.* Why, all delights are vain; but that most vain,
Which, with pain purchased, doth inherit pain:
As, painfully to pore upon a book
To seek the light of truth; while truth the while
Doth falsely blind the eyesight of his look:
Light, seeking light, doth light of light beguile:
So, ere you find where light in darkness lies,
Your light grows dark by losing of your eyes.
Study me how to please the eye indeed,
By fixing it upon a fairer eye;
Who dazzling so, that eye shall be his heed,
And give him light that it was blinded by.
Study is like the heaven's glorious sun,
That will not be deep-search'd with saucy looks;
Small have continual plodders ever won,
Save base authority from others' books.
These earthly godfathers of heaven's lights,
That give a name to every fixed star,
Have no more profit of their shining nights
Than those that walk and wot not what they are.
Too much to know, is to know nought but fame;
And every godfather can give a name."

All this points most palpably to the earnest, though
vague and impossible, theories set forth by Chapman in " The Shadow of Night "; the learning and
philosophy which he there endeavors to extol is
most certainly " hid and barr'd from common

sense "; it is so filled also with phrases and similies borrowed from obscure classics, with what Biron calls,

> " Base authority from others' books,"

that Chapman, conscious of their obscurity, and to explain the borrowed conceits, appends a glossary which often but makes the darkness darker. In both of these " Hymns," but especially in the second one, " Hymnus in Cynthiam," as he calls it, he rolls off the names of the stars and constellations with great glibness and volubility, and sometimes, not content with one name, gives us several for the same heavenly body: for the moon he gives us " Cynthia, Lucinia, Ilythia, Prothyrea, Diana, Luna, and Hecate," proving himself a veritable

> " Earthly godfather of heaven's lights."

So, all through this play, such hints and parallels are numerous. In the first passage in Act IV. scene 3, where Biron,—at the invitation of the King and his fellows who have fallen away from their vows,—to prove their " loving lawful " and their " faith not torn,"—speaks for over eighty lines in praise of love and light and a joyous life, Shakespeare brings his heavy guns to bear upon the gloomy brotherhood of night, and in two lines in particular unmistakably paraphrases two of Chapman's own lines, clearly indicating him and his theories as the object of his attack. I shall quote a few lines of Biron's speech and a few from " The

Shadow of Night," to show the antithesis and the paraphrase:

> "*Biron.* But love, first learned in a lady's eyes,
> Lives not alone immured in the brain;
> But, with the motion of all elements,
> Courses as swift as thought in every power,
> And gives to every power a double power,
> Above their functions and their offices.
> It adds a precious seeing to the eye;
> A lover's eyes will gaze an eagle blind;
> A lover's ear will hear the lowest sound,
> When the suspicious head of theft is stopp'd:
> Love's feeling is more soft and sensible
> Than are the tender horns of cockled snails;
> Love's tongue proves dainty Bacchus gross in
>   taste:
> For valour, is not Love a Hercules,
> Still climbing trees in the Hesperides?
> Subtle as Sphinx; as sweet and musical
> As bright Apollo's lute, strung with his hair;
> And when Love speaks, the voice of all the gods
> Make heaven drowsy with the harmony.
> Never durst poet touch a pen to write
> Until his ink were temper'd with Love's sighs."

Chapman's " Shadow of Night ":

> " Since day, or light, in any quality,
> For earthly uses do but serve the eye;
> And since the eye's most quick and dangerous use,
> Enflames the heart, and learns the soul abuse;
> Since mournings are preferr'd to banquettings,

And they reach heaven, bred under sorrow's
    wings;
Since Night brings terror to our frailties still,
And shameless Day doth marble us in ill,
All you possess'd with indepressed spirits,
Endued with nimble, and aspiring wits,
Come consecrate with me to sacred Night
Your whole endeavours, and detest the light.
No pen can anything eternal write,
That is not steep'd in humour of the Night."

In these two extracts, as in numerous others I
could quote, a very plain antithesis is seen, but I
have selected this particular passage from Chapman
for comparison, because it contains even more than
antithesis; if the two last lines of each of these extracts be compared, paraphrase also is plainly discernible, in which Shakespeare refutes Chapman in
almost his own words.

Chapman:

" No pen can anything eternal write
That is not steep'd in humour of the Night."

Shakespeare:

" Never durst poet touch a pen to write
Until his ink were temper'd with Love's sighs."

Another palpable proof of the truth of my contention I will adduce; one which did not occur to me
till long after I had become possessed of the idea,
but which lends it strong confirmatory evidence.

In working out the proof of my theory I have

kept by me, for reference, Mr. Halliwell-Phillipps'
facsimile reprint of the first folio of Shakespeare's
plays.

In Act IV. scene 3 Biron, praising the beauty of
Rosaline, who is represented as being of dark complexion, says:

"*Biron.*   Where is a book?
That I may swear beauty doth beauty lack,
If that she learn not of her eyes to look:
No face is fair that is not full so black.
"*King.* O paradox! Black is the badge of hell,
The hue of dungeons, and the school of night."

This expression "*the school of night*" has always puzzled commentators, and appeared to all of
them so senseless that, to give meaning to an apparently meaningless line, the following emenda-
tions have, at different times, been proposed:
"scowl of night," "shade of night," "seal of
night," "scroll of night," "shroud of night," "soul
of night," "stole of night." The Cambridge editors have proposed "shoote of night" for "suit."
None of these changes add a particularly strong
meaning to the line, nor give a fit figure to the expression, and it appears very patent to me that this
is one of the many instances in which Shakespeare,
since the days of Steevens and Malone, has been
misimproved by the critics. The reading of this
line as it appears in the first folio, and also in the
first quarto, in the light of my theory, as referring
to the ideas of Chapman evolved in " The Shadow

of Night," is full of pith and point. To show the
aptness of this phrase in this connection I shall
quote a few extracts from this extraordinary poem:

" Since day, or light, in any quality,
   For earthly uses do but serve the eye;
   And since the eye's most quick and dangerous
      use,
   Enflames the heart, and learns the soul abuse;
   Since mournings are preferred to banquettings,
   And they reach heaven, bred under sorrow's
      wings;
   Since Night brings terror to our frailties still,
   And shameless Day doth marble us in ill,
   All you possess'd with indepressed spirits,
   Endued with nimble, and aspiring wits,
   Come consecrate with me to sacred Night
   Your whole endeavours, and detest the light.
   No pen can anything eternal write.
   That is not steep'd in humour of the Night."

" Day of deep students, most contentful night."

" Men's faces glitter, and their hearts are black,
   But thou (great mistress of heaven's gloomy rack)
   Art black in face, and glitter'st in thy heart."

" Rich-taper'd sanctuary of the blest,
   Palace of ruth, made all of tears, and rest,
   To thy black shades and desolation
   I consecrate my life."

" Ye living spirits then, if any live,
    Whom like extremes do like affections give,
    Shun, shun this cruel light, and end your thrall,
    In these soft shades of sable funeral."

" Kneel then with me, fall wormlike on the ground,
    And from the infectious dunghill of this round,
    From men's brass wits and golden foolery,
    Weep, weep your souls, into felicity:
    Come to the house of mourning, serve the Night
    To whom pale Day . . .
    Is but a drudge," etc., etc.

There is certainly a distinct enough mental pose exhibited in this poem, as shown in these selections, to warrant the application of the word " school," and Chapman so often applies the word " black " in his praise of the night as sovereign and mistress of his philosophy, that the full gist of Shakespeare's reference becomes clear when we transpose the line and give the plain prose meaning: black is the hue of the school of night.

Though Shakespeare attacks Chapman as the spokesman of this " School of Night " and the most eloquent exponent of its theories, there were, no doubt, others like Chapman, so filled with the pride of " The New Learning " that they could see little merit in the literary production of one of Shakespeare's " Smalle Latine and lesse Greeke," and who, in all probability, took sides with Chapman in this dispute. Years after Shakespeare's death we find Ben Jonson, himself a scholar of even greater parts than Chapman, defending himself from the accusation of having attempted to belittle Shakespeare. We may, then, assume that the rivalry and hostility between Chapman and Shakespeare was no hidden thing, but well known to the literary world, and that each poet had his friends and champions, the scholastic element, to a large extent, probably siding with Chapman. The term " school of night," then, while plainly indicating Chapman and his poems, evidently embraced those others of like views who, while not openly attacking Shakespeare as does Chapman, may have given their countenance to that poet's invectives.

In Ben Jonson's allusions to Shakespeare's " Smalle Latine and lesse Greeke " in his verses prefixed to the first folio some critics have found what they have conceived to be a recrudescent glimmer of Jonson's alleged enmity to Shakespeare during our poet's life. While Jonson and Shakespeare may at times have crossed swords during the period in which Jonson collaborated in dramatic work with Shakespeare's arch-enemy Chapman, they were never really bad friends in the sense that Chapman and Shakespeare were, but it is well known that Jonson and Chapman were for many years at daggers drawn, and we know that the last thing to which Chapman put his hand, and which was left unfinished by his death, was a bitter attack upon Jonson. With the knowledge of Chapman's enmity to Shakespeare in mind, added to the fact that, in 1623 (the date of the issue of the first folio), Jonson and Chapman were avowed enemies, Jonson's allusion to Shakespeare's " Smalle Latine and lesse Greeke " takes on quite a new significance. Let us examine the lines:

" And though thou had'st small Latin, and less
   Greek,
 From thence to honour thee I would not seek
 For names; but call forth thundering Æschylus,
 Euripides, and Sophocles to us;
 Pacuvius, Accius, him of Cordova, dead,
 To life again, to hear thy buskin tread
 And shake a stage: or, when thy socks were on,
 Leave thee alone, for the comparison
 Of all that insolent Greece, or haughty Rome,
 Sent forth, or since did from their ashes come."

Here Jonson, while admitting to the full the charge which Chapman constantly brings against Shakespeare, *i. e.,* his ignorance of the classics, yet challenges for Shakespeare a comparison with the best dramatic writers that Rome or Greece produce and with the line:

  " Or since did from their ashes come,"

throws his gage directly into the teeth of Chapman and the classicist clique. We may then reasonably impute to the hand of Chapman, and not Jonson, those strokes which have been recognized as leveled at Shakespeare in " Eastward Hoe! " and one or two other plays in which Jonson, Marston, and Chapman are known to have collaborated at an earlier period.

With this slight digression, which I have introduced here in preference to using footnotes, I will
return to a consideration of Shakespeare's allusions
to Chapman in the play under discussion.

A careful reading of " Love's Labor's Lost " will
plainly show many passages quite lacking in either
sense, point, or wit, unless they had a topical meaning. I have previously shown that, in the 21st
Sonnet, Shakespeare undoubtedly refers to and
criticises Chapman's " Amorous Zodiac." In this
poem Chapman, after describing in detail the physical beauties of a naked woman through twenty-eight
verses, concludes with the two following verses as
L'Envoi:

" Dear mistress, if poor wishes heaven would hear,
  I would not choose the empire of the water;
  The empire of the air, nor of the earth,
  But endlessly my course of life confining,
  In this fair Zodiac for ever shining,
  And with thy beauties make me endless mirth.

" But, gracious love, if jealous heaven deny
  My life this truly-blest variety;
  Yet will I thee through all the world disperse;
  If not in heaven, amongst those braving fires,
  Yet here, thy beauties, which the world admires,
  Bright as these flames, shall glister in my verse."

The first of these verses, if accepted as having
been written by Chapman to an actual woman,
would reveal that prosy and stilted moralist as a

most reprehensible person. The incongruity and humor of the thing appeal to Shakespeare, and we find many veiled, though, when analyzed, rather broad allusions to it in "Love's Labor's Lost"; Shakespeare, however, true to the demands of his art, puts his vulgarisms into the mouths of the homespun yokels Costard and Dull.

Many idioms and phrases which we find in Shakespeare may still be found in common use, and retaining their Elizabethan meaning, in primitive and remote communities, though they have now quite ceased to be used or even understood in more polite circles. In several of the plays, but especially in "Romeo and Juliet," and "Love's Labor's Lost," I find the word "goose" used in a vulgar sense. I have heard this word used with exactly the same meaning in England, Ireland, Australia, and America; an examination of the plays mentioned will reveal the sense intended by Shakespeare.

The use of the word in "Love's Labor's Lost," and every allusion to "goose" or "geese," and especially Costard's mistake in supposing the word "L'Envoi" to be synonymous, are directed by Shakespeare at the apparent sensuousness of Chapman's L'Envoi to the "Amorous Zodiac."

The first use of this term is in Act I. scene 1, where Shakespeare, speaking through the mouth of Biron, attacks Chapman and his poems, "The Shadow of Night" and those published in the next year.

" *Biron.* Why, all delights are vain; but that
    most vain,
Which, with pain purchased, doth inherit pain:
As, painfully to pore upon a book
To seek the light of truth; while truth the while
Doth falsely blind the eyesight of his look:
Light, seeking light, doth light of light beguile:
So, ere you find where light in darkness lies,
Your light grows dark by losing of your eyes.
Study me how to please the eye indeed,
By fixing it upon a fairer eye;
Who dazzling so, that eye shall be his heed,
And give him light that it was blinded by.
Study is like the heaven's glorious sun,
That will not be deep-search'd with saucy looks:
Small have continual plodders ever won,
Save base authority from others' books.
These earthly godfathers of heaven's lights,
That give a name to every fixèd star,
Have no more profit of their shining nights
Than those that walk and wot not what they are.
Too much to know, is to know nought but fame;
And every godfather can give a name.
    " *King.* How well he's read to reason against
        reading!
    " *Dum.* Proceeded well, to stop all good pro-
        ceeding!
    " *Long.* He weeds the corn, and still lets grow
        the weeding.

> " *Biron.* The spring is near, when green geese
>   are a-breeding.
> " *Dum.* How follows that?
> " *Biron.*   Fit in his place and time.
> " *Dum.* In reason nothing.
> " *Biron.*   *Something, then, in rhyme.*"

Farther on in the play, in Act III. scene 1, there
is another similar allusion, where the word goose is
used. Costard with his usual obtuseness confounds
it with the word " L'Envoi," which he imagines is
synonomous.

Armado says:

" Sirrah Costard, I will enfranchise thee.

> " *Cost.* O, marry me to one Frances: *I smell
>   some l'envoy, some goose, in this.*"

The play on these words " goose " and " l'envoy "
in this passage is entirely without point unless it
had some topical meaning.

When Armado, amused at Costard's mistake in
confounding " salve " and " l'envoy," says:

" Doth the inconsiderate take salve for l'envoy,
and the word l'envoy for salve? "

Moth replies:

" Do the wise think them other? is not l'envoy a
   salve? "

apparently alluding to the Latin parting salutation,
" salve."

Armado answers:

" No, page, it is an epilogue or discourse, to make
  plain
  Some obscure precedence that hath tofore been
    sain.
I will example it:
  The fox, the ape, and the bumble-bee,
  Were still at odds, being but three.
There's the moral.   Now the l'envoy.
  Until the goose came out of the door
  And stayed the odds by adding four.
    " *Moth. A gool l'envoy, ending in the goose;
    would you desire more?*

If Chapman's " Amorous Zodiac " be read with
the L'Envoi, and the L'Envoi compared with Costard's and Moth's references, the allusions intended
by Shakespeare will, I believe, be recognized.

The last passage in this play in which the word
" goose " or " geese " appears is as follows, when,
Longaville having read his sonnet, Biron says:

" This is the *liver vein,* which makes flesh a deity,
  A green goose a goddess."

I shall in the next chapter show that this is a
palpable allusion to Chapman.   If this be admitted,
the claims I make for the previous passages where
the same term appears will, I believe, be justified.

CHAPTER VI.

CHAPMAN DISPLAYED AS THE ORIGINAL OF HOLOFERNES.

THAT Holofernes is a caricature of some one pedantic original, and not merely a type of pedants in general, has long been the opinion of the best Shakespearean critics. The strokes with which this character is drawn are too intimate and personal for any other conclusion. Mr. Warburton and Dr. Farmer suggested that John Florio, a well-known Anglo-Italian of that day, was Shakespeare's original for this character; their only grounds for this supposition being the somewhat flowery and bombastic preface with which Florio introduced his " World of Words " to the public, upon the issue of that work in 1598. This theory necessarily assigns the production of " Love's Labor's Lost " to a period subsequent to the publication of Florio's book, which alone proves its inconsistency. We may reasonably infer that Shakespeare held Florio in good estimation; we know that he made use of his translations in some of his plays and that one of the few authentic autographs which we have of Shakespeare's was found in a copy of Florio's translation of Montaigne's " Essays," which is now preserved in the British Museum. It is quite likely that Florio and Shakespeare were intimate, as both were, to some extent, protégés of the Earl of South-ampton.

I am fully convinced that Shakespeare has cari-catured George Chapman in the character of Holo-fernes.

Whoever will read Chapman's "Shadow of Night," "Ovid's Banquet of Sense," and the son-net-sequence called "A Coronet for His Mistress Philosophy" with their dedications and glossaries, and will compare them with those parts of "Love's Labor's Lost" in which Holofernes appears, will find such an original for the character there repre-sented as shall not be matched in the whole range of Elizabethan literature; especially when this re-markable likeness is supported by the other evi-dences in this play and the Sonnets which I have already adduced.

Every fault and foible caricatured in Holofernes will be found in these poems and dedications of Chapman's; the bombastic verbosity and tautology, the erudition gone to seed, the overweening scorn of ignorance, the extravagant similes and far-fetched conceits, and the pedantic Latinity, are all not only clearly indicated, but, I believe, I can show, *actually parodied in the play*. Even the alliteration of the "Playful Princess" doggerel is noticeable in these poems, but particularly so in "The Shadow of Night," where it often spoils otherwise fine lines.

A few of Holofernes' speeches, compared with extracts from the poems and dedications I have mentioned, will prove the caricature.

Holofernes is first introduced into the play, dis-

Could Holofernes have been a characterization of James Starkey? Isn't he somewhat as laughable as Malvolio

cussing the age and quality of a deer which has been killed by the Princess; thus:

"*Holo.* The deer was, as you know, sanguis, in blood; ripe as the pomewater, who now hangeth like a jewel in the ear of Caelo, the sky, the welkin, the heaven; and anon falleth like a crab on the face of terra, the soil, the land, the earth.

Nath. Truly, Master, Holofernes, *the epithets are sweetly varied, like a scholar at the least;* but, sir, I assure ye, it was a buck of the first head."

Compare this with the following extract from the dedication to " Ovid's Banquet of Sense ":

" Obscurity in affection of words and indigested conceits, is pedantical and childish; but where it shroudeth itself in the heart of his subject, *uttered with fitness of figure and expressive epithets,* with that darkness will I still labor to be shadowed."

And again:

" *Dull.* 'Twas not a haud credo; 'twas a pricket.
" *Holo.* Most barbarous intimation! yet a kind of insinuation, as it were, in via, in way, of explication; facere, as it were, replication, or rather, ostentare, to show, as it were, his inclination, after his undressed, unpolished, uneducated,. unpruned, untrained, or, rather, unlettered, or, ratherest, unconfirmed fashion, to insert again my haud credo for a deer."

Compare this effort of Holofernes with the following extract from the dedication to " Ovid's Banquet of Sense ":

"It serves not a skilful painter's turn, to draw the figure of a face only, to make known who it represents; but he must limn, give lustre, shadow and heightening; which though ignorants will esteem spiced and too curious, yet such as have the judicial perspective will see it hath motion, spirit and life."

And again:

"*Dull.* I said the deer was not a haud credo; 'twas a pricket.

"*Hol.* Twice sad simplicity, bis coctus!
O thou monster Ignorance, how deformed dost thou
      look!

"*Nath.* Sir, he hath never fed of the dainties that are bred in a book; he hath not eat paper as it were; he hath not drunk ink: his intellect is not replenished; he is only an animal, only sensible in the duller parts:

"And such barren plants are set before us, that we
      thankful should be,
   Which we of taste and feeling are, for those parts
      that do fructify in us more than he."

Compare the attitude of these scholars, Holofernes and Nathaniel, with the following from Chapman's dedication to "Ovid's Banquet of Sense":

"Such is the wilful poverty of judgements, sweet Matthew, wandering like passportless men, in contempt of the divine discipline of poesy, that a man may well fear to frequent their walks. The profane multitude I hate, and only consecrate my strange poems to those searching spirits whom learning hath made noble, and nobility sacred," etc.

Also

" I know that empty and dark spirits will complain of palpable night; but those that beforehand have a radiant and light-bearing intellect, will say they can pass through Corinna's garden without the help of a lantern."

This same attitude towards the ignorant multitude is also expressed in a footnote which he makes to the glossary of " The Shadow of Night ":

" For the rest of his own invention, figures and similes touching their aptness and novelty he hath not laboured to justify them, because he hopes they will be proved enough to justify themselves, and prove sufficiently authentical to such as understand them; for the rest, God help them."

In comparing these extracts with the caricature in the play, we see the contemptuous and disdainful spirit of the dedications plainly pilloried, the " expressive epithets " reproduced, and the " profane multitude " indicated in the person of Dull.

In one or two other extracts which I shall now quote, I am quite convinced that Shakespeare parodies parts of these dedications and glossaries; for instance:

" *Dull.* You two are book-men: can you tell me
    by your wit

What was a month old at Cain's birth, that's not five
    weeks old as yet?
"*Hol.* Dictynna, goodman Dull; Dictynna, good-
    man Dull.
"*Dull.* What is Dictynna?
"*Nath.* A title to Phœbe, to Luna, to the moon."

In Chapman's gloss to "The Shadow of
Night" he elucidates what he pretends to consider
an enigmatical passage in that poem; he speaks of
the moon as,—

"Nature's bright eyesight and the night's fair
    soul,"

a line which, when considered as poetry, scarcely
needs elucidation; from which, even one not lacking in charity, might well infer that the following
gloss savors more of pedantry than of a desire to
give light.

When this gloss is compared with Dull's conun-
drum, and Holofernes' answers, the parody is, I
think, apparent:

"1. He gives her that periphrasis—viz., Nature's
bright eyesight, because that by her store of humours issue is given to all birth: and thereof is she
called Lucina and Ilythia, quia præest parturienti-
bus cum invocaretur, and gives them help: which
Orpheus in a Hymn of her praise expresseth and
calls her besides Prothyrea, ut sequitur:

Κλῦθί μοι, ὦ πολύσεμνε θεα, etc.

" Audi me veneranda Dea, cui nomina multa:
  Prægnantum adjutrix, parientum dulce levamen,
  Sola puellarum servatrix, solaque prudens:
  Auxilium velox teneris Prothyræa puellis."

And a little after, he shows her plainly to be Diana,
Ilythia, and Prothyræa, in these verses:

" Solam animi requiem te clamant parturientes,
  Sola potes diros partus placare labores
  Diana, Ilythia gravis, sumus et Prothyræa."

" 2. He calls her the soul of night, since she is
the purest part of her according to common conceit.

" 3. Orpheus in these verses of Argonauticus,
saith she is thrice-headed, as she is Hecate, Luna
and Diana, ut sequitur.

" Cumque illis Hecate properans horrenda cucurrit
  Cui trinum caput est, genuit quam Tartarus olim."

There were many, no doubt, even amongst the
foremost verse-writers of that day, to whom the
gloss just quoted was not more intelligible than was
Holofernes' " Dictynna " and Nathaniel's " Phœbe "
and " Luna " to the by no means dull-witted
" Dull." The parody here displayed, we may assume, would not be lost upon an audience composed
of a class more or less interested in current verse.
The voluminous supply of poetry at that period
would certainly seem to indicate a considerable public demand.

I shall adduce one more parallel which savors strongly of parody.

Nathaniel having read Dumain's canzonette aloud, Holofernes' holds forth as follows:

" *Hol.* You find not the apostrophes, and so miss the accent: let me supervise the canzonet. Here are only numbers ratified; but, for the elegancy, facility, and golden cadency of poesy, caret. Ovidius Naso was the man: and why, indeed, Naso, but for smelling out the odoriferous flowers of fancy, the jerks of invention? Imitari is nothing: *so doth the hound his master, the ape his keeper, the tired horse his rider.*"

Compare this with the following extract from " Ovid's Banquet of Sense."

" The profane multitude I hate, and only consecrate my strange poems to those searching spirits, whom learning hath made noble, and nobility sacred; endeavouring that material oration which you call schema; varying in some rare fiction from popular custom, even for the pure sakes of ornament and utility; this of Euripides exceeding sweetly relishing with me; lentem coquens ne quicquam dentis addito.

" But that poesy should be as pervial as oratory, and plainness her special ornament, were the plain way to barbarism, and *to make the ass run proud of his ears, to take away strength from lions, and give camels horns.*

" That Energia, or clearness of representation,

required in absolute poems, is not the perspicuous delivery of a low invention; but high and hearty invention expressed in most significant and unaffected phrase."

If one not acquainted with these extracts from Chapman's dedications, and "Love's Labor's Lost," were to be told that one was a satire on the spirit of the other, he would verily be at a loss to know which was meant for sense, and which for nonsense. The unnecessary Latinity of Chapman and the pseudo-Latinity of Shakespeare in these extracts, the triple phrases in each,—the hound, the horse and the ape in one and the ass, the lion and the camel in the other,—the introduction of Euripides by Chapman and of Ovidius Naso by Shakespeare, all most strongly suggest direct parody.

When examined more critically there is something even stronger than parody in this passage. Seeing that Shakespeare is here caricaturing Chapman as Holofernes, and that he has very evidently parodied a passage from his dedication to "Ovid's Banquet of Sense," we may infer that Chapman makes a stroke at Shakespeare in the following words:

"*But that poesy should be as pervial as oratory and plainness her special ornament, were the plain way to barbarism, and to make the ass run proud of his ears, to take away strength from lions, and to give camels horns.*"

Shakespeare, recognizing Chapman's intention,

not only plainly parodies this passage, but through the mouth of Holofernes names Ovid, and attacks Chapman's poem as being a mere imitation of that poet.

"Let me supervise the canzonet," says Holo-fernes—it will be seen that this term is applica-ble to the form of verse which Chapman uses in "Ovid's Banquet of Sense." Holofernes then con-tinues,

used in the sonnets

"Here are only numbers ratified; but for the ele-gancy, facility, and golden cadence of poesy, caret. Ovidius Naso was the man: and why, indeed, Naso, but for smelling out the odoriferous flowers and fancy, the jerks of invention? *Imitari is nothing: so doth the hound his master, the ape his keeper, the tired horse his rider.*"

Shakespeare here practically says that Chapman, in "Ovid's Banquet of Sense," has merely "rati-fied numbers," that is, that he has only built the structure of the verse, but has borrowed his flowers of fancy or imagery, and his invention, from Ovid; and as Chapman accuses him of being too *"per-vial"* and *"plain,"* saying that *"plainness is the way to barbarism, to make the ass run proud of his ears, to take away strength from lions, and to give camels horns;"* so Shakespeare accuses him of lack of originality and imitation of Ovid; and parodying Chapman's passage just quoted, says: *"Imitari is nothing, so doth the hound his master, the ape his keeper, and the tired horse his rider."*

The play upon Ovid's surname "Naso" is a reference to one of the heads under which Chapman divides this poem in the " argument " which he prefixes to it; the heads are, " Auditus, Olfactus, Visus, Gustus, Tactus."

In playing upon " Naso " where he says : "and why, indeed, Naso, but for smelling out the odoriferous flowers of fancy," etc., he very evidently alludes to Chapman's " Olfactus," which that poet explains as follows :

" Olfactus. Then the odours she used in her bath breathing a rich savour, he expressed the joy he felt in his sense of Smelling."

There are numerous other passages in this play, very evidently of an indicative nature, which a closer examination will, no doubt, show to be directed at Chapman; one, in particular, I felt sure pointed at him, and that it was introduced into the play for no other purpose; for unless meant indicatively, it has no special point or wit. In Act V. scene 1 Armado addresses Holofernes as follows :

" *Arm.* Arts-man, pre-ambulate, we will be singled from the barbarous. Do you not educate youth at the charge-house on the top of the mountain?

" *Hol.* Or Mons, the hill.

" *Arm.* At your sweet pleasure, for the mountain.

" *Hol.* I do, sans question."

Not being able to find any record of Chapman's

occupation previous to his publication of "The Shadow of Night" (1594), in the meager records which we have of his life, and taking Mr. Swinburne as my authority for the paucity of that knowledge, I supposed it hopeless to look for any indication which could connect Chapman with this allusion to Holofernes' avowed occupation; I had passed this by, suggesting, however, that if other Shakespearean students, having access to sources impossible to me, cared to follow up my theory, they would probably find that Chapman, some time during the hidden years of his life, between 1574 and 1594, and perhaps for a while later, had earned his livelihood as a schoolmaster, and that the school at which he taught would be found to have been located, as indicated in this passage, somewhere on an eminence. In Chapman's "Tears of Peace," however, I find a passage which plainly shows us Chapman's abode during at least a part, and perhaps the whole of this period; and which also lends strong point to this allusion I notice in "Love's Labor's Lost." In this poem Chapman pictures himself as in a deep reverie; when a spirit appears to him of which he asks:

> "'O thou, that, blind, doth see
> My heart and soul, what may I reckon thee,
> Whose heavenly look shows not, nor voice sounds man?'
> 'I am,' said he, 'that spirit Elysian,
> That in thy native air, and *on the hill*
> *Next Hitchin's left hand,* did thy bosom fill

With such a flood of soul, that thou were fain,
With explanations of her rapture there,
To vent it to the echoes of the vale;
When, meditating of me, a sweet gale
Brought me upon thee; and thou did'st inherit
My true sense, for the time then, in my spirit;
And I, invisibly, went prompting thee
To those fair greens where thou dids't English
  me:'
Scarce he had utter'd this, when well I knew
It was my Prince's Homer."

Here we see that Chapman lived on a hill near
the village of Hitchin, in Hertfordshire, before
coming to London, and I have very little doubt that,
if those who can look into this matter will do so,
and supposing that any records exist by which it
may be proved, that Chapman will be found to have
taught a school while there. His whole style, and
particularly his earlier style, very strongly suggests
the pedagogue; his dogmatic and overbearing manner, towards all but scholars like himself, bespeaks
the bachelor village schoolmaster of thirty-six. It
takes much of the grace of God to preserve a proper
proportionate sense of his own importance in any
man who lives, as no doubt Chapman did, for about
fifteen years, as the high court of appeal in all literary, and in fact, in all other matters, for a rural com-
munity. Further evidence confirms this avowal of
Chapman's as to his abode during these years, and
possibly refers also to the avocation which I have

assigned him. William Browne, in "Britannia's Pastorals," alludes to him as:

"The learned shepherd of fair *Hitching Hill.*"

All through this play there are undoubted topical and indicative allusions, which, though dark now to us, were full of point to an Elizabethan audience. In the flouting of the characters in the impromptu play of the "Nine Worthies," the gibes directed at Holofernes, who takes the part of "Judas Maccabæus," are much more pointed than at the other characters; they have a sharper touch; the "Judas," the "ass" and the "kissing traitor," I am inclined to believe, have an intended sting and that they refer to some smallness or treachery of Chapman's against Shakespeare.

In the following passage, where Biron, Boyet, Dumain, and Longaville each expend their wit upon Holofernes, we fail at this day to find any wit whatever; and unless these taunts had an indicative or topical value, it is hard to see where the wit came in, even in that day. I shall show in a later chapter where Chapman several times indicates Shakespeare, by alluding in a scurrilous manner to his falcon crest: it occurs to me as possible, that Shakespeare, in the following lines, refers to the rather vainglorious use which Chapman makes of a medallion—with a picture of his own head in the center and this legend on the rim "Georgius Chapmanus Homeri Metaphrastes"— as an illustration to the title-page of the earlier issues of his Homeric translations.

" *Hol.* I will not be put out of countenance.

" *Biron.* Because thou hast no face.

" *Hol.* What is this?

" *Boyet.* A cittern-head.

" *Dum.* The head of a bodkin.

" *Biron.* A death's face in a ring.

" *Long.* The face of an old Roman coin, scarce seen.

" *Boyet.* The pommel of Cæsar's falchion.

" *Dum.* The carved bone face on a flask.

" *Biron.* Saint George's half-cheek in a brooch.

" *Dum.* Ay, and in a brooch of lead.

" *Biron.* Ay, and worn in the cap of a tooth drawer—and now forward; for we have put thee in countenance.

" *Hol.* You have put me out of countenance.

" *Biron.* False: we have given thee faces.

" *Hol.* But you have out-faced them all.

" *Biron.* An thou wert a lion, we would do so.

" *Boyet.* Therefore, as he is an ass, let him go."

The indicative value which I suggest as possible for these lines is not at all incompatible with the dates which I assign for the play, as these lines, if meant in this manner as well as the more bitterly satirical tone of this whole scene, very probably belongs to the period of the revision of this play by Shakespeare in 1598, when it was also published, very shortly after Chapman's issue of the first seven books of Homer in that year. The references to Achilles and Hector, further on in this same scene, very evidently belong also to the period of revision, as I shall prove later that Shakespeare wrote "Troilus and Cressida" in this year as a satire upon Chapman's work, and shall also give good reasons for believing that the revision of "Love's Labor's Lost" and the production of "Troilus and Cressida" occupied our poet's attention at about the same time.

In the next chapter I shall endeavor to show the reason for Shakespeare's attack upon Chapman in "Love's Labor's Lost," at the period of its production in 1595.

CHAPTER VII.

CHAPMAN'S ATTACKS UPON SHAKESPEARE IN 1594 AND 1595.

It is a rather curious fact that both Shakespeare and Chapman should have reached such an advanced age before publishing any of their poems. At the age of thirty Shakespeare published "Venus and Adonis"; at the age of thirty-five Chapman published his first poem, "The Shadow of Night." Shakespeare's poem met with almost immediate success—a success, too, that was not of a day; as we find that in the eight years following its first appearance it went into seven editions, and into five more editions in the next twenty or twenty-five years. Chapman's "Shadow of Night" was published in 1594, one year later than "Venus and Adonis," and did not see a second print for over forty years (in 1639). In the same year that Chapman published "The Shadow of Night" Shakespeare issued his second poem "Lucrece," which, in turn, met with almost as flattering a reception as "Venus and Adonis." The dedication to "Lucrece" contains strong evidence that Shakespeare reaped something more tangible than mere popularity from his first effort; the passage: "the warrant I have of your honourable disposition, and not the worth of my untutored lines," etc., lends good

Did Southampton intercede with Queen E after the death of Harrington Feb 1st 1593/4 ?

color to the report which we have from Nicholas
Rowe (Shakespeare's earliest biographer) as to
Southampton's munificence to our poet. The fame
of this munificence brought many worshipers to this
young nobleman's shrine. In 1595 Gervase Markham, in a sonnet addressed to Southampton, apos-
trophizes him as follows:

"Thou glorious laurel of the Muses' hill
   Whose eye doth crown the most victorious pen;
   Bright lamp of virtue in whose sacred skill
   Lives all the bliss of ear-enchanting men."

There can be little doubt but that these lines refer
to Shakespeare; they show, however, a very different spirit from Chapman's advances in the same
field. We have proof positive, in an extant sonnet
of Chapman's, that he sought the patronage of
Southampton at a later date (in 1609). I shall now
endeavor to show that he sought it in 1594 or 1595,
for his poems of those years; and that he sought it
again in 1596 or 1597 for his first Homeric translations, and that the references to Chapman which
Professor Minto discovered in certain of Shakespeare's Sonnets referred to this latter period. That
he was unsuccessful in both attempts we are assured from the fact that his dedications to Southampton, which Shakespeare mentions in certain of
his Sonnets, never saw print.

In "The Shadow of Night," published later
than "Venus and Adonis" and "Lucrece," I find
references to patrons who reward "fools," in much

the same strain as in the poems of Chapman published in the following year, where similar references undoubtedly indicate Shakespeare, as I shall prove.

The literary world at this date (1594) was, no doubt, ringing with the praises of Shakespeare's published poems; his early Sonnets to Southampton were also being read in manuscript. The fact of Southampton's patronage and friendship was now, no doubt, well known, therefore, when we find Chapman, whom we prove to have been an avowed enemy of Shakespeare, working himself into a heat over the recent successes of a poet whom he calls a fool, we may take it for granted whom he means. The following quotation from "The Shadow of Night" is exceedingly suggestive:

" Wealth fawns on fools; virtues are meat for vices;
   Good gifts are often given to men past good
   And noblesse stoops sometimes beneath his blood."

This seems to lend color to Nicholas Rowe's rumor of Southampton's munificence to our poet and seems also to indicate, not only Southampton's patronage of Shakespeare, but also the fact of his close intimacy and friendship as revealed in the Sonnets. It also calls to mind several of Shakespeare's Sonnets, wherein he seems to defend himself and his friend from such attacks, when he complains of the meanness of his own state and fears that his friend and patron will be besmirched by such open recognition of their friendship.

SONNET 26.

" Till whatsoever star that guides my moving,
  Points on me graciously with fair aspect,
  And puts apparel on my tattered loving
  To show me worthy of thy sweet respect:
  Then may I dare to boast how I do love thee."

And again in Sonnet 36:

" In our two loves there is but one respect,
  Though in our lives a separable spite,
  Which though it alter not love's sole effect,
  Yet doth it steal sweet hours from love's delight.
  I may not evermore acknowledge thee,
  Lest my bewailed guilt should do thee shame,
  Nor thou with public kindness honour me,
  Unless thou take that honour from thy name."

There are many of the Sonnets written in this
strain; it is noticeable, too, that in these lines
Shakespeare bewails, not his standing as a poet, but
his social condition, and when we find him in 1596
applying, through his father, to the college of Heralds, for the confirmation of an ancient grant of
arms to his family, we get some idea of what he
meant in the lines:

" Till whatsoever star that guides my moving,
  Points on me graciously with fair aspect,
  And puts apparel on my tatter'd loving,
  To show me worthy of thy sweet respect," etc.

It is very probable that Shakespeare made use
of his crest even before the date of the ratification

of this grant, and was moved to secure this recognition by the slurs which Chapman, and perhaps others also, cast at his gentility. Spenser, in 1594, in "Colin Clout's Come Home Again," very probably describes Shakespeare, in a passage which I shall quote, indicating him in the first line as "Ætion,"—derived from the Greek *Aetŏs*, an eagle, which he uses as a reference to his crest; and in the last line the name Shakespeare certainly fits the description given: we know of no other contemporary poet to whom either indication can apply and certainly none to whom both could refer:

"And there, though last not least is Ætion;
A gentler shepherd may nowhere be found,
Whose Muse full of high thoughts' invention
Doth like himself heroically sound."

I shall show in a later chapter that Chapman also indicates Shakspeare by several scurrilous allusions to this crest.

Towards the end of "The Shadow of Night" Chapman evidently alludes to Southampton in a passage from which unfortunately, at the most telling point, a line has slipped out: speaking of his hobby, "beauty of the mind," as contrasted with mere physical beauty, he says:

"He is the Ganymede, the bird of Jove,
Rapt to her sovereign's bosom for his love,
His beauty was it, not the body's pride,
That made him great Aquarius stellified,"

and in the gloss he explains this passage as follows:

" The beauty of the mind being signified in Ganymede, he gives a man's shape unto it."

He then continues:

" If wisdom be the mind's true beauty, then,
And that such beauty shines in virtuous men,
If those sweet Ganymedes shall only find "—

and here a line has slipped out, but the word
" find " would indicate a line ending in the word
mind. The context attacks poets who solicit the
favor of these " Ganymedes "—

" Love of Olympus, are these wizards wise,
That naught but gold, and his dejections prize? "
etc.

Thomas Nash, in some lines which are supposed
to refer to Southampton, uses this expression of
Chapman's " Jove's Eagle-born Ganymede," and
in 1595 Richard Barnfield dedicated a sonnet-
sequence containing twenty sonnets to a young
nobleman whom he indicates by this same name,
" Ganymede." Southampton has been suggested
as the original in this instance also.

In "A Coronet for his Mistress Philosophy," published in 1595, in all probability after the production of Shakespeare's first sonnet-sequence, Chapman makes the central idea the beauty of the
mind, in contradistinction to mere physical beauty.
I have already shown that Chapman and his poem
entitled " The Amorous Zodiac " are indicated in
the 20th and 21st Sonnets. Professor Minto's sug-

gestion as to the identity of the "rival poet" scarcely needs the support of my findings, but with that support becomes, I believe, unassailable. In the 69th and 70th Sonnets the reference to Chapman and his beauty of the mind idea, as shown in "The Shadow of Night" and "A Coronet for his Mistress Philosophy," when supported by the references already noted, becomes fairly plain.

SONNET 69.

" Those parts of thee that the world's eye doth view
    Want nothing that the thought of hearts can
        mend;
    All tongues, the voice of souls, give thee that due,
    Uttering bare truth, even so as foes commend.
    Thy outward thus with outward praise is
        crown'd;
    But those same tongues, that give thee so thine
        own,
    In other accents do this praise confound
    By seeing farther than the eye hath shown.
    They look into the beauty of thy mind,
    And that, in guess, they measure by thy deeds;
    Then, churls, their thoughts, although their eyes
        were kind,
    To thy fair flower add the rank smell of weeds;
      But why thy odour matcheth not thy show,
      The solve is this, that thou dost common grow."

The 70th Sonnet is clearly a continuation of the theme discussed in the 69th.

SONNET 70.

" That thou art blamed shall not be thy defect,
For slander's mark was ever yet the fair;
The ornament of beauty is suspect,
A crow that flies in heaven's sweetest air.
So thou be good, slander doth but approve
Thy worth the greater, being woo'd of time;
For canker vice the sweetest buds doth love,
And thou present'st a pure unstained prime.
Thou hast passed by the ambush of young days,
Either not assail'd, or victor being charged;
Yet this thy praise cannot be so thy praise,
To tie up envy evermore enlarged:
   If some suspect of ill mask'd not thy show,
   Then thou alone kingdoms of hearts shouldst
   owe."

A comparison of these two Sonnets with their contexts, 68 and 71, will show that they are of a different nature and period, and that they are a separate exercise upon a particular subject such as are the 20th and 21st Sonnets. The following lines from the 70th Sonnet,

" And thou present'st a pure unstained prime.
Thou hast passed by the ambush of young days,
Either not assail'd or victor being charged,"

as I have hitherto suggested, denote a period anterior to the indiscretion of Southampton with the poet's mistress recorded in the 33d, 34th, and 35th and 40th, 41st, and 42d Sonnets. I would therefore give these two Sonnets a very early date, and place them shortly after the first sequence, and at about the same period as the 20th and 21st Sonnets. I find them to be a direct criticism of " A Coronet for his Mistress Philosophy," as were the 20th and 21st Sonnets of " The Amorous Zodiac."

Though Shakespeare does not in the 69th and 70th Sonnets so definitely indicate one poet, he uses an expression which, I believe, is meant to single out Chapman. He says:

" All tongues, the voice of souls, give thee that
       due."

This expression, *" tongues, the voice of souls,"* seems to point very directly at that poet. I do not find in any other poet of that day a similar use of the figure, which leads me to suppose that Chapman is here indicated.

In " Ovid's Banquet of Sense " Chapman says:

" Alas! why lent not heaven *the soul a tongue*
Nor language nor peculiar dialect."

And again:

" Or turn me into swound, possess me whole
Soul to my life and essence to my *soul.*"

And again:

" Her body doth present those fields of peace
Where *souls* are feasted with the *soul* of ease."

And, in contradistinction to his high soul, he speaks of rival poets as follows:

"Hell-descending gain
The *soul* of fools that all their *soul* confounds,
The art of peasants and our nobles' stain,
The bane of virtue and the bliss of sin,
Which none but fools and peasants glory in."

*ie
greed*

In the "Coronet for his Mistress Philosophy" he often uses similar "soulful" expressions; for instance:

"But my love is the cordial of *souls,*
Teaching by passion what perfection is,
Spirit to flesh and *soul* to spirit giving,
Love flows not from my liver, but her living."

And again:

"Virtue is but the merit and reward,
Of her removed and *soul-infused* regard."

Again, in the same poem, in a verse which I shall show to be an attack upon Shakespeare, he says:

"Not the weak disjoint
Of female humours; nor the Protean rages
Of pied-faced fashion, that doth shrink and swell,
Working poor men like waxen images,
And makes them apish strangers where they dwell,
Can alter her; titles of primacy,
Courtship of antic gestures, brainless jests,
Blood without soul, of false nobility,
Nor any folly which this world infests," etc.

And in the dedication to "The Shadow of Night," in the same passage to which Professor

Minto suggests that Shakespeare refers in the 86th Sonnet, Chapman says:

"Now what a supererogation in wit this is, to think Skill so mightily pierced with their loves, that she should prostitutely show them her secrets when she will scarcely be looked upon by others but with invocation, fasting and watching. Yea, not without having drops of their *souls*," etc.

I think it will be granted that the frequent use of the idea in these extracts warrants the assumption that Shakespeare indicates Chapman in the 69th Sonnet.

In Sonnet 141 Shakespeare again has Chapman in mind.

SONNET 141.

"In faith, I do not love thee with mine eyes,
  For they in thee a thousand errors note;
  But 'tis my heart that loves what they despise,
  Who, in despite of view, is pleased to dote;
  Nor are mine ears with thy tongue's tune de-
      lighted;
  Nor tender feeling, to base touches prone,
  Nor taste, nor smell, desire to be invited
  To any sensual feast with thee alone:
  But my five wits nor my five senses can
  Dissuade one foolish heart from loving thee,
  Who leaves unsway'd the likeness of a man,
  Thy proud heart's slave and vassal wretch to be:
      Only my plague thus far I count my gain,
      That she that makes me sin awards me pain."

A comparison of this Sonnet with " Ovid's Banquet of Sense " will reveal the references suggested.

Thus we see that Shakespeare indicates Chapman in a more or less critical and unfriendly manner in the 20th, 21st, 38th, 69th, and 70th Sonnets, also in the series from 78 to 86, as well as the 141st. The indications already shown in " Love's Labor's Lost " are also fairly definite.

We have no positive proof, in extant dedications, that Chapman sought Southampton's patronage previous to the year 1609, yet we have much evidence in the above-mentioned Sonnets that he did so, both in the years 1594 and 1595 for his earliest poems, and also, a year or two later, for his Homeric translations. Chapman having sought this patronage and being unsuccessful, it stands to reason he would not publish his rejected dedications as monuments of his repulse; therefore, the " dedicated words," of which Shakespeare speaks in the 82d Sonnet, were undoubtedly still in manuscript at the date of his expostulation in that Sonnet; so, in writing of Chapman's dedications of the earlier period (1594-1595) as follows:

" All tongues, the voice of souls, give thee that due,
  Uttering bare truth, even so as foes commend.
  Thy outward thus with outward praise is
        crown'd;
  But those same tongues, that give thee so **thine**
        own,
  In other accents do this praise confound,
  By seeing farther than the eye hath shown,"

Shakespeare evidently indicates some poem of Chapman's which he had seen in manuscript and that has not come down to us, or else that has been published in some other form; that this latter is the case, I shall give my reasons for believing. We know that "The Shadow of Night," issued in 1594, was the first published poem of Chapman's; and that "Ovid's Banquet of Sense," "The Amorous Zodiac," and "A Coronet for his Mistress Philosophy," issued in 1595, were the second published efforts of his Muse; yet we find that he rages and fumes both in these poems and in their dedications, over his lack of patronage. It is reasonable to infer that he would not do this unless he had sought such patronage and been repulsed. The poems of both these years are dedicated to his friend Matthew Roydon, a poor scholar like himself; but the disgruntled tone of these dedications argues that Chapman had previously sought a more shining mark than his friend Roydon as sponsor for the children of his brain. There can be little doubt but that Chapman was numbered amongst the many suitors who were drawn at this time, by the fame of Shakespeare's success, to seek some share of Southampton's bounty. I have shown how Gervase Markham in this year (1595), approaching this young nobleman, alludes in a most propitiatory manner to Shakespeare as "the most victorious pen." Chapman, either on account of a previous enmity to Shakespeare or because of his innate envy, instead of praising the nobleman's favorite, covertly slurs him; he, however, does Shakespeare

the honor of imitating him, or at least he endeavors
to do so. Assuming, no doubt, that it was the sensuous nature of Shakespeare's poems ("Venus and
Adonis," and "Lucrece") which charmed the
young patron and caught the public fancy; but
scornful of Shakespeare's limpid diction and blind
to the imaginative beauties which relieve the sensuousness of these two poems, Chapman forthwith
trips his elephantine Muse to like measures; its
gambols, however, suggest Æsop's fabled donkey
that would fain be a lapdog. While there are many
fine lines in these poems of Chapman's, as a whole
they are meandering, conceited, and strained.

In "Venus and Adonis," sensuous and unnatural
as is the theme, we have the "freshness of the early
world"; we have an ideal Greek god and an ideal
Greek goddess, in an idealized landscape; we have

> "The gleam,
> The light that never was on sea or land,
> The consecration and the poet's dream."

The sensuousness is idealized.

"All breathing human passion far above,
  That leaves a heart high-sorrowful and cloy'd,
  A burning forehead, and a parching tongue."

We forget it, carried away by the beauty of the
verse.

In "Ovid's Banquet of Sense" we have simply a
naked woman and a "peeping Tom"; a lady of the
Roman court, disrobed for bathing, in a trim
garden where spouts an artificial fountain; and a
man (Ovidius Naso) lurking behind bushes, men-

tally dissecting and analyzing the senses, one by
one. By and by Ovid reveals himself and talks
erotic metaphysics with this unblushing female
through about twenty verses of the poem.

"The Amorous Zodiac" is a weaker effort in the
same direction; both poems are filled with what
Mr. Swinburne calls "the dry rot of scholastic sensuality." The very assumption of purity, and the
high moral pose which Chapman endeavors to com-
bine with his sensuous subject, fail utterly of their
purpose, and what, in Ovid's hands, had been mere
Pagan sensuousness becomes, under his touch,
analytic obscenity. The subjects treated of by
Chapman in these two poems were utterly foreign
to him and his Muse, and there can be little doubt
that, in choosing these subjects, he was trying
either to do the popular thing in order to gain fame
speedily, or else to show how much better a poet of
his erudition and morality could treat the same subjects that had won an unlearned actor such fame as
Shakespeare had achieved with "Venus and
Adonis" and "Lucrece."

I have already shown that Shakespeare attacks
Chapman in "Love's Labor's Lost," indicating these
poems of 1594 and 1595; in the following lines from
that play I believe he refers to Chapman's efforts
to be sensuously poetic.

Act V. scene 2, "Love's Labor's Lost":

"*Prin.* None are so surely caught, when they are
    catch'd,
As wit turn'd fool: folly, in wisdom hatch'd,

Has wisdom's warrant and the help of school,
And wit's own grace to grace a learned fool.
   " *Ros.* The blood of youth burns not with such
        such excess
As gravity's revolt to wantonness.
   " *Mar.* Folly in fools bears not so strong a note,
As foolery in the wise, when wit doth dote;
Since all the power thereof it doth apply
To prove by wit, worth in simplicity."

These lines are spoken by the Princess, Rosaline, and Margaret, criticising Biron, who has the reputation of being a wit; but Biron is quite a young man; he is described in the play in the following terms:

" Biron they call him; but a merrier man,
  Within the limit of becoming mirth,
  I never spent an hour's talk withal:
  His eye begets occasion for his wit;
  For every object that the one doth catch,
  The other turns to a mirth-moving jest,
  Which his fair tongue, conceit's expositor,
  Delivers in such apt and gracious words,
  That aged ears play truant at his tales,
  And younger hearings are quite ravished;
  So sweet and voluble is his discourse."

So that the expressions used in the lines previously quoted; " a learned fool " and " foolery in the wise," and also the lines spoken by Rosaline,

" The blood of youth burns not with such excess
  As gravity's revolt to wantonness,"

?

though in the play directed at Biron, are not at all descriptive of that character's age or bearing; they are very evidently directed at Chapman's freakish attempt at sensuousness in these two poems. To anyone that makes a study of Chapman's other poems—" The Shadow of Night," " A Coronet for his Mistress Philosophy," " The Tears of Peace," the " Penitential Hymns," " Eugenia," " A Hymn to our Saviour on the Cross," " Epicedium," " Pro Vere Autumni Lachrymæ," etc., etc.—his two sensuous poems will be seen to be a very peculiar breaking away from his ordinary and usual strains, and quite out of accord with the man's scholastic and rather puritanical mentality.

Never a Puritan

In the third poem of Chapman's published in 1595, entitled " A Coronet for his Mistress Philosophy," I find what I conceive to be a distinct and spiteful attack upon Shakespeare. Regarding this sonnet-sequence of Chapman's an idea occurs to me which I offer for what it is worth. Looking at it in the light which I shall suggest, it certainly gives some meaning to the reference which Shakespeare makes in the 69th Sonnet to a dedicatory poem of Chapman's, addressed to Southampton at this date, in which that poet is indicated as praising not only the nobleman's physical beauty, but also the beauty of his mind. I have hitherto suggested that " Ovid's Banquet of Sense " and " The Amorous Zodiac," written in imitation of Shakespeare's two sensuous poems, were offered to Southampton along with the dedication referred to in the 69th Sonnet. I am very strongly of the opinion that this poem (" A Coronet for his Mistress Philosophy ") *is that identical dedicatory poem.* Shakespeare's expostulations having induced Southampton to refuse these poems, Chapman altered this latter poem into an address to " his Mistress Philosophy," and also into a virulent attack upon the rival who was the cause of his repulse. Many lines in this poem seem to suggest such a change : being addressed in the first place to a young man, it contains many of Chapman's slurs at femininity and female natures, which seem quite out of place when we find the poem addressed to a feminine abstraction, " his Mistress Philosophy." The first three verses of this poem show little alteration, and if the gender of the pronouns be changed and " he " and " his " substituted for " she " and " her," in these verses, the poem may be recognized as having the fulsome dedicatory touch usual with Chapman ; however, even in its present state, it plainly reveals an attack upon Shakespeare.

" Ovid's Banquet of Sense " has evidently also been somewhat altered. There can be little doubt, from the tone of Chapman's two dedications to Roydon, that he had previously sought a wealthier patron for these poems, so that, when we find two verses in the poem itself breathing the same disgruntled spirit as the dedication, we may infer that they were introduced after his repulse. The last two verses evidently belong to the poem in its original form ; the two verses preceding these, however, are, in all likelihood, of a later time. I shall quote these verses :

" In these dog-days how this contagion smothers
The purest blood with virtue's diet fined,
Nothing their own unless they be some other's
Spite of themselves, are in themselves confined,
And live so poor they are of all despised.
Their gifts held down with scorn should be di-
vined,
And they like mummers mask, unknown, un-
prized :
A thousand marvels mourn in some such breast,
Would make a kind and worthy patron blest.

" To me, dear sovereign, thou art patroness,
And I, with that thy graces have infused,
Will make all fat and foggy brains confess
Riches may from a poor verse be deduced :
And that gold's love shall leave them grovelling
here,
When thy perfections shall to heaven be mused,
Deck'd in bright verse, where angels shall appear,
The praise of virtue, love and beauty singing,
Honor to noblesse, shame to avarice bringing."

I will now, in a general way, analyze the sonnet-
sequence " A Coronet for his Mistress Philosophy,"
and show what I believe to be covert references to
Shakespeare, as well as a few instances where
Shakespeare, in some of the Sonnets and in
" Love's Labor's Lost," refers to this poem.

Though Chapman in this sonnet-sequence addressed Muses collectively, it is not difficult to perceive that he had one figure in mind. Shakes-

peare's undoubted pre-eminence at this date, as
shown by the lines of Gervase Markham which I
have quoted, should be borne in mind in considering Chapman's indications. "Venus and Adonis"
and "Lucrece," with the first sonnet-sequence, had
all been produced at this date. In all of these
poems Shakespeare very plainly sings "Love's sensual empery." This sonnet-sequence of Chapman's
seems to refer more particularly to Shakespeare's
early Sonnets to his patron than to the other two
poems, though they also are indicated. In Shakespeare's first sonnet-sequence, he certainly praises
his friend's exterior graces; so that when Chapman writes,

> "Muses that sing Love's sensual empery,
>   And lovers kindling your enraged fires
> At Cupid's bonfires burning in the eyes,
> Blown with the empty breath of vain desires,
> You that prefer the painted cabinet
> Before the wealthy jewels it doth store ye,
> That all your joys in dying figures set,
> And stain the living substance of your glory,
> Abjure those joys, abhor their memory,
> And let my love the honour'd subject be
> Of love, and honour's complete history;
> Your eyes were never yet let in to see
>   The majesty and riches of the mind,
>   But dwell in darkness; for your god is blind,"

he very plainly indicates a poet or poets who praise
a man's beauty, and whom he accuses of being ob-

livious to the beauties of the mind. Chapman would scarcely be referring to the amorous verses of poets who praised their mistresses; even he himself, tiresome old pedant that he was, in extolling his mistress or imaginary mistress, found that in her worthier of his eulogy than her mind.

In "The Amorous Zodiac" he most decidedly preferred

> "The painted cabinet
> Before the wealthy jewels it did store him,"

and

> "All his joys in dying figures set."

A few extracts from Shakespeare's first sonnet-sequence will show the continuous praise of his patron's outward graces to which Chapman refers.

SONNET 1.

> "Thou that art now the world's fresh ornament
> And only herald to the gaudy spring."

SONNET 2.

> "Thy youth's proud livery, so gazed on now."

SONNET 3.

> "Thou art thy mother's glass, and she in thee
> Calls back the lovely April of her prime."

SONNET 4.

> "Unthrifty loveliness, why dost thou spend
> Upon thyself thy beauty's legacy?"

SONNET 5.

" Those hours that with gentle work did frame
The lovely gaze where every eye doth dwell."

SONNET 6.

" Be not self-will'd, for thou art much too fair
To be death's conquest and make worms thine
heir."

SONNET 14.

" Or else of thee this I prognosticate:
Thy end is truth's and beauty's doom and date."

SONNET 17.

" If I could write the beauty of your eyes
And in fresh numbers number all your graces,
The age to come would say ' This poet lies;
Such heavenly touches ne'er touch'd earthly
faces.' "

SONNET 19.

" O, carve not with thy hours my love's fair brow,
Nor draw no lines there with thine antique pen;
Him in thy course untainted do allow,
For beauty's pattern to succeeding men."

All through this sequence Shakespeare, in this
strain, sings of his patron's beauty, not once referring to his mental attributes, so that when Chapman writes:

" You that prefer the painted cabinet
Before the wealthy jewels it doth store ye,
That all your joys in dying figures set,

And stain the living substance of your glory,
Abjure those joys, abhor their memory,
And let my love the honour'd subject be
Of love, and honour's complete history;
Your eyes were never yet let in to see
The majesty and riches of the mind,"

Harrington

there can be little doubt but that he refers to
Shakespeare, and that Shakespeare, recognizing the
intention, answers in the 69th Sonnet, as follows:

" Those parts of thee that the world's eye doth view
    Want nothing that the thought of hearts can
        mend;
    All tongues, the voice of souls, give thee that due,
    Uttering bare truth, even so as foes commend.
    Thy outward thus with outward praise is
        crown'd;
    But those same tongues, that give thee so thine
        own,
    In other accents do this praise confound
    By seeing farther than the eye hath shown.
    They look into the beauty of thy mind."

Where else

In the next verse Chapman continues his attack
in much the same strain:

" But dwell in darkness, for your God is blind,
    Humour pours down such torrents on his eyes;
    Which, as from mountains, fall on his base kind,
    And eat your entrails out with ecstasies.
    Colour, whose hands for faintness are not felt,
    Can bind your waxen thoughts in adamant;

And with her painted fires your heart doth melt,
Which beat your soul in pieces with a pant.
But my love is the cordial of souls,
Teaching by passion what perfection is,
In whose fix'd beauties shine the sacred scrolls,
And long-lost records of your human bliss,
    Spirit to flesh, and soul to spirit giving,
    Love flows not from my liver, but her living."

To Chapman's thrusts at Shakespeare in this
verse I think I can show our poet's answers, not
only in the Sonnets, but in " Love's Labor's Lost."
Chapman here says:

" *Colour, whose hands for faintness are not felt,*
Can bind your waxen thoughts in adamant;
And with her *painted fires* your heart doth melt,
Which beat your soul in pieces with a pant."

Compare this with Biron's words in the play, only
a few lines after the mention of " The School of
Night," and written, no doubt, while Shakespeare
had Chapman still in mind:

" Her favour turns the fashion of the days,
For native blood is counted painting now;
And therefore red, that would avoid dispraise,
Paints itself black, to imitate her brow."

And again in Sonnet 83:

" I never saw that you did painting need,
And therefore to your fair no painting set;
I found, or thought I found, you did exceed
The barren tender of a poet's debt:

And therefore have I slept in your report,
That you yourself, being extant, well might show
How far a modern quill doth come too short,
Speaking of worth, what worth in you doth grow.
This silence for my sin you did impute,
Which shall be most my glory, being dumb:
For I impair not beauty, being mute,
When others would give life, and bring a tomb.
　There lives more life in one of your fair eyes
　Than both your poets can in praise devise."

Both of these references of Shakespeare's may
point to these lines of Chapman's, but that in
" Love's Labor's Lost " undoubtedly does. In the
latter lines of this Sonnet Chapman says:

" But my love is the cordial of souls,
　Teaching by passion what perfection is,
　In whose fix'd beauties shine the sacred scrolls,
　And long-lost records of your human bliss,
　Spirit to flesh, and soul to spirit giving,
　Love flows not from my liver, but her living."

There are two expressions in this extract to which
I can show that Shakespeare refers in the 69th Sonnet: the words *" the voice of souls"* have no possible meaning unless a satirical or indicative one;
they very evidently point to Chapman's frequent
use of this figure which we find used in the above
passage. The last two lines of this extract,
Shakespeare refers to satirically in " Love's Labor's
Lost "; if any other meaning can be given to the
expression which Shakespeare uses, than an indic-

ative reference to this Sonnet of Chapman's, it has yet to be advanced.

In Act IV. scene 3 Longaville having read his Sonnet:

Morley's plea to the Queen!

" Did not the heavenly rhetoric of thine eye,
 ' Gainst whom the world cannot hold argument,
 Persuade my heart to this false perjury?
 Vows for thee broke deserve not punishment.
 A woman I forswore; but I will prove,
 Thou being a goddess, I forswore not thee:
 My vow was earthly, thou a heavenly love;
 Thy grace being gain'd cures all disgrace in me.
 Vows are but breath, and breath a vapour is:
 Then, thou, fair sun, which on my earth doth
          shine,
 Exhalest this vapour vow; in thee it is:
 If broken then, it is no fault of mine,
 If by me broke, what fool is not so wise
 To lose an oath to win a paradise?"

Biron comes in with

" This is the *liver vein, which* makes *flesh a deity.*"

Compare this with Chapman's

" *Spirit to flesh* and *soul to spirit* giving
 Love flows not from *my liver, but her living.*"

In the sixth verse of this sequence Chapman works himself into great wrath:

" Her look doth promise and her life assure;
 A right line forcing a rebateless point,

Not proper comparison for the LLL extract was a plea to the Queen while the Chapman sonnet praises the Queen in double personalization with Philosophy

In her high deeds, through everything obscure,
To full perfection; not the weak disjoint
Of female humours; nor the Protean rages
Of pied-faced fashion, that doth shrink and swell,
Working poor men like waxen images,
And makes them apish strangers where they
    dwell,
Can alter her, titles of primacy,
Courtship of antic gestures, brainless jests,
Blood without soul, of false nobility,
Nor any folly that the world infests
    Can alter her who with her constant guises
    To living virtues turns the deadly vices."

Let us analyze this Sonnet. The words,

> "Not the weak disjoint
Of female humours,"

certainly seem out of place, as I have previously
suggested, when we find these verses apparently addressed to a feminine figure.

> "The Protean rages
Of pied-faced fashion, that doth shrink and swell,
Working poor men like waxen images,
And makes them apish strangers where they dwell,"

possibly refers to Shakespeare's growth out of the
mere actor's sphere, and to his friendship with
Southampton; "titles of primacy" takes on point
when we consider Gervase Markham's reference, of
this date, to Shakespeare as "the most victorious
pen." Others besides Markham, no doubt, spoke

of Shakespeare in much the same strain at this period. A few years later, in 1598, Meres gives him an equally high and much more clearly defined standing when he says:

"The Muses would speak Shakespeare's fine filed phrase if they could speak English: among the English he is the most excellent in both kinds for the stage, that is, comedy and tragedy." He further says, "the sweet witty soul of Ovid lives in mellifluous and honey-tongued Shakespeare."

The remainder of this sonnet,

"Courtship of antic gestures, brainless jests,"

is evidently a fling at Shakespeare as a comedian;

"*Blood without soul*, of false nobility,"

a slur upon his gentility; the "false nobility" probably calling in question his right to the use of the Eagle and Spear crest, by which it has been shown that Spenser indicated our poet, and by which it shall be shown later that Chapman again indicates him. The expression here used, "blood without soul," when considered as a stroke at Shakespeare's quality, accounts for the retort which he makes at Chapman in the 69th Sonnet where he says:

"All tongues, *the voice of souls*," etc.

In the 9th and 10th sonnets of this sequence Chapman even more definitely indicates Shakespeare and more bitterly assails him:

" For words want art, and art wants words to praise
      her;
Yet shall my active and industrious pen
Wind his sharp forehead through those parts that
      raise her,
And register her worth past rarest women.
Herself shall be my Muse; that well will know
Her proper inspirations; and assuage—
With her dear love—the wrongs my fortunes show,
Which to my youth bind heartless grief in age.
Herself shall be my comfort and my riches,
And all my thoughts I will see her convert;
Honour and error which the world bewitches,
Shall still crown fools, and tread upon desert,
    And never shall my friendless verse envy
    Muses that Fame's loose feathers beautify.

Poets who don't write for the stage?

" Muses that Fame's loose feathers beautify,
And such as scorn to tread the theatre,
As ignorant: the seed of memory
Have most inspired, and shown their glories there
To noblest wits, and men of highest doom,
That for the kingly laurel bent affair
The theatres of Athens and of Rome,
Have been the crowns and not the base impair.
Far, then, be this foul cloudy-brow'd contempt
From like-plumed birds: and let your sacred
      rhymes
From honour's court their servile feet exempt,
That live by soothing moods, and serving times:
    And let my love adorn with modest eyes,
    Muses that sing Love's sensual emperies."

The construction, grammar, and sense of this last sonnet are strange and wonderful. Chapman has evidently tried to put the full point and sting of the whole sequence into the last verse, and grammar and construction have been secondary to his wrath. Let us first take the indications in the 9th sonnet pointing at Shakespeare:

" Herself shall be my comfort and my riches,
 And all my thoughts I will on her convert;
 Honour and error, which the world bewitches,
 Shall still crown fools, and tread upon desert."

" Herself," his Mistress Philosophy, shall be his comfort and his riches, the antithesis of "honour and error " which " still crown fools,"—Shakespeare,— and " tread upon desert,"—Chapman. " Honour," I suppose, means Southampton; " Error," the applauding public " altogether hide-bound with affection to great men's fancies," which calls a poem like " Venus and Adonis " into eight editions in as many years, and lets a gem like " The Shadow of Night " lie hidden.

" And never shall my friendless verse envy
 Muses that Fame's loose feathers beautify."

What does Chapman mean by " *Fame's loose feathers*"? I would opine, such pieces of classical fiction as the legend of " Venus and Adonis " and the story of " Lucrece," which Shakespeare uses as he finds them in stray translations: not being able, as was Chapman, with his superior classical knowledge, to pluck the whole birds of Grecian mythology and Roman history. In this line Chapman not only indicates our poet, but sneers at his lack of learning.

In the next verse Chapman, repeating the last line of the preceding verse, as he does all through the sequence, addresses

" Muses that Fame's loose feathers beautify,
And such as scorn to tread the theatre,
As ignorant,"

and tells them:

" The seed of memory
Have most inspired, and shown their glories there
To noblest wits, and men of highest doom,
That for the kingly laurel bent affair
The theatres of Athens and of Rome,
Have been the crowns and not the base impair."

The punctuation in this passage is evidently wrong; there should be some stop after " affair."

The sense I make of this passage is as follows:

Muses who beautify the loose feathers of Fame and who scorn, as ignorant, the dramatic profession, know ye, the seed of memory have most inspired, and shown their glories there to noblest wits and men of highest doom, who, for the kingly laurel strove in endeavor. For such men the theaters of Athens and of Rome have been the crowns, and not the base impair.

He then continues:

" Far, then, be this foul cloudy-brow'd contempt
From like-plumed birds."

By " like-plumed birds " Chapman here very evidently means the class of men of whom he has just
been writing, *i. e.*, actors, or writers for the stage.

" And let your sacred rhymes
From honour's court their servile feet exempt,
That live by soothing moods, and serving times."

Here is proof that he is not addressing the sonneteers of the day; he would not write of the
amorous sonnet as a " sacred rhyme." By this expression he evidently means poems or rhymes on
sacred, that is classical subjects, and I believe,
intends to indicate " Venus and Adonis " and
" Lucrece."

" From honour's court " means the courtship of
men of honour, *i. e.*, title and position.

" Their servile feet exempt
That live by soothing moods, and serving times "

probably refers to Shakespeare's dedications of his
poems to Southampton.

The last line of this Sonnet gives the same indication as the first line of the whole sequence :

" Muses that sing Love's sensual emperies."

In this poem we have, singled out for attack, a
poet who sings of love and its emperies; who
praises his friend's physical beauty and not the
beauty of his mind; who remodels and beautifies

fragments from classical lore; who is given titles of primacy, that is, who is greeted as foremost amongst poets; who is applauded by the public, and rewarded by a titled patron; who is an actor and yet scorns the actor's profession and who writes soothing dedications. If these indications do not point to Shakespeare, I do not know any other contemporary poet to whom all this could have been applied in the year 1595. We have many suggestions in the Sonnets that the theatrical profession was repugnant to Shakespeare at this period, however much his ideas on that subject may have changed in later years with his increase in wealth and his enhanced standing in the profession, as well as the comparative importance and respectability which the dramatic profession attained during these years. The English stage previous to Shakespeare's time was extremely crude, and in the estimation of the public, and before the law, actors ranked little better than vagabonds and traveling tinkers.

When we consider the personal references contained in these verses, we can see the reason for Shakespeare's personalities against Chapman in " Love's Labor's Lost " and also his satirical references to him in the 20th and 21st and 69th and 70th Sonnets. Several of the Sonnets in the series 78 to 86 probably refer also to Chapman's attempts upon Southampton's favor at this date; but I am inclined to believe that most of them point to a slightly later period, which I shall endeavor to indicate in the next chapter.

CHAPTER VIII.

THE references to a " rival poet " in the Sonnets, from which Professor Minto's happy inference regarding Chapman in that connection was drawn, are to be found in the 86th Sonnet. In his " Characteristics of the English Poets " (1885) Professor Minto asks: " Who was the ' rival poet ' ? " and then continues:

" So complete is the parallel of the course of true friendship to the course of true love that even the passion of jealousy finds a place. Nine Sonnets, 78 to 86, are occupied with the pretensions of other poets, and one poet in particular, to the gracious countenance of his patron.

" In the 80th Sonnet he cries:

" ' O how I faint when I of you do write
Knowing a better spirit doth use your name.'

Who was this ' better spirit '? I hope I shall not be held guilty of hunting after paradox if I say that every possible poet has been named but the right one, nor of presumption if I say that he is so obvious that his escape from notice is something little short of miraculous. The 86th Sonnet supplies ample means of identification:

" ' Was it the proud full sail of his great verse,
    Bound for the prize of all too perfect you,
    That did my ripe thoughts in my brain inhearse,
    Making their tomb the womb wherein they
        grew?
    Was it his spirit, by spirits taught to write
    Above a mortal pitch, that struck me dead?
    No, neither he, nor his compeers by night
    Giving him aid, my verse astonished.
    He, nor that affable familiar ghost
    Which nightly gulls him with intelligence,
    As victors, of my silence cannot boast;
    I was not sick of any fear from thence:
      But when your countenance fill'd up his line,
      Then lack'd I matter; that enfeebled mine.'

"The allusions to supernatural assistance are here very pointed. Chapman was a man of overpowering enthusiasm, ever eager in magnifying poetry and advancing fervid claims to supernatural inspiration. In 1594 he published a poem called 'The Shadow of Night,' which goes far to establish his identity with Shakespeare's rival; in the dedication, after animadverting severely on vulgar searchers after knowledge, he exclaims, 'Now what a supererogation in wit this is, to think Skill so mightily pierced with their loves, that she should prostitutely show them her secrets, when she will scarcely be looked upon by others but with invocation, fasting, and watching, yea, not without having drops of their souls like an heavenly familiar,' etc.

"Here we have something like a profession of the familiar ghost that Shakespeare so saucily laughs at."

In these words Professor Minto gave the clew to my findings, the only mistake he makes being in supposing that, in these nine Sonnets, others besides this one particular poet are indicated.

I have conclusively shown that Chapman is even more distinctly indicated in four Sonnets of an earlier date; viz.: 20, 21, 69, and 70 (1595). To the bulk of the Sonnets in the apparent sequence from 78 to 86 I assign a later date. Shakespeare's protestations are here more pronounced, and his allusions to the "rival poet" more respectful, than in the earlier years. He is evidently threatened by a more powerful weapon in the rival's hands. In 1598 Chapman published his translation of seven books of Homer's Iliad, and a little later in the same year, another book of the Iliad which he entitled "Achilles' Shield," dedicating them both to the Earl of Essex, Southampton's intimate friend, and connection by marriage.

Dedicated to Earl of Essex

These translations were licensed for publication in 1596 or 1597; in the time intervening between their entry in the "Stationer's Register" and their actual issue, Chapman, no doubt, sought a suitable patron to whom to dedicate them. I am fully convinced that it was an attempt of Chapman's upon Southampton's favor at this time that called forth Shakespeare's protest in the bulk of the Sonnets from 78 to 86 and even beyond them, as I am very

no proof

much inclined to place all of this group of Sonnets, from 78 to 96, at this date.

I would, however, omit Sonnet 81, which evidently belongs to another sequence, as I have previously pointed out. I believe I shall plainly prove these Sonnets of Shakespeare's to have been written previous to 1598, when Chapman published his first translations, as I shall show in a poem of Chapman's, published with these translations, very palpable references made by him to the attack which Shakespeare makes upon him in these particular Sonnets.

We may infer from this that these Sonnets of Shakespeare's were written while Chapman's translations were still in manuscript, and while Southampton was considering whether or not he would accept their dedication. Southampton probably left England at this time, leaving Shakespeare in doubt on that point; and our poet was probably not cognizant that his remonstrances had been successful, till Chapman's translations appeared with the dedication to the Earl of Essex. These Sonnets of Shakespeare's reveal argument; there is a question-and-answer tone about them, as though Southampton had intimated that he was not tied to Shakespeare's Muse, in answer to which Shakespeare says:

SONNET 82.

"I grant thou wert not married to my Muse,
And therefore mayst without attaint o'erlook
The dedicated words which writers use
Of their fair subject, blessing every book.

Thou art as fair in knowledge as in hue,
Finding thy worth a limit past my praise;
And therefore art enforced to seek anew
Some fresher stamp of the time-bettering days.
And do so, love; yet when they have devised
What strained touches rhetoric can lend,
Thou truly fair wert truly sympathized
In true plain words by thy true-telling friend;
  And their gross painting might be better used
  Where cheeks need blood; in thee it is abused."

A little later Southampton seems to have suggested that his learned eulogist praised him more highly than did Shakespeare, and our poet answers:

" You to your beauteous blessings add a curse,
  Being fond on praise, which makes your praises
    worse."

In this the young nobleman was possibly playing upon the feelings of his protégé, to induce him to display his poetic versatility. However, we are quite assured that Southampton did not accept Chapman's dedications, but probably feeling rather kindly disposed than otherwise towards his presumably flattering suitor, and at the same time not wishing to offend Shakespeare, to whom, we may safely conclude, he bore as strong a friendship as a man in his position—an only and, I suppose, a spoiled child, of great place and wealth, flattered from his cradle—could bear to anyone inferior in station; he very likely introduced Chapman to the notice of Essex, to whom we see that Chapman's translations were finally dedicated. In this same year we find proof of Southampton's influence with Essex, who was then chief of the college of Heralds, in the fact that Shakespeare at this date finally secured the confirmation of his long-sought honor of arms.

utter Rot

That Chapman was fully conscious of the fact that the repulse he met with, in seeking Southampton's favor, was due to Shakespeare's objections, he plainly shows in a poem of this date.

Appended to a translation of the 18th book of the Iliad, published this year (1598) under the name of "Achilles' Shield," there is a poem addressed as follows: "To my admired and soul-loved friend, master of all essential and true knowledge, M. Harriots."

In the poem Chapman sings the same high praise of learning, and castigates the pretensions of "ignorants," in much the same terms as I have shown in "A Coronet for his Mistress Philosophy." Taking the date of this poem into consideration, and in the light of the references I find in the poem, I am fully convinced that it is Chapman's revenge for the repulse he has recently met with in soliciting Southampton's favor, as well as his answer to a satire which Shakespeare produced this year upon his Homer-worship in "Troilus and Cressida." There can be no doubt but that Chapman, at the time of writing this poem, had read the Sonnets by which Shakespeare had wrought on Southampton to refuse his dedications.

Chapman received nothing from Essex!

In the first passage in which I notice references

to Shakespeare in this poem to Harriots, Chapman says:

"When, absurd and vain,
Most students in their whole instruction are,
But in traditions more particular;
Leaning like rotten houses, on out beams,
And with true light fade in themselves like dreams."

Here we find the same idea expressed which Chapman voices in "A Coronet for his Mistress Philosophy," where he indicates Shakespeare's lack of classical knowledge in the line:

"Muses that Fame's loose feathers beautify."

He here accuses Shakespeare of being "absurd and vain" in his whole instruction, but particularly so in his knowledge of traditions, that is, ancient history and mythology; he says he uses "out beams" of knowledge, intimating by that term that he makes use of stray translations. In the use of this word "traditions," Chapman is not making a mere general charge of ignorance, but is definitely alluding to his version of the story of "Troilus and Cressida," which I shall show in a later chapter that Shakespeare produced this year as an attack upon Chapman's Homer-worship. Shakespeare's proved sources for this play were Chaucer's poem "Troylus and Cryseyde," Lydgate's "Troye Book," and Caxton's "Recuyell of the Historie of Troye." It is to this fact that Chapman refers when he says,

> " Absurd and vain,
> Most students in their whole instruction are,
> But in traditions more particular;
> Leaning like rotten houses, on out beams,"

contrasting Shakespeare's play, done from translations, with his own great work, which he asserts
he takes directly from the Greek.

Chapman continues this passage as follows:

> " True learning hath a body absolute,
> That in apparent sense itself can suit,
> Not hid in airy terms, as if it were
> Like *spirits* fantastic, *that put men in fear,*
> And are but bugs form'd in their foul conceits."

In these lines he distinctly refers to Shakespeare's attack upon his spirit-taught Muse in the
86th Sonnet:

> " Was it his *spirit, by spirits* taught to write
> Above a mortal pitch, that struck me dead?
> No, neither he, nor his compeers by night
> Giving him aid, my verse astonished.
> He, nor that affable *familiar ghost*
> Which nightly gulls him with intelligence,
> As victors, of my silence cannot boast;
> I was not sick of any *fear from thence.*"

Chapman claims that learning has an absolute
body and is not hid in airy terms

> " Like spirits fantastic that put men in fear,"

[handwritten margin notes:] Southwell taught by Bruno Derbyshire Spondanus

[handwritten margin note:] Thomas Pon

and in using these terms, shows very plainly in the next line that he is quoting someone who has used a like simile, when he says:

" And are but *bugs* formed in their foul conceits."

This word " bug," for spirit or ghost, is still used with variations of pronunciation in this same sense in many parts of the United Kingdom even at this day, and upon the Continent many forms of the same word still exist; the " pucca " of Welsh, the " pooka " of Irish, and the " bock " of German folk-lore have, I believe, the same origin; and the " boogie," which children fear, is of the same stock. I am inclined to the opinion that Shakespeare's " Puck " is also connected with this family.

Chapman continues his praise of learning and his scolding of ignorance, thus:

" Not made for sale, glazed with sophistic sleights,
   But wrought for all times proof, strong to bid prease
   And shiver ignorants, like Hercules,
   On their own dung-hills; but our formal clerks,
   Blown for profession, spend their souls in sparks,
   Framed of dismember'd parts that make most show,
   And like to broken links of knowledge go."

In the first line of the extract he echoes back the slur which Shakespeare casts at him in the 21st Sonnet where he refers to 'Chapman's avowed intention to publish " The Amorous Zodiac," and says of his own Sonnets,

" I will not praise that purpose not to sell."

The remainder of this extract bears the usual stamp of his anti-Shakespearean passages: " ignorant" and " dung-hill" are words which he often uses against our poet.

The last four lines of the extract,

> " But our formal clerks,
> Blown for profession, spend their souls in sparks,
> Framed of dismember'd parts that make most show
> And like to broken links of knowledge go,"

almost spell the word sonnets.

In the following passage I quote, Chapman evidently refers again to Shakespeare's Sonnets to his patron:

> " When thy true wisdom by thy learning won,
> Shall honour learning while there shines a sun;
> And thine own name in merit, far above
> *Their tympanies of state, that arms of love,*
> *Fortune, or blood shall lift to dignity."*

He speaks of the Sonnets as "tympanies of state." Shakespeare very probably refers to this passage in the 124th Sonnet, where he says:

> " *If my dear love were but the child of state,*
> *It might for Fortune's bastard be unfather'd,*
> As subject to Time's love or to Time's hate,
> Weeds among weeds, or flowers with flowers
>   gather'd.
> No, it was builded far from accident."

These lines of Chapman,

" Their tympanies of state, that arms of love,
  Fortune, or blood shall lift to dignity,"

being published in 1598, may also refer to Southampton's recent success in securing for his protégé
his coveted badge of gentility. This takes on
special point when we recall Chapman's slur three
years before, in " A Coronet for his Mistress Philosophy," upon Shakespeare's

" Blood without soul, of false nobility."

Further on in this poem, I find a still clearer allusion to some of the Sonnets contained in the group
78 to 96; Chapman says:

" Then past anticipating *dooms and scorns*
  Which for self-grace *each ignorant suborns,*
  Their glowing and amazed eyes shall see
  How short of thy soul's strength my weak words
      be."

In these lines Chapman refers to those Sonnets
in which Shakespeare seems to fear the waning of
his friend's regard, " anticipating " both " dooms
and scorns "; which Chapman asserts he " suborns "
for " self-grace." I shall quote:

SONNET 88.

" When thou shalt be disposed to set me light,
  And place my merit in the eye of *scorn,*
  Upon thy side against myself I'll fight,

And prove thee virtuous, though thou art for-
    sworn.
With mine own weakness being best acquainted,
Upon thy part I can set down a story
Of faults conceal'd wherein I am attainted;
That thou in losing me shalt win much glory:
And I by this will be a gainer too;
For bending all my loving thoughts on thee,
The injuries that to myself I do,
Doing thee vantage, double-vantage me.
    Such is my love, to thee I so belong,
    That for thy right myself will bear all wrong."

SONNET 89.

" Say that thou didst forsake me for some fault,
And I will comment upon that offence;
Speak of my lameness, and I straight will halt,
Against thy reasons making no defence.
Thou canst not, love, disgrace me half so ill,
To set a form upon desired change,
As I'll myself disgrace; knowing thy will,
I will acquaintance strangle, and look strange;
Be absent from thy walks; and in my tongue
Thy sweet beloved name no more shall dwell,
Lest I, too much profane, should do it wrong,
And haply of our old acquaintance tell.
    For thee, against myself I'll vow debate,
    For I must ne'er love him whom thou dost
    hate."

In these two Sonnets we have the " scorns " which

Chapman accuses Shakespeare of suborning for " self-grace " very plainly displayed.

I shall now show the dooms of which he speaks:

SONNET 92.

" But do thy worst to steal thyself away,
  For term of life thou art assured mine;
  And life no longer than thy love will stay,
  For it depends upon that love of thine.
  Then need I not to fear the worst of wrongs,
  When in the least of them *my life hath end.*
  I see a better state to me belongs
  Than that which on thy humour doth depend:
  Thou canst not vex me with inconstant mind,
  Since that *my life* on thy revolt doth lie.
  O, what a happy title do I find,
  Happy to have thy love, *happy to die!*
      But what's so blessed-fair that fears no blot?
      Thou mayst be false, and yet I know it not."

Here we have the " dooms." Shakespeare says that life will stay no longer than his friend's love; there can be little doubt but that Chapman refers to these particular Sonnets.

Chapman, continuing his attack, says:

" And that I do not like our poets prefer,
  For profit, praise, and keep a squeaking stir
  With *call'd-on Muses* to unchild their brains
  Of wind and vapour."

In these lines he again accuses Shakespeare of

seeking pelf, as he does in many passages in the earlier poems, and in the line

" With call'd-on Muses to unchild their brains "

refers to those Sonnets of Shakespeare's in which he invokes his Muse as follows :

SONNET 78.

" So oft have I *invoked thee for my Muse*
  And found such fair assistance in my verse,
  As every alien pen hath got my use
  And under thee their poesy disperse.
  Thine eyes, that taught the dumb on high to sing
  And heavy ignorance aloft to fly,
  Have added feathers to the learned's wing
  And given grace a double majesty.
  Yet be most proud of that which I compile,
  Whose influence is thine and born of thee :
  In others' works thou dost but mend the style,
  And arts with thy sweet graces graced be ;
      But thou art all my art, and dost advance
      As high as learning *my rude ignorance.*"

SONNET 79.

" Whilst I alone did call upon thy aid,
  My verse alone had all thy gentle grace ;
  But now my gracious numbers are decay'd,
  And my sick Muse doth give another place.
  I grant, sweet love, thy lovely argument
  Deserves the travail of a worthier pen ;
  Yet what of thee thy poet doth invent

He robs thee of, and pays it thee again.
He lends thee virtue, and he stole that word
From thy behaviour; beauty doth he give,
And found it in thy cheek: he can afford
No praise to thee but what in thee doth live.
    Then thank him not for that which he doth say,
    Since what he owes thee thou thyself dost pay."

Both these Sonnets belong to the same period as the other Sonnets which Chapman has indicated in this poem; they were both also written as an attack upon him, as were most of the other Sonnets to which he refers.

There are several other Sonnets in which Shakespeare very distinctly calls upon his Muse to which these lines of Chapman might refer, but I do not think that they were written at this date. In the 100th Sonnet Shakespeare says:

"*Where art thou, Muse,* that thou forget'st so
    long,"

and again

"*Return, forgetful Muse,* and straight redeem,"

and yet again,

"*Rise, resty Muse,* my love's sweet face survey,"

and in the 101st Sonnet he says:

"*O truant Muse,* what shall be thy amends,"

also,

" *Make answer, Muse,* wilt thou not haply say,"

and so on.

In the next lines of this poem of Chapman's which I shall quote, he probably refers to his recent repulse in seeking Southampton's patronage:

" Though all the rotten spawn of earth reject me.
  For though I now consume in poesy,
  Yet Homer being my root I cannot die."

In the following passage I find the first, last, and only admission upon Chapman's part that Shakespeare had any merit whatever:

" And though to rhyme and give a verse smooth
      feet,
  Uttering to vulgar palates passions sweet,
  Chance often in such weak capricious spirits,
  As in naught else have tolerable merits,
  Yet where high poesy's native habit shines,
  From whose reflections flow eternal lines,
  Philosophy retired to darkest caves
  She can discover," etc.

This admission is grudging, but it is very descriptive of Shakespeare's style, as we would imagine it judged by Chapman's mind. This poem concludes with what looks like a paraphrase of one of Shakespeare's own lines:

" But as ill-lines new filled with ink undried
  An empty pen with their own stuff applied

Can blot them out: so shall their wealth-burst
    wombs
Be made with empty pen their honours' tombs."

Chapman, in writing these lines, possibly had the
following line of Shakespeare's in mind:

" Making their tomb the womb wherein they grew."

This is from the 86th Sonnet, to which I have
shown that Chapman has hitherto referred in this
poem. It is rather difficult to tell exactly what
Chapman means in this last passage; he possibly
refers to the nobleman who has rejected him, and
predicts for him the same lack of future fame from
Shakespeare's pen that Shakespeare in the 83d Sonnet predicts for his patron if sung by Chapman,
when he says:

" For I impair not beauty, being mute,
    When others would bring life, and give a tomb."

It seems fairly evident, from the parallels which
I have here shown, that Chapman had read many
of Shakespeare's Sonnets while they were in manuscript. In this poem his references, however, are
all to the particular sequence or series which refer
to the " rival poet " and to those which immediately
follow them. Chapman very evidently recognized
them as being directed against himself.

The evidences of Chapman's hostility to Shakespeare are somewhat more definite in this poem to
Harriots than in the poems of 1594 and 1595. I

have already shown that Shakespeare answers Chapman's covert sneers and criticisms of the earlier years, in several of the Sonnets and in " Love's Labor's Lost," and that he attacks that poet's theories, which he attempts to evolve in " The Shadow of Night "; but Chapman has advanced now beyond the nebulous stage of vague theorizing, and in the year 1598 challenges the approval of the world as a translator of Homer. In his various introductory poems and prefaces he claims a very exalted plane, not only for Homer, but even for the heroes of that poet's epics; and for his own work of translation he assumes a greatness beside which he attempts to make all contemporary literary efforts pale into insignificance. I shall now show that Shakespeare takes issue with Chapman in " Troilus and Cressida," and as he attacked his old and vague ideals in "Love's Labor's Lost," so, in this later play, he satirizes the new gods of his worship.

CHAPTER IX.

SHAKESPEARE'S SATIRE UPON CHAPMAN IN "TROILUS AND CRESSIDA," IN 1598.

IN many important respects "Troilus and Cressida" stands apart from all of Shakespeare's plays. Its history, as well as its matter, has been a most fruitful source of speculation for the critics. Previous to its final inclusion in the folio of 1623 it seems to have had a most checkered career. The theory here evolved, regarding the personal relations of Shakespeare and Chapman, throws a very strong and new light both upon the play and its history.

The first actual mention which we have of it is in the year 1603, when it was entered for publication in the "Stationers' Register" in the following terms: "Master Roberts Feb'y 7th 1603. Entered for his copy in full court holden this day, to print when he hath got sufficient authority for it, the book of Troilus and Cressida as it is acted by the Lord Chamberlain's men." No publication followed this entry; we may, therefore, assume that the authority to print was denied by the Lord Chamberlain. This qualifying clause, "When he hath got sufficient authority for it," appears in the "Stationers' Register," against entries for plays for publication made by this man Roberts, seven times

Hugh Holland's alias according to Trinity College Admissions was "Roberts" — was he related to the printer

between the year 1598 and 1603. In every instance
the plays are those which have been acted by the
Lord Chamberlain's men; we find a like clause entered occasionally against other publishers in those
years, but the entry of the clause against Roberts
*outnumbers the entries against all other publishers
during that period.* In 1598 a William Jones
entered Chapman's " Blind Beggar of Alexandria "
for publication, and against this entry appear the
words: " Upon condition that it belong to no other
man." From this we may infer that applicants for
entry of plays had to prove their ownership of the
plays to be entered, and failing to do so, that entry
was either refused or qualified as in the case of
Roberts' applications. This would certainly seem
to imply that Roberts had come by the manuscripts
of these plays dishonestly, and that he failed to
secure the necessary license to publish, through his
inability to prove ownership. Roberts at this
period, and for several years later, owned the right
or contract to print the players' bills for this company. This connection placed him in a very ad-
vantageous position to secure old manuscripts, or
to copy new ones. Roberts sold this right in 1613
to William Jaggard, who, with his son, ten years
later, printed the first folio edition of Shakespeare's
plays.

It has been supposed by some critics that the
play of " Troilus and Cressida," entered in 1603 in
the " Stationers' Register " by Roberts, was not
Shakespeare's, but one of Dekker and Chettle's, of
the same name. In Henslow's papers there are

entries of moneys advanced to these writers in 1599 for a promised play of this name.

This play was produced a short time after the date of these entries, under the name of " Agamemnon "; the name, no doubt, being changed because of the previous production of Shakespeare's " Troilus and Cressida." However, that Roberts' entry in 1603 refers to Shakespeare's " Troilus and Cressida " is fully proved by the fact *that all the other entries made by this man, at this period, were of plays previously produced by the Lord Chamberlain's company;* the manuscripts of which he secured through his business connection with the theater ; and also by the fact that license to publish was in every case refused by the Lord Chamberlain.

was this proven ?

After the year 1603 the next actual mention that we have of this play is in 1609, when it was published by Bonian and Walley, twice in the same year. The title-page of the first issue reads : " The Historie of Troylus and Cresseida. As it was acted by the King's Majesty's servants at the Globe. Written by William Shakespeare. London. Imprinted by G. Eld for Richard Bonian and Henry Walley and are to be sold at the Spred Eagle in Paules Church Yeard, Over against the great North doore. 1609." The title-page of the second issue differs somewhat from the first, although the text of the play in both issues is identical; it reads as follows :

(1)

" The Famous Historie of Troylus and Cresseid. Excellently expressing the beginning of their loves, with the conceited wooing of Pandarus Prince of

(2)

Licia. Written by William Shakespeare. London. Imprinted by G. Eld for R. Bonian and H. Walley, and are to be sold at the Spred Eagle in Paules Church-yeard, over against the great north doore. 1609."

It is now generally recognized that these were not really two editions, but one edition in which for some reason the title-page was changed. The second issue of 1609, besides contradicting the assertion made in the first issue, that it had been " acted by the King's servants," differs from all the quarto editions of Shakespeare's plays in that it was published with a prefatory address, as follows:

" A NEVER WRITER TO AN EVER READER.

" NEWS.

" Eternal reader, you have here a new play, never staled with the stage, never clapper-clawed with the palms of the vulgar, and yet passing full of the palm comical; for it is a birth of your brain that never undertook anything comical vainly: and were but the vain names of comedies changed for titles of commodities or of plays for pleas, you should see all those grand censors that now style them such vanities flock to them for the main grace of their gravities; especially this author's comedies that are so framed to the life, that they serve for the most common commentaries of all the actions of our lives, showing such a dexterity and power of wit, that the most displeased with plays are pleased with his comedies. And all such dull and heavy-witted worldlings as were never capable of the wit of a comedy, coming by report of them to his representations have found that wit that they never found in themselves, and have parted better witted than they came; feeling an edge of wit set upon them more than ever they dreamed they had brain to grind it on. So much and such savoured salt of wit is in his comedies, that they seem (for their height of pleasure,) to be born in that sea that brought forth Venus. Amongst all there is none more witty than this; and had I time I would comment upon it, though I know it needs not (for so much as will make you think your testern well bestowed); but for so much worth as even poor I know to be stuffed in it, it deserves such a labour as well as the best comedy in Terence or Plautus. And believe this, that when he is gone and his comedies out of sale, you will scramble for them and set up a new English Inquisition. Take this for a warning and at the peril of your pleasure's loss and judgements, refuse not nor like this the less for not being sullied with the smoky breath of the multitude; but thank fortune for the scape it hath made amongst you since by the grand possessors' wills I believe you should have prayed for them rather than been prayed. And so I leave all such to be prayed for (for the states of their wits' health) that will not praise it. Vale."

This play was not again printed till 1623, when it was included in the folio; but even there it still

seems to have been beset by accident; it stands apart
from the other plays, in that no mention is made
of it in the catalogue, and that it occupies a place by
itself between the Histories and the Tragedies. It
seems to have been the first intention of the publishers to have included it in the Tragedies following " Romeo and Juliet." All of its pages except
the first six are unnumbered, and those six run
from 79 to 84. " Romeo and Juliet " ends with 79,
but pages 77 and 78 are missing. " Timon of
Athens," which evidently takes the place of " Troilus and Cressida," ends with page 98, and " Julius
Cæsar," following it, begins with page 109.
"Troilus and Cressida" would just fill the lacking
number of pages. The reason for this change in
position must remain a matter of conjecture. A
comparison of the quarto edition of 1609 with the
text of the play as it appears in the folio shows
plainly that the folio edition is a revision or a com-
pilation made from the quarto and an older and
unrevised copy of the play, which was probably
used in the theater, and the manuscript of which
was, no doubt, held by Hemminge and Condell.
As the copyright of the quarto was owned by
Bonian and Walley or their successors, the publishers of the folio may have had some difficulty in
securing its use for their publication, which was not
adjusted till the remainder of the plays, including
the catalogue, were printed. This seems more reasonable than the suggestion that it was removed
from the Tragedies to the Histories owing to a
doubt as to its class, as, in that event, the catalogue

of plays would have record of it, either in one class or the other.

The title-page of both the issues of the quarto in 1609 reads, "The Historie of Troylus and Cresseida"; the title-page of the folio reads, "The Tragedy of Troylus and Cresseida"; yet there can be no doubt but that much of the new matter of the revision of 1609 is included in the text of the folio; consequently, the title-page of the folio was probably taken from an earlier and unrevised manuscript, which was, as I have suggested, the property of Hemminge and Condell and the version used in the theater previous to 1609.

A very casual reading of " Troilus and Cressida " fully establishes the fact of revision, and I am inclined to believe, of more than one revision.

To those students of Shakespeare who have followed the development of the poet's style and art in his plays, the characteristics of the early plays are plainly discernible in " Troilus and Cressida," as well as the matured style of his later years, but should the internal evidence of style and matter not be sufficient to some minds to definitely settle the fact of the early production of this play, we have one distinct outside reference that puts it beyond peradventure. In the old play of " Histrio-Mastix " written about 1598, and generally accredited to Marston, appears the following passage:

"*Troylus.* Come, Cressida, my cresset light,
Thy face doth shine both day and night,
Behold, behold thy garter blue

Thy knight his valiant elbow wears,
That when he *Shakes* his furious *Speare,*
The foe, in shivering fearful sort.
May lay him down in death to snort.

" *Cressida.* O knight, with valour in thy face,
Here take my skreene, wear it for grace ;
Within thy helmet put the same,
Therewith to make thy enemies lame."

This passage obviously refers to an incident in Shakespeare's play in Act V. scene 2, where Cressida parts with Troilus' love token to Diomed.

The play upon the name of Shakespeare in the line,

" That when he *Shakes* his furious *Speare,"*

alone proves that the reference is to Shakespeare's play. Thus we see that " Troilus and Cressida," though not published before 1609, was in existence and had probably been acted previous to 1599.

Another piece of evidence exists which, if looked at critically, appears to be a reference to " Troilus and Cressida " in or about 1598. In the list of Shakespeare's plays which Meres gives us in 1598, he mentions " Henry IV."; whether or not the second part of this play is included in this mention is still a matter of conjecture. There can be no doubt, however, that the Second Part of " Henry IV." preceded " Henry V.," and we have fairly definite proof that this latter play was acted in 1599, and probably written also in that year. The proof to which I allude is the well-known reference to the Earl of Essex' expected return from the Irish wars, in the following passage in the Chorus to Act V.:

" Were now the general of our gracious empress,
    As in good time he may, from Ireland coming,
    Bringing rebellion broached on his sword,
How many would the peaceful city quit
To welcome him! "

Now in the Epilogue to Henry IV. Part II. we have an allusion to some play of Shakespeare's that was evidently produced, last preceding this one. When the date is borne in mind, and the nature of the allusion considered, it seems to refer very plainly to " Troilus and Cressida." I do not know of any other play of Shakespeare's, which, from any known data or plausible inference, we can assign to this period, and make fit the allusion, which is as follows:

" Be it known to you, as it is very well, I was lately here in the end of a displeasing play, to pray your patience for it and to promise you a better. I meant indeed to pay you with this."

In the list of extant plays of Shakespeare's which Meres gives us early in 1598, in his " Palladis Tamia," " Troilus and Cressida " is not mentioned; we may infer, then, that it was produced sometime between the middle of 1598 and the spring of 1599. It has been sometimes claimed that " Troilus and Cressida " was Shakespeare's contribution to, or share in, what is commonly known as the "War of the Theatres," and that he personified Jonson in the character of Ajax, and Marston or Dekker as Thersites. This play, as I have before suggested, shows plain evidence of revision, and perhaps of more than one revision: Shakespeare may have altered it somewhat, in 1600 or 1601, for the purpose suggested; but, whether he did so or not, it was not originally produced with this intention. We have very strong evidence that Shakespeare took no sides in this quarrel, and even if he did, "Troilus and Cressida" was produced, as has been proved, previous to its inception. That it was written in 1598, as a satirical attack upon Chapman's Homerworship, I am convinced and believe I can prove, and also that it was revised by the poet himself, and published in 1609, in answer to a new attack of Chapman's of that date. I have already pointed out that "Love's Labor's Lost" was written in 1594-95, in answer to Chapman's slurs at Shakespeare, in his publications of that period, and how later, in 1598, it was revised and published, in answer to Chapman's new attempts upon his patron's favor with his seven books of Homer. The titlepage of the quarto of 1598 reads: "Newly corrected and augmented by William Shakespeare," but, without this evidence, we can plainly see the traces of revision in the play; we may, therefore, conclude that Shakespeare was fully cognizant of its publication, and that he revised it with this intention. So with "Troilus and Cressida," it was written in 1598 as a travesty upon Chapman's fulsome laudation of Homer and his Greek heroes, which is so strongly displayed in the prefaces and addresses to the seven books of the Iliad, issued that year; and was revised and published in 1609, upon the publication of Chapman's " Tears of Peace," in which poem he not only attacks Shakespeare, but also prepares his public for the twelve books of Homer; which he issued later in the same year with a great flourish of trumpets.

It is impossible, now, to definitely divide the earlier play from the revised portions of the later period, or to show all the satirical passages which distinctly indicate each period, though many indicative passages may be shown which are palpably of the earlier year.

In attempting to separate the satirical allusions of each period, I am guided not only by the more openly personal touches which show the earlier years, or more formative stage of Shakespeare's art, and the greater frequency of rhyme which indicates the early plays of the Sonnet period, but also by the strong light of the personal theory of the Sonnets as touching the " dark lady," who, I believe, is here introduced in the character of Cressida, as she was introduced in 1594-95 in " Love's Labor's Lost " in the character of Rosaline.

Nonsense

I have already shown the touches of satire in " Love's Labor's Lost," but they are little more than touches. It was produced in the springtide of the poet's infatuation for this woman; the shafts of Chapman's envy and malice scarcely penetrated the armor of life's gladness with which this exultant passion at that period clothed him, and his satire hides itself in playful comedy. Fame was fresh and love was young; the world smiled upon him, and his idol, Southampton, called him friend; but in 1598 the times are changed, or changing. Sonnets 78 to 96 reveal the strength of his rival and show a waning of his friend's love. He is evidently left in doubt as to Southampton's intentions regarding Chapman, and a period of coolness follows.

Many of the Sonnets from 100 onwards, written sometime later, show plainly that there has been an estrangement between the poet and his friend.

Shakespeare's love for the "dark lady" has lost now its ideality; he is disillusioned; he has come to see that fickleness is inherent with her; that she is absolutely sensuous and a light-o'-love.

Sonnet 140 foreshadows the catastrophe:

" If I might teach thee wit, better it were,
   Though not to love, yet, love, to tell me so;
   As testy sick men, when their deaths be near,
   No news but health from their physicians know;
   For, if I should despair, I should grow mad,
   And in my madness might speak ill of thee:
   Now this ill-wrestling world is grown so bad,
   Mad slanderers by mad ears believed be.
     That I may not be so, nor thou belied,
      Bear thine eyes straight, though thy proud heart
        go wide."

This is the beginning of the end; the end itself is pictured in Cressida's faithlessness.

Sonnet 129, on the sexual passion, is evidently of this period; we find it almost paraphrased in Act I. scene 2 of " Troilus and Cressida ":

> " Women are angels wooing:
> Things won are done; joy's soul lies in the doing:
> That she beloved knows nought that knows not
>   this:
> Men prize the thing ungained more than it is;
> That she was never yet, that ever knew
> Love got so sweet as when desire did sue:
> Therefore this maxim out of love I teach
> Achievement is command; ungained, beseech."

His love proves false, his friend grows cold, and his rival gains in power. These changes have come rapidly; Shakespeare, so recently smiled upon in all his goings, is not prepared for them; it is too sudden to be calmly digested. His mind has not yet resolved adversity; the matured wisdom of the period of " The Tempest " has yet to be attained: his opponent angers him—his unnatural views of life, his Greek idolatry, and his constant and spiteful abuse disgust him, and he vents his anger and disgust in satire.

" Troilus and Cressida " is a satire pure and simple, and Shakespeare's conception is not attained if it is read in any other light.

In Roberts' entry the play is called " The book of Troilus and Cressida "; the quartos name it a " Historie "; the folio a " Tragedy "; and the prefa-

tory address a " Comedy." What it was in Shakespeare's eyes, we may judge from the prefatory address in the second issue of the quarto in 1609.
There can be little doubt, from the tone of this address, that the writer of it was fully in Shakespeare's
confidence as to the purport of the play as it appeared in that year. Nearly all critics have taken
this play seriously as a Tragedy or History. Her-
man Ulrici recognizes the satire; he supposes it
to be an impersonal satirical tragedy reflecting upon
the classicist cult in general. It is rather suggestive, then, that the writer of the prefatory address
should so plainly indicate the satire, and practically
tell the public that there is a hidden meaning in the
play if they will seek it; he several times mentions
it as a comedy and says: " So much and such
savoured salt of wit is in his comedies, that they
seem for the height of pleasure to be born in the
sea that brought forth Venus. Amongst all there
is none more witty than this, and had I time I
would comment on it; but for so much worth as
even poor I know to be stuffed in it, it deserves such
a labour as well as the best comedy in Terence or
Plautus," etc., etc. This is very strange language
to use in speaking of what so many critics have accepted as a dark and bloody tragedy. Whoever
was the writer of this address, I doubt if he would
so plainly have seen what has escaped the eyes of
many later critics, if he had not been taken into the
confidence of the writer of the play. The words,
" but for so much worth as even poor I know to be
stuffed in it," bespeak a knowledge deeper than that

which would have come from his own unaided reading.

This writer seems also to defend Shakespeare from the very attack made by Chapman, which I believe induced him to revise and publish the play in 1609. He says:

"And were but the vain names of comedies changed for titles of commodities, or of plays for pleas, you should see all those grand censors that now style them such vanities, flock to them for the main grace of their gravities, and all such dull and heavy-witted worldlings as were never capable of the wit of a comedy, coming by report of them to his representation, have found that wit that they never found in themselves, and have parted better witted than they came, feeling an edge of wit set upon them, more than ever they dreamed they had brain to grind it on."

Though the writer generalizes here, and uses the plural all through the passage, he merely does as Chapman does in his attacks upon Shakespeare, but that that poet in his wrath sometimes gets his numbers mixed; he at times begins a sentence as if indicating a class, using the plural " those," and " they," and ends his sentence as if indicating an individual, using the singular " he," " him," and " his "; his venom proving too strong for his grammar, which, notwithstanding his erudition, often becomes involved when he grows argumentative.

The fact that the writer of the prefatory address

Privy Council?

refers to the "*grand censors*" whom he attacks, as "*Never*" having been "*capable of the wit of a comedy,*" warrants the assumption that the person or persons he had in mind were writers who had at least tried their hands at matter of that nature; and were in all probability rival dramatists. This prefatory address, however, did not appear until 1609, when it was printed in the second issue of the play in that year; and of course may be read as applicable only to the satire of that date.

Those touches of satire directed against Chapman that are indicative of the earlier period, and which it is now possible to trace, are milder, though more personal, than the satire of the later period.

The love episodes, with the faithlessness of Cressida, are undoubtedly of the earlier year. From the evidence of the Sonnets I am led to the belief that Shakespeare's connection with the "dark lady," which had now lasted from three to four years, had a disagreeable ending about this time, and that its culmination is depicted in Cressida's perfidy.

The character of Achilles, as given us by Shakespeare, belongs also, I believe, to 1598, and was the central point of Shakespeare's satire upon Chapman's Greek worship at that date. In dedicating

Now, you've admitted it!

the seven books of the Iliad to the Earl of Essex, Chapman lauds that nobleman's "Achillean virtues," and compares him to that character. This dedication, or an equally fulsome one, was, no

no proof nor reason to suggest it!

doubt, first addressed to Southampton, and was the cause of Shakespeare's Sonnets against Chapman at that time, and also the reason for the satire in

"Troilus and Cressida," which he probably wrote while still in doubt as to whether or not his patron intended to accept Chapman's advances. The fact that there are no extant dedications from Chapman to Southampton, of this or the earlier period in 1594 or 1595, proves that Shakespeare was successful in his expostulations with Southampton, in defeating Chapman's encroachments. I have already proved that Chapman must have read Shakespeare's series of Sonnets, 78 to 96, at about this time, and certainly while they were still in manuscript; the references which he makes to them in his poem to Harriots are in two or three instances very plain. It is, therefore, reasonable to infer that Shakespeare had also seen Chapman's dedications and poems in manuscript this year while they were in Southampton's hands, and previous to their publication.

The character of "Achilles," which Chapman so belauds, becomes in Shakespeare's play that of a brutal coward and bully. The play was, no doubt, produced very shortly after the publication of Chapman's Iliad, and its intention very evidently at once recognized by that poet, as within a few months of the issue of the seven books of the Iliad he produced, separately, a single book—the 18th Iliad, under the title of "Achilles' Shield"; dedicating it also, very fulsomely, to Essex. *Both the title and dedication of this publication denote a defensive attitude.* It is very evident that his gods have been attacked, and that he issued this book as a defense, as well as a counter-attack upon his assailant. He never before or afterwards published a book of the

Rubbish

Iliad singly. To "Achilles' Shield" he appended the poem to his friend Harriots wherein he attacks Shakespeare, and clearly indicates him as the contemner of his hero Achilles, whom he defends. The passages indicating Shakespeare in that poem will, I believe, convince all of their indicative intention who will compare them critically with those Sonnets of Shakespeare's to which I have suggested that they allude. It will be noticed that Shakespeare, in his version of the story of Achilles, represents him as sulking in his tent from wounded vanity, and also because of an intrigue in which he is involved with Polyxena, one of Priam's daughters; against which version of the story Chapman issued the 18th book of the Iliad, in order to give Homer's version of Achilles' reasons for inaction. In attacking Shakespeare in the poem which he appends to this book, he very evidently alludes to the inaccuracy of Shakespeare's sources when he says:

> "Absurd and vain,
> Most students in their whole instructions are,
> But in traditions more particular;
> Leaning like rotten houses on out beams."

To the earlier period, also, I would assign a certain passage in which the sense very obviously points at Chapman, and in which his name is, I think, actually mentioned. I assign this passage to 1598, because it reveals a too strongly personal and subjective phase of Shakespeare's art to be attributed to the later period. It seems, too, to be practically a repetition of a very similar indicative passage which I find in "Love's Labor's Lost"; which latter play was revised and published that year, with the same intention that "Troilus and Cressida" was written: both were intended as travesties upon Chapman and his ideas. In each of these passages in the two plays, the word "Chapmen" is used, and in both instances the sense of the passage, as well as the actual word, points at Chapman; the sense, too, when applied to the context in the play, appears in both cases somewhat strained.

These two are the only plays of which we have any proof that they were revised by Shakespeare himself for publication.

The title-page of the quarto of "Love's Labor's Lost" states clearly that it was "revised and augmented by William Shakespeare," and the text of the play plainly shows extensive alterations. The prefatory address, as well as the title-page of the second issue of the quarto of 1609, state that the play is practically a new one; having been written and revised by Shakespeare. These are also the only plays in which caricature or satire is strongly suggested; they are the only plays in which this word "Chapmen" is used; not once again in all his poems or plays can it be found. In the light of all this it will hardly be denied that the word was used by Shakespeare as a personality.

We will first consider the passage in "Love's Labor's Lost" in which this word appears.

In the 21st Sonnet I have conclusively proved that Shakespeare refers satirically to Chapman's poem entitled " The Amorous Zodiac," and that he compares the purely private character of his own Sonnets to his patron with the avowed purpose to publish which Chapman acknowledges in his poem, when he says:

" Yet will I thee, through all the world disperse,
   If not in heaven among those braving fires
   Yet here, thy beauty, which the world admires,
   Bright as those flames shall glister in my verse."

Against which Shakespeare in the 21st Sonnet says:

" And then believe me, my love is as fair
   As any mother's child, though not so bright
   As those gold candles fix'd in heaven's air;
      Let them say more that like of hearsay well;
      I will not praise that purpose not to sell."

When this stroke, which Shakespeare makes at Chapman's mercenary motives, is compared with the passage from " Love's Labor's Lost," as follows,

              " My beauty, though but mean,
   Needs not the painted flourish of your praise;
   Beauty is bought by judgment of the eye,
   Not uttered by base sale of chapmen's tongues,"

the same idea is found to be repeated, and the word " chapmen " is merely used to give the intended personal point, it has no relation whatever to the play as shown in the context. Lord Boyet, the

[handwritten marginal note:] Here he uses the common saying to give a clue to his name!

Princess' attendant, to whom she addresses these words in answer to his flattering praise of her personal charms, is certainly no " chapman," nor is he making any " base sale."

Again, when in " Troilus and Cressida " the word " chapmen " is used, in a somewhat different sense, it indicates Chapman in a new light in 1598.

Diomed, addressing Paris and speaking of Helen, says:

"*Diomed.* She's bitter to our country: hear me,
    Paris:
For every false drop in her bawdy veins
A Grecian's life hath sunk; for every scruple
Of her contaminated carrion weight,
A Trojan hath been slain: since she could speak,
She hath not given so many good words breath
As for her Greeks and Trojans suffered death.
    Paris. Fair Diomed, *you do as chapmen do,*
Dispraise the thing that you desire to buy:
But we in silence hold this virtue well,
We'll not commend what we intend to sell."

No poet at that time, and in fact all through his life, so persistently sought the patronage of the great as Chapman; and none so bitterly condemned a like spirit in other poets. No poet so eagerly sought fame, yet none so abused and belittled it: in this way he constantly " *dispraised the thing* " that he " *desired to buy.*" It is this trait of Chapman's to which Shakespeare alludes in the first two lines of Paris' speech.

In the next two lines,

" But we in silence hold this virtue well,
  We'll not commend what we intend to sell,"

Shakespeare makes a thrust at the fulsomely lauda-
tory commendations which Chapman gives his own
works in the prefaces, poems, and addresses with
which he usually heralds his publications.

A critical reading of this play will, I believe,
justify my contention that the satirical indications
here noted belong to the earlier period.

In considering the satirical nature of the play
relative to the period of 1609, I shall, in the next
chapter, first show Shakespeare's reasons for the
enlargement and publication of his satire in that
year.

CHAPTER X.

ALL of Chapman's original poems, from the earliest to the latest, reveal in that poet a most abnor-
mal self-consciousness; he seems to find it impossible ever to forget himself or his woes.

The very thing not in Shakespeare

This fault, inherent with him, grows stronger
with the years; the plaintive self-pitying note we
find in the poems of 1594 and 1595 becomes, in his
poem to Harriots in 1598, a savage snarl, and by
1609 develops, in "The Tears of Peace," into rancorous and abusive misanthropy.

His ill success in winning patronage and friends
for his undoubtedly great works was, no doubt, in a
large measure due to his unfortunate disposition.
He seems to have had a most overweening sense of
his own importance; to have been absolutely tactless,
and quite destitute of a sense of humor.

?

In his early poems he abuses his rivals and scorns
the ignorant multitude; in his later poems he runs
amuck, and all classes and conditions come within
the measure of his wrath.

In his poem to Harriots he breaks out in this wise:

" Continue then your sweet judicial kindness
    To your true friend, that though this lump of
        blindness

189

This scornful, this despised, inverted world,
Whose head is fury-like with adders curl'd
And all her bulk a poison'd porcupine,
Her stings and quills darting at worths divine,
Keep under my estate with all contempt,
And make me live even from myself exempt,
Yet if you see some gleams of wrestling fire
Break from my spirit's oppression, showing desire
To become worthy to partake your skill,—
Since virtue's first and chief step is to will,—
Comfort me with it, and prove you affect me,
Though all the rotten spawn of earth reject me."

This passage is fairly representative of the misanthropic strain which runs through all his original
verse, and many passages can be shown of even a
bitterer tone. While he abuses the world in general
so bitterly, he reserves the very dregs of his spleen
for his great rival. We may almost trace the
growth of Shakespeare's fortune and estate, as well
as of his literary prestige, by chronologically following and noting the tone of Chapman's invectives
against him.

In 1609 Chapman produced what was up till that
time the most ambitious literary effort of his life;
the translation of twelve books of the Iliad, which
he issued under the title of "Homer, Prince of
Poets." So conscious is he of the importance of
his work that, not content with the fulsome poetical
and prose dedications to Prince Henry, he, in sixteen sonnets, calls upon as many noblemen to the
following of Homer and incidentally to the patron-

age of Chapman. A few months previous to this publication he issued a poem called "The Tears of Peace," dedicating it also to Prince Henry of Wales. This poem was meant as a precursor to, or advertisement for, his coming twelve books of the Iliad.

In this poem, as well as in the prose dedications to his Homeric translations, and also in two of the sixteen dedicatory sonnets, he covertly indicates and scurrilously attacks Shakespeare.

Nonsense

Shakespeare did not wait for the publication of the Iliad, but, recognizing the intended personalities of Chapman in "The Tears of Peace," immediately revised and published "Troilus and Cressida" as a counter-attack. It is rather suggestive that Shakespeare used the same publishers to issue this play that Chapman had shortly before employed to publish his "Tears of Peace." The prefatory address, which very evidently makes allusions to Chapman's strictures on Shakespeare's plays in "The Tears of Peace," in all likelihood emanated from these publishers.

In "The Tears of Peace" Chapman commences with an induction, in which he introduces the spirit of Homer and the spirit of Peace, and also pictures himself as being in the spirit; he then follows with an invocation in which he first calls upon the nine Muses, then upon Henry, Prince of Wales; he beseeches the Prince to dry the eyes of the mournful Muses and of weeping Peace, which shed tears of

> " The precious blood
> Of Heaven's dear Lamb that freshly bleeds in them."

He then invokes the Prince to

> " Deign to raise
> The heavy body of my humble Muse
> That thy great Homer's spirit in her may use
> Her topless flight, and bear thy fame above
> The reach of mortals and their earthly love;
> To that high honour his Achilles won,
> And make thy glory far outshine the sun."

Shakespeare has been accused of being too fulsome in his praise of his patron's grace and merits in certain of his Sonnets. The most flattering of his Sonnets sinks into commonplace greeting when compared with this incongruous and impious nonsense. After indulging in this tearfully sentimental religiosity, he commences " The Tears of Peace " proper; wherein, while apparently chanting a psalm of pious resignation, extolling peace, poverty, and contentment, and deprecating fame and fortune as things of little moment to his religious and philosophic soul, he most extravagantly belauds his coming publication and abuses and berates the world and all that therein is. He also spitefully attacks and indicates Shakespeare.

In this poem there are many fine lines and passages; in fact, Chapman here reaches in many places a higher point of poetic excellence than in any of his original verse: he is also clearer and more logical than usual, and holds more consistently to his argument. In it he evidently eased his soul of all that he tried, but failed, to utter some years before in " The Shadow of Night."

The envious and misanthropic state of Chapman's mind at this period, as revealed in this poem, and the broad and general slurs which he casts at Shakespeare, cannot be fully shown by extracts; it is infused into the spirit of the whole poem, which must be read for it to be fully apprehended.

In a few passages which I shall quote, his indications are fairly definite. Representing the spirit of Peace as speaking, he says:

" Of men there are three sorts that most foes be
  To Learning and her love, themselves and me.
  Active, Passive, and Intellective men,
  Whose self-loves, learning and her love disdain.
                    . . . Your Passive men—
  So call'd of only passing time in vain—
  Pass it in no good exercise, but are
  In meats and cups laborious, and take care
  To lose without all care their soul-spent time.
  And since they have no means nor spirits to
        climb,
  Like fowls of prey, in any high affair,
  See how like kites they bangle in the air
  To stoop at scraps and garbage, in respect
  Of that which men of true peace should select,
  And how they trot out in their lives the ring
  With idly iterating oft one thing—
  A new-fought combat, an affair at sea,
  A marriage, or a progress, or a plea.
  No news but fits them as if made for them,
  Though it be forged, but of a woman's dream;

*also deprecating himself for who was it took
on "The old Joyner of Aldgate" to his worsening.*

And stuff with such stolen ends their manless
      breasts—
Sticks, rags, and mud—they seem mere puttocks'
      nests."

(margin: You are oversensitive!)

This passage, critically read, reveals not only Chapman's usual and characteristic slings at Shakespeare's lack of learning, but shows expressions purposely used to indicate our poet, and in the last lines almost names his plays; it actually does name the well-known materials from which he constructs them. Besides these indications, it also gives strong corroborative evidence of the truth of the persistent rumors which have come down to us of Shakespeare's sociable habits; and throws a side light upon those merry meetings where conviviality, tempered by wit and wisdom, fired the spirits of Shakespeare, Ben Jonson, and their compeers, to the wit combats recorded by Beaumont in the lines:

(margin: Alltogether unproven material)

" What things have we seen
Done at the Mermaid! heard words that have been
So nimble, and so full of subtle flame,
As if that everyone from whence they came,
Had meant to put his whole wit in a jest,
And had resolved to live a fool the rest
Of his dull life."

To Chapman's dyspeptic soul this was " passing time in vain "; being " in meats and cups laborious," and " passing without all care their soul-spent time." In the next lines of this passage Chapman harps on

(margin: He was Server in ordinary)

Feathers of an Eagle stuck on a goose

his old theme of Shakespeare's ignorance of the classics and his general lack of learning, as follows:

" And since they have no means nor spirits to
   climb,
Like fowls of prey, in any high affair,
See how like _kites_ they bangle in the air
To stoop at scraps and garbage, in respect
Of that which men of true peace should select."

I have hitherto shown that Chapman refers to Shakespeare's " small Latin and less Greek " in other poems, where he writes of

" Muses that Fame's loose feathers beautify,"
and of those who are
    " Absurd and vain
. . . in their whole instructions . . .

Leaning like rotten houses on out beams,"

indicating by these expressions the stray translations from which Shakespeare borrowed the plots of certain of his poems and plays.

In the passage just quoted from " The Tears of Peace " he used the terms " scraps and garbage " in the same disdainful sense, and alluded to the miscellaneous and fragmentary sources of the plots of Shakespeare's plays, in contradistinction to his own continuously followed theme and purpose of Homeric translation.

The next passage is so plainly leveled at Shakespeare that it does not need elucidation:

> " And how they trot out in their lives the ring
>   With idly iterating oft one thing—
> *A new-fought combat, an affair at sea,*
> A *marriage,* or a *progress,* or a *plea.*
> No news but fits them as if made for them,
> Though it be forged, but of *a woman's dream;*
> And stuff with such stolen ends their manless
>   breasts—
> Sticks, rags, and mud—they seem mere *puttocks'*
>   nests."

Here we have a list of the well-known stock materials of Shakespeare's plays. There is no other
Elizabethan writer to whom this stroke can be applied, as no other writer of that day used all these
materials, and as Chapman says " iterated " them.
In this passage, however, our poet is indicated by a
veiled allusion, as well as this very palpable reference to his plays. In an earlier chapter I have
shown that Spenser very evidently alludes to Shakespeare under the name of " Ætion," in the lines:

> " And there, though last not least, is Ætion;
>   A gentler shepherd may nowhere be found:
> Whose Muse, full of high thoughts' invention,
>   Doth like himself heroically sound."

Besides making a very palpable allusion to the
name of Shakespeare in the last line of this passage,
Spenser here indicates Shakespeare's well-known
falcon crest by the use of the word " Ætion," which
is derived from the Greek āĕtos, an eagle. In the
passage from Chapman just analyzed, that poet indi-

cates Shakespeare in the same manner, but that he uses *as mean types of the falcon family* as he can find—"kite" and "puttock." If this was the only place where Chapman used these or synonymous terms, the indication I suggest might be deemed strained; but when we see the same idea twice again used, and *avowedly used in an indicative sense,* in another attack which Chapman makes upon our poet, it passes mere coincidence and lays bare the intended point.

In the preface to the complete edition of the Iliad published in 1611, Chapman says:

"But there's a certain envious *windsucker* that hovers up and down engrossing all the air with his luxurious ambitions, and buzzing into every ear my detraction; affirming I turn Homer out of the latin only, that sets all his associates and the whole rabble of my maligners on the wing with him to hear about my impair and poison my reputation. One that as he thinks whatever he gives to others he takes from himself, so that whatsoever he takes from others he adds to himself; one that in this kind of robbing doth like Mercury, but stole good, and supplied it with counterfeit bad still; one like the two gluttons Philoxenus and Gnatho, that would spit upon the dishes they loved, that no man might eat but themselves; for so this *kestrel,* with too hot a liver and lust after his own glory, and to devour all himself, discourageth all appetite to the fame of another. *I have stricken; single him if you can.*"

Scaliger

Here is a distinct challenge: "Single him if you can." These words prove that Chapman in this passage has given some indication by which his foe may be discerned. He commences by calling him a "windsucker" and ends by naming him a "kestrel." Now a windsucker, a kestrel, a puttock, and a kite are practically the same thing; they are all mean species of the falcon family, and the words are undoubtedly used in both passages derisively, and to indicate Shakespeare, as referring to his falcon crest. Chapman would not use these terms four times unless with an indicative object; when he grows merely abusive he can use, and does use, much nastier epithets.

They are not!

In this poem, "The Tears of Peace," there are many other less indicative allusions to Shakespeare which a critical reading will reveal. It was written, as I have already noted, as a precursor to his twelve books of the Iliad, which were published a few months later in the same year.

In two of the sixteen dedicatory sonnets to this publication I find what I believe to be an intended thrust at Shakespeare. Among the noblemen whose favor he seeks he addresses both the Earl of Southampton and the Earl of Pembroke. These being the only two noblemen of whom we have any definite record of their having shown favor to Shakespeare, it is interesting to notice that, in the prefatory lines to each of the sonnets addressed to these noblemen, Chapman uses a characteristic expression, indicative of his feeling towards Shakespeare, which is *not to be found in any of the other sonnets, writ-*

How fortunate

ten at the same time, and with the same avowed
object, to the other noblemen whom he addresses.
We have seen in previous poems and dedications
how often Chapman refers to and indicates Shakespeare by the use of the terms " ignorants," and
" ignorance." " Ignorance and impiety " is a common charge of his against our poet. The induction to the sonnet to Southampton reads:

" To the right valorous and virtuous Lord, the
Earl of Southampton, etc.

" The Muses' great herald, Homer, especially
calls to the following of our most forward Prince,
in his sacred expedition against *Ignorance and Im-*
piety."

The address to the sonnet to Pembroke reads:

" To the learned and most noble patron of learning, the Earl of Pembroke," etc.

" Against the two Enemies of Humanity and Religion (*Ignorance and Impiety*) the awaked spirit of
the most knowing and divine Homer, calls to attendance of our heroical Prince, the most honoured
and uncorrupted hero, the Earl of Pembroke," etc.

Seeing that these words, " Ignorance and Impiety," occur, out of all the sixteen dedications,
only in those addressed to the two noblemen whom
we know showed favor to Shakespeare, and that the
same term is constantly used in other attacks against
our poet, it is but reasonable to infer that Shakespeare is here again intended.

The charge of "ignorance," which Chapman makes against Shakespeare, is found in the earliest as well as the latest attacks; but the charge of "impiety" commences only after the production of Shakespeare's satire in "Troilus and Cressida" upon Chapman's Homer-worship. It will be noticed that Chapman, in many places, makes most absurd and incongruous claims for the sanctity of Homer and his Greeks.

I shall now endeavor, in a general way, to outline the satire in the play of "Troilus and Cressida," which belongs to the period of its revision and publication in 1609.

In the years that have elapsed between the production of the play in 1598 and its revision and publication in 1609, Shakespeare has thoroughly mastered the dramatic art. He no longer uses mere personalities to indicate Chapman, as in "Love's Labor's Lost" and in those parts of "Troilus and Cressida" which we can assign to the same period. In 1609 the hostility between the two poets was, no doubt, a matter of wider public cognizance, and the shafts they aimed at each other, even when not so personal, were better understood than in the earlier period of their rivalry. Chapman's inordinate praise of Homer has by now developed with him almost into a religion. He never speaks of him but as "divine Homer," and he even begins to claim a like moral pre-eminence, not only for the characters in Homer's Iliad, but also some shadow of it for himself. I shall quote a passage from "Troilus and Cressida" which I believe is of this period and is intended by Shakespeare to indicate this pose of Chapman's mind. Hector, speaking of Helen, says to Troilus :

" *Hect.* Brother, she is not worth what she doth
  cost
The holding.
 " *Tro.* What's aught, but as 'tis valued?
 " *Hect.* But value dwells not in particular will;
It holds its estimate and dignity
As well wherein 'tis precious of itself
As in the prizer; *'tis mad idolatry*
To make the service greater than the god;
And the will dotes, that is attributive
To what infectiously itself affects,
Without some image of the affected merit."

Atcheson
could have
learned here!

While I believe this passage to be a side stroke at Chapman, it is so veiled that it reads perfectly into the sense of the context, in which Priam's sons argue the merits of the cause of the war. This argument between the brothers is very evidently of the later period, and strongly shows the falsity of Chapman's claims for the moral and religious worth with which he tries to invest Homer and his heroes. Hector says :

" If Helen then be wife to Sparta's king,
 As it is known she is; these moral laws
 Of nature and of nations speak aloud
 To have her back return'd : thus to persist
 In doing wrong, extenuates not wrong,
 But makes it much more heavy. Hector's opinion

Is this in way of truth: yet, ne'ertheless,
My spritely brethren, I propend to you
In resolution to keep Helen still;
For 'tis a cause that hath no mean dependence
Upon our joint and several dignities.
    " *Tro.* Why, there you touch'd the life of our
        design:
Were it not glory that we more affected
Than the performance of our heaving spleens,
I would not wish a drop of Trojan blood
Spent more in her defence. But, worthy Hector,
She is a theme of honour and renown;
A spur to valiant and magnanimous deeds,
Whose present courage may beat down our foes,
And fame in time to come canonize us:
For, I presume, brave Hector would not lose
So rich advantage of a promised glory
As smiles upon the forehead of this action
For the wide world's revenue."

Here Shakespeare plainly divests Helen and the
cause of the war of all the moral altitude claimed by
Chapman, and attributes to the characters the same
mere thirst for martial glory which fired the breasts
of warriors in his own day.

In this play Shakespeare has woven his satire so
intimately into the subject, and with such masterly
objective art, that hitherto, even to the most analytic
critics, the idea of satire has been merely a matter
of supposition, and many have failed entirely to perceive it.

In all his plays Shakespeare follows the narrative

very closely, as it appears in the sources from which
he works. "Troilus and Cressida" is no exception to this rule. There can be little doubt that, for
the general outline of his play, Shakespeare used
Chaucer's poem of "Troylus and Cryseyde." He
also made some use of Lydgate's "Troye Book," and
Caxton's "Recuyell of the historyes of Troye," but
there are no incidents used in this play, which are
found in these two latter sources, that are not also
to be found in Chaucer's poem. Chapman's translation of the seven books of Homer, published in 1598,
is also mentioned by many critics as one of Shakespeare's sources. The only feature of the play directly traceable to this work of Chapman's is the
character of Thersites, and in using this character,
I am convinced that Shakespeare intentionally castigates Chapman with a rod of his own making. I
do not think that this character was used in the
earlier play of 1598, but, if it was, it was enlarged
and deepened, upon the revision of the play in 1609,
as a personal attack upon Chapman. Thersites, as
shown us by Chapman in a short passage in the 2d
book of the Iliad, is a deformed and foul-mouthed
jester. As depicted by Shakespeare, the physical
deformity is scarcely noticed, but a misanthropic,
spiteful, and envious, though strong and analytic,
mentality appears. He becomes satire and misanthropy personified. Coleridge, who was quite un-
conscious of the personalities, and oblivious of the
satire intended by Shakespeare, describes Thersites
as the "admirable portrait of intellectual power, de-
serted by all grace; wise enough to detect the weak

head, and fool enough to provoke the armed fist of his betters." In Shakespeare's play none are too high nor too sacred to be free from the venom of his tongue. Achilles, Hector, Agamemnon himself, and even old Nestor, all come in for his abuse; he even abuses himself; he berates Trojans and Greeks, individually and collectively, the war, and the object of the war, with all the scurrilous invective of an analytic and inventive, but distorted and envious, mentality.

In personifying Chapman's repellent disposition and envious nature in this character, the subtlety and strength of the attack revealed against that poet exceed, in satirical point and force, anything of a like nature in our tongue.

If the personal touches in Chapman's original poems, from the earliest to the latest, be followed, a most abnormally envious, self-centered, and misanthropic individuality, accentuating in bitterness with the years, will be displayed. *The character of Thersites, extravagant caricature as at first sight it may appear, pales into a resemblance very near to portraiture, when compared with the personality there to be found.* Much of the force and sting of the satire lies in the fact that Shakespeare uses Chapman's own personality in this character, to cast in clear relief the moral obliquity and low ethical standards of the gods of that poet's own ardent worship and fulsome praise.

Chapman claims supremacy for Homer, not only as a poet, but as a moralist, and, as I have hitherto noticed, extends his claims for moral altitude to in-

THERSITES
"
Skaliger

Could Thersites have been an early portrayal of James Starkey? See Newe Mieta — also what about Nicholas wh wh

clude the heroes of his epics. Shakespeare divests the Greek heroes of the glowing, but misty, nimbus of legend and mythology, and presents them to us in the light of common day, and as men in a world of men. In a modern Elizabethan setting he pictures these Greeks and Trojans, almost exactly as they appear in the sources from which he works. He does not stretch the truth of what he finds, nor draw willfully distorted pictures, and yet, the Achilles, the Ulysses, the Ajax, etc., which we find in the play, have lost their demigodlike pose. How does he do it? The masterly realistic and satirical effect he produces comes wholly from a changed point of view. He displays pagan Greek and Trojan life in action—with its low ideals of religion, womanhood, and honor; with its bloodiness and sensuality—*upon a background from which he has eliminated historical perspective.* Thus, in the light of Christian civilization and chivalric ideals, Achilles becomes a disgruntled bully and coward; Ajax a frothy boaster; Patroclus a pimp; Nestor a dotard; Diomed a libertine; Agamemnon a mock king; Ulysses a Machiavellian opportunist; and Helen and Cressida wantons. The satirical effect is vastly enhanced, and its intention revealed, by the introduction of the character of Thersites, which runs as a scornful and gibing commentary through the whole play.

While Shakespeare was, no doubt, moved in the first place to this satire by personal considerations incidental to his enmity to Chapman, I cannot but believe that, in Chapman's exorbitant claims for

" divine Homer," and in the incongruous religiosity with which he invested Homer's heroes, and the high moral plane upon which he placed them, Shakespeare's sane and judicial mind not only recognized the falsity and sham, but, to some extent, apprehended the evil effect which such an extravagant admiration and indiscriminate acceptance of old-world and pagan ideals might have, not only upon our budding English literature, but even upon English life.

After the death of Shakespeare, and indeed for some time before it, the classicist movement inaugurated by the Renaissance gained by slow, but sure, stages upon our distinctively English literature and threatened for a long period to quite engulf it, but the healthy growth which it had already attained in Elizabethan days, and the established status which the dominant pen of Shakespeare, and the fine discrimination of the translators of the authorized version of the Bible had given our English tongue, enabled it in time to reassert itself, strengthened and beautified by the classicist purgation through which it had passed.

It is curious and interesting, then, to notice almost at the inception of the classicist movement the unavowed, but real champions of these divergent schools, moved apparently by a personal enmity, locking horns in combat, unconsciously, but none the less really, over an issue which it took two more centuries to decide.

CHAPTER XI.

CONCLUSION.

I DOUBT if any reader who has followed the arguments and proofs which I have adduced in the foregoing pages will fail to see that the patron, the rival, and the mistress of the Sonnets, were living actualities. The identity of the patron and rival, I believe, is definitely proved; I have not attempted to prove that of the " dark lady," but think that it may yet be done. In 1594, on September 3, a poem called " Willobie his Avisa " was licensed for publication. In the following prefatory verses to that poem we have one of the earliest extant mentions of Shakespeare's name.

" In Lavine land, though Livy boast
  There hath been seen a constant dame ;
  Though Rome lament that she have lost
  The garland of her rarest fame ;
  Yet now we see that here is found,
  As great a faith in English ground.
  Though Collatine have dearly bought
  To high renown a lasting life
  And found, that, most in vain have sought
  To have a fair and constant wife
  Yet Tarquin pluckt his glittering grape
  And Shakespeare paints poor Lucrece' rape."

Here we have Shakespeare mentioned by name. Two of the characters in the story of this poem have initials which coincide exactly with those of Shakespeare and Southampton: " Henry Willobie and W. S." The libelous nature and intention of the poem is revealed in the fact that, upon its second issue in 1596, it was condemned by the public censor and withdrawn from print.

I am strongly of the opinion, held by many critics, that this poem refers to Shakespeare and Southampton, and to their acquaintance with the " dark lady " of the Sonnets, who is here given the name of " Avisa," but I do not agree with those same critics in the opinion that this poem refers to the period of the affair with the " dark lady " revealed in the Sonnets, but am inclined to believe that it alludes to an earlier period of Shakespeare's acquaintance with this woman, which antedates this affair by nearly two years.

Shakespeare's attack upon Chapman's " Amorous Zodiac," in the 20th and 21st Sonnets, and his references to the " Coronet for his Mistress Philosophy," in the 69th and 70th Sonnets, which I date shortly after the issue of these poems in 1595, were all anterior to Sonnets 30, 31, and 32, 40, 41, and 42, which reveal Southampton's culpability. The following lines from the 70th Sonnet are undoubtedly of an earlier time:

" And thou present'st a pure unstained prime.
Thou hast passed by the ambush of young days,
Either not assail'd, or victor being charged."

If the " H. W. and W. S." of " Willobie his
Avisa " denote Shakespeare or Southampton, the
story there told refers to the earlier stages of the
poet's friendship with the " dark lady." In the
early verses of this poem " Avisa " is unmarried; in
the later verses she is married.

Her home, while she was still unmarried, is described as being somewhere in the country, as follows :

" At east of this a castle stands ;
  By ancient shepherds built of old ;
  And lately was in shepherds' hands ;
  Though now by brothers bought and sold.
  At west side springs a crystal well,
  There doth this chaste Avisa dwell.

" In sea-bred soil, on Tempe downs ;
  Whose silver spring from Neptune's well,
  With mirth salutes the neighbouring towns," etc.

The latter verses, which show her as married, de-
scribe quite a different residence, which is evidently
in London.

" See yonder house, where hangs the badge
  Of England's saint, when captains cry
  Victorious laud to conquering rage,
  Lo there my hopeless help doth lie ;
  And there that friendly foe doth dwell,
  That makes my heart thus rage and swell."

Her connections, now, are also described as of
" meanest trade," consequently, " the badge of Eng-

land's saint " cannot be armorial, but is, very probably, the sign of an inn.   Avisa, then, has married
an innkeeper; the inn is known as the George, or
the St. George and Dragon.

This will probably account for the fact that
Shakespeare and Southampton, nobleman and
player, could alike meet her on the same social footing.   The very intimate knowledge of tavern life
which Shakespeare shows us in many of his plays
was, no doubt, the fruit of his experience.   The
story in this poem shows no indiscretion upon the
part of Avisa; both H. W. and W. S. are represented
as being unsuccessful in their intrigues and assaults.
This poem, upon its first publication in 1594, was
allowed to pass unchallenged; in 1596, however
(in which year I date Southampton's infidelity to
Shakespeare, during the latter's absence in Stratford), upon its second issue, it was immediately condemned by the public censor as libelous.   This
action of the censor shows that the object of the
libel at this date felt the stroke and complained, and
shows also that the complainant was a man of some
consequence, to have secured such speedy action
from his protest.   Many of Shakespeare's Sonnets to
the " dark lady " show a much more advanced stage
in their affair than that shown in " Willobie
his Avisa."   Southampton's indiscretion was evidently a very temporary thing, and his repentance and apology seem to follow closely upon
the avowal of his fault.   I believe that Shakespeare
wrote " The Two Gentlemen of Verona " in 1594,
and that the experiences of Proteus and Valentine

to some extent portray the facts in his own and his friend's ease.

Assuming, then, that Avisa and the " dark lady " are one and the same person, it is not impossible that research might yet reveal her identity. The allusions to her early and later homes which we get in this poem, and which were evidently used with indicative intention, may yet be followed out. It is possible, then, that the identity of the " dark lady " is not an insoluble mystery. There is not much to be gained, however, even could we definitely identify this woman.

The female characters of Shakespeare's plays which are more plainly his own ideal conceptions of womanhood differ from this recurring sensuous and fleshly personality—which first appears in " Love's Labor's Lost " as Rosaline, and later in " Troilus and Cressida " as Cressida, and afterwards as Cleopatra—only in the added sensuousness; she always retains, to some extent, that captivating elusiveness of all Shakespeare's women. I have used the expression " his own ideal conception of womanhood," but no man, not even Shakespeare, ever evolved from his own consciousness such witchery of femininity as his female characters reveal. To have attained such mastery of this subject, he must have closely studied, not women, but a woman, and that woman a very " daughter of Eve "; one who, even in her faults and vices, preserved an " infinite variety " of charm.

" Whence hast thou this becoming of things ill,
That in the very refuse of thy deeds,

There is such strength, and warrantise of skill,
That in my mind, thy worst, all best exceeds? "

This woman appears as Rosaline in the initiatory
stages of the poet's enslavement in 1594 or 1595
(though I think I perceive a few added touches of
the date of the revision of this play in this character). She shows as Cressida when the bloom of
love is worn away and the ideal is lost in lust, and
as Cleopatra some time afterwards, when the whole
affair has become a reminiscence: "would I had
never seen her!" says Antony. "O, sir," replies
Enobarbus, "you had then left unseen a wonderful
piece of work; which not to have been blessed
withal, would have discredited your travel."

Whatever the real facts concerning Shakespeare's
connection with this woman may have been, there
can be no doubt that he loved her and idealized her
with his love, and that, finally, his ideal was shat-
tered; but to her influence upon his mind we owe
some of his greatest and most inspired work. No
one can read "Romeo and Juliet" without feeling
and knowing that the writer had experienced the
full force of what he pictured; no one but a lover
could have written what Mr. Gollancz calls "This
song of songs of romantic passion."

It has not been my intention, in treating of this
matter, either to exaggerate or palliate our poet's
fault, but to portray him as he was, and as I believe
he himself would prefer to be shown. "Paint the
wart," said Cromwell to his flattering limner. "I
am that I am," says Shakespeare, alluding to those

who gossiped of his frailties. Let us, then, take him as we find him; neglecting nothing that will enable us to better understand and appreciate his great genius.

The character of Southampton must necessarily interest us on account of his friendship for, and favor shown to, Shakespeare. The faults of this young nobleman's character were largely due to his environment from infancy. Heir to vast estate, and an only son, to whom, at an early age, were lost the firm control and careful guidance of his father; petted and spoiled, no doubt, as a child, and indulged as a youth; he presents withal, in manhood, a noble figure, and reveals a generous and lovable nature. He was a typical Elizabethan, fully imbued with the virile spirit of the time; a man of action, though hampered, by his wealth and position, in individual effort. He entered, like Raleigh, into the colonizing schemes of the day, as the names of Southampton River, Hampton Hundreds, and Hampton Roads in Virginia, bear record. He was a liberal patron of the arts and a true lover of literature.

A single-minded and high-tempered man of strong passions, with no capacity for the intrigue of politics, he was yet drawn into its maelstrom by his fidelity to his friends. A favorite at the Court of James, though no courtier nor timeserver, he sacrificed his prospects, by opposing the encroachment of the kingly power upon the rights of the people. As a sailor, he won renown in action against the Spanish fleet while still a youth, and he ended his days as a soldier, fighting in the cause of European

Protestantism, surviving his great protégé by but eight years. The debt which the world owes him, for his encouragement and favor to Shakespeare, has never been fully realized.

In turning from a consideration of Southampton's character to that of Chapman, I do not feel that I can be entirely just to the latter. Southampton is often represented as a pleasure-loving and pampered young aristocrat of somewhat loose principles. George Chapman, as a man, is usually taken at his own valuation; that is, as a saintly, learned, and dignified philosopher, and a contemner of vice. This was undoubtedly his pose, but I am drawn strongly to the belief that he was more or less of a humbug. He protested most vociferously against the imputation that he had translated Homer out of the Latin, and attempted to prove by most inconclusive arguments that he used the Greek only. The Rev. Richard Hooper, who writes rather sympathetically than otherwise regarding Chapman, in the preface to his edition of Chapman's Iliad (1875), asserts that Chapman undoubtedly used the Latin of Scapula in nearly all his translations.

In 1594, in his first poem, " The Shadow of Night," he takes a very lofty pose, scorning and contemning the sensuous trivialities of other poets. His poem, however, won him little fame, and nothing more substantial. In the next year, suiting himself, as he supposes, to his public, he out-Herods Herod, in the first and only effort he makes at sensuous verse. Failing in this also, he reassumes his high moral altitude, and begins to tell the world of

RUBBISH

other great things he will do. As a dramatist, his comedies are dismal failures, and his tragedies cloudy blood and thunder. As a poet, his intense egotism kills his art by precluding objectivity.

utterly untrue

He at various times succeeded in securing the favor of patrons, but seems always to have failed in holding their interest. Where his own unfortunate disposition did not lose them, fate seemed to be against him. Late in 1598 he appears to have interested the Earl of Essex; two years later Essex went to the block. In 1609 Prince Henry of Wales showed him some favor and seemed inclined to continue it; three years later this young prince died. The nobleman who favored him for the longest period, the Earl of Somerset, was himself a social pariah; but in this case Chapman's lamentable lack of common sense and tact lost him forever the favor of the Court.

Is all this Chapman's fault?

Chapman outlived Shakespeare by many years, and died as he had lived, scorning humanity, abusing and abused.

If you don't know, why write this?

His great translations, however, have kept and will, no doubt, keep his name alive.

It has often been remarked that the greatest of all our English poets is to us only a name. This is true in more senses than one: applied to a grasp of his personality, it is true with even students of Shakespeare; applied to a knowledge of his works, it is true with respect to a great many people who consider themselves well read. It has grown into habit with such people to acknowledge Shakespeare's preeminence and let it rest there. The woeful lack of even an elementary knowledge of the poet and his works is exemplified by the comparatively large amount of interest which has been evoked, in recent years, by an attempted recrudescence of what has been called the " Baconian theory."

The interest which this theory temporarily evoked has, however, been sufficient to kill it, so that it has, after all, done more good than harm, in bringing many people to a study of the poet's works who would otherwise have neglected them.

None can fail to expand their mental horizon who study Shakespeare, and they who arouse in themselves an abiding interest in his works have enlarged and intensified their lives. Ben Jonson truly said: " He is not of an age, he is for all time." He is not only perennial, but all-pervading; he arouses as much interest when translated into foreign tongues as in his own; but to the man of his own blood and tongue he is more than a poet or dramatist; he is the poet and dramatist *par excellence*.

As a people, we are supposed to lack artistic sense; Frenchmen shrug their shoulders at our paintings; Germans and Italians smile askance at our music; sculpture does not flourish with us. We undoubtedly have and have had great painters, great composers, and even sculptors, but in these branches of art our excellence is not inherent—it is borrowed; other peoples are our masters. Our highest ideal in art is not expressed by color, nor in marble, nor yet with notes of music; the former are too sensuous and material for our northern imagination, music is too vague for our practical nature. What, then, is our natural material? The truest medium by which we best express our highest ideal of beauty and of truth? The English language! With this we satisfy, not only the sense, in the harmonious combination of beautiful words, but also the sense of sense—intellectual beauty, in the expression of the idea.

Poetry is the Englishman's art.

Less sensuous than the pleasure-loving romance peoples, more practical than the theoretical and dreamy Teuton; that blending of Celt and Norse-Teuton—that being of initiative and will, which we call the Anglo-Saxon—expresses his highest ideal of beauty, not with dead pigments, nor in cold marble, nor yet by beautiful, but indefinite, sound, but with living and breathing words. So Shakespeare wrought with our material,—the word, which is the voice of the spirit of deeds and of things,—subordinating, with truest art, beauty to use, till use became beauty. This, then, is the secret of Shakespeare's unchallenged place in our national life: he is the concrete embodiment of the artistic ideal of our forceful and virile race. What all vaguely feel, he not only felt, but expressed. The dim and nebulous glimmerings of beauty which come at times to all of us, and pass unuttered, found life and expression in his pen.

The most remarkable thing about the genius of Shakespeare is his wonderful sanity; his perceptive and reflective faculties were equally developed; nothing escaped his eye, and his mind digests to use, and transmutes to beauty, all that comes into his vision. He has no touch of the madness allied to wit which we so often find in such extremely sensitive and susceptible natures. He was one with nature; his genius was not a sport, it was a development; it grew as a tree grows, strengthening and spreading with the years, taking more of the sun and the light, yet ever striking its roots deeper into the heart of things. Placed by his fate in a position where he came in contact with all classes, and where he could acquire a varied experience of life, he had not only the power to put on record what he saw and felt of common life, but also to clearly, yet beautifully, express the subtlest shades of most ardent and inspired thought.

His pervasive mind felt and saw all things, not only in detail and outline, but innately and in spirit. He did not, like Chapman, stand apart from the world in brooding and scornful disdain, but entered into it; he gave himself to the world, and the world gave itself to him. He was of no school—nature was his book and school. Book-learning he used as mere scaffolding and framework, upon which to build that which he derived from nature.

The inevitable sadness of human life, the natural result of infinite aspiration linked to finite mortality, never develops with him into a worship of sorrow, but sounds low and sweet like a minor chord, lending proper harmony to the great song of life he sings.

THE POEMS OF
GEORGE CHAPMAN.

Surrounding the portrait:

M.DC.XVI. GEORGIVS

EVASI

ÆTA: LVII.

CHAPMANVS

HOMERI METAPHRASTES

Optimus Sic sese, qui novit cuncta Magistro,
Prospiciens rerum fines Meliora sequutus
            De Homero Redivivo Hes

    Doven Kingdome proud, whist Greece, should Homer tall,
    And now one Chapman, owndsEim, from them all.   *Scotiæ Nobilis.*
Eruditorum Poetarum huius Ævi, facile Principi Dno Georgio Chapman:
Homero (velit nolit Invidia) Redivivo.   *I. M.*   *Jessellam hanc*
Χαρистηριον. D. D.
        Ille simul Musas et Homerum scripserit ipsum,
        Qui scribit Nomen, (Magne Poeta) tuum

THE POEMS OF GEORGE CHAPMAN.

THE SHADOW OF NIGHT.

[1594.]

TO

MY DEAR AND MOST WORTHY FRIEND

MASTER MATTHEW ROYDON.

IT is an exceeding rapture of delight in the deep search of knowledge (none knoweth better than thyself, sweet Matthew) that maketh men manfully indure the extremes incident to that Herculean labour: from flints must the Gorgonean fount be smitten. Men must be shod by Mercury, girt with Saturn's adamantine sword, take the shield from Pallas, the helm from Pluto, and have the eyes of Græa (as Hesiodus arms Perseus against Medusa) before they can cut off the viperous head of be-numbing ignorance, or subdue their monstrous affections to most beautiful judgment.

How then may a man stay his marvailing to see passion-driven men, reading but to curtail a tedi-ous hour, and altogether hidebound with affection to great men's fancies, take upon them as killing censures as if they were judgment's butchers, or as if the life of truth lay tottering in their verdicts.

Now what a supererogation in wit this is, to

think Skill so mightily pierced with their loves, that she should prostitutely shew them her secrets, when she will scarcely be looked upon by others but with invocation, fasting, watching; yea, not without having drops of their souls like an heavenly familiar. Why then should our *Intonsi Catones* with their profit-ravished gravity esteem her true favours such questionless vanities, as with what part soever thereof they seem to be something delighted, they queamishly commend it for a pretty toy? Good Lord how serious and eternal are their idolatrous platts for riches! No marvel sure they here do so much good with them. And heaven no doubt will grovel on the earth (as they do) to imbrace them. But I stay this spleen when I remember, my good Matthew, how joyfully oftentimes you reported unto me, that most ingenious Darby, deep-searching Northumberland, and skill-embracing heir of Hunsdon had most profitably entertained learning in themselves, to the vital warmth of freezing science, and to the admirable lustre of their true nobility, whose high-deserving virtues may cause me hereafter strike that fire out of darkness, which the brightest Day shall envy for beauty. I should write more but my hasting out of town taketh me from the paper, so preferring thy allowance in this poor and strange trifle, to the passport of a whole City of others, I rest as resolute as Seneca, satisfying myself if but a few, if one, or if none like it.

By the true admirer of thy virtues and perfectly vowed friend,

G. CHAPMAN.

HYMNUS IN NOCTEM.

GREAT goddess, to whose throne in Cynthian fires,
This earthly altar endless fumes expires;
Therefore, in fumes of sighs and fires of grief,
To fearful chances thou send'st bold relief,
Happy, thrice happy type, and nurse of death,
Who, breathless, feeds on nothing but our breath,
In whom must virtue and her issue live,
Or die for ever;—now let humour give
Seas to mine eyes, that I may quickly weep
The shipwrack of the world: or let soft sleep
(Binding my senses) loose my working soul,
That in her highest pitch she may control
The court of skill, compact of mystery
Wanting but franchisement and memory
To reach all secrets: then in blissful trance,
Raise her, dear night, to that perseverance,
That in my torture, she all Earth's may sing,
And force to tremble in her trumpeting
Heaven's crystal temples; in her powers implant
Skill of my griefs, and she can nothing want.

Then like fierce bolts, well ramm'd with heat and
    cold
In Jove's artillery, my words unfold,
To break the labyrinth of every ear,
And make each frighten'd soul come forth and
    hear.

Let them break hearts, as well as yielding airs,
That all men's bosoms (pierced with no affairs
But gain of riches) may be lanced wide,
And with the threats of virtue terrified.

Sorrow's dear sovereign, and the queen of rest,
That when unlightsome, vast, and indigest,
The formless matter of this world did lie,
Fill'd'st every place with thy divinity,
Why did thy absolute and endless sway
License heaven's torch, the sceptre of the day,
Distinguish'd intercession to thy throne,
That long before, all matchless ruled alone?
Why lett'st thou Order, orderless disperse
The fighting parents of this universe?
When earth, the air, and sea, in fire remain'd;
When fire, the sea, and earth, the air contain'd;
When air, the earth, and fire, the sea enclosed;
When sea, fire, air, in earth were indisposed;
Nothing, as now, remain'd so out of kind,
All things in gross, were finer than refined,
Substance was sound within, and had no being;
Now form gives being, all our essence seeming,
Chaos had soul without a body then.
Now bodies live without the souls of men,
Lumps being digested; monsters in our pride.

And as a wealthy fount that hills did hide,
Let forth by labour of industrious hands,
Pours out her treasure through the fruitful strands,
Seemly divided to a hundred streams,
Whose beauties shed such profitable beams,

And make such Orphean music in their courses,
That cities follow their enchanting forces;
Who running far, at length each pours her heart
Into the bosom of the gulfy desart,
As much confounded there and indigest,
As in the chaos of the hills comprest:
So all things now (extract out of the prime)
Are turn'd to chaos, and confound the time.

A step-dame Night of mind about us clings,
Who broods beneath her hell-obscuring wings,
Worlds of confusion, where the soul defamed,
The body had been better never framed,
Beneath thy soft and peaceful covert then
(Most sacred mother both of gods and men),
Treasures unknown, and more unprized did dwell;
But in the blind-born shadow of this hell,
This horrid step-dame, blindness of the mind,
Nought worth the sight, no sight, but worse than
        blind,
A Gorgon, that with brass and snaky brows
(Most harlot-like) her naked secrets shows;
For in th' expansure, and distinct attire
Of light, and darkness, of the sea, and fire;
Of air, and earth, and all, all these create,
First set and ruled, in most harmonious state,
Disjunction shows, in all things now amiss,
By that first order what confusion is:
Religious curb, that managed men in bounds,
Of public welfare, loathing private grounds
(Now cast away by self-love's paramours),
All are transform'd to Caledonian boars,

That kill our bleeding vines, displough our fields,
Rend groves in pieces; all things nature yields
Supplanting: tumbling up in hills of dearth,
The fruitful disposition of the earth,
Ruin creates men: all to slaughter bent,
Like envy, fed with others' famishment.

And what makes men without the parts of men,
Or in their manhoods, less than childeren,
But manless natures? All this world was named
A world of him, for whom it first was framed,
Who (like a tender cheveril) shrunk with fire
Of base ambition, and of self-desire,
His arms into his shoulders crept for fear
Bounty should use them; and fierce rape forbear,
His legs into his greedy belly run,
The charge of hospitality to shun.
In him the world is to a lump reversed
That shrunk from form, that was by form dis-
        persed,
And in nought more than thankless avarice,
Not rendering virtue her deserved price:
Kind Amalthea was transferr'd by Jove,
Into his sparkling pavement, for her love,
Though but a goat, and giving him her milk;
Baseness is flinty, gentry soft as silk,
In heavens she lives, and rules a living sign
In human bodies: yet not so divine,
That she can work her kindness in our hearts.

The senseless Argive ship, for her deserts,
Bearing to Colchos, and for bringing back

The hardy Argonauts, secure of wrack,
The fautor, and the god of gratitude,
Would not from number of the stars exclude.
A thousand such examples could I cite
To damn stone-peasants, that like Typhons fight
Against their Maker, and contend to be
Of kings, the abject slaves of drudgery.
Proud of their thraldom: love the kindest least,
And hate, not to be hated of the best.

If then we frame man's figure by his mind,
And that at first, his fashion was assign'd,
Erection in such god-like excellence
For his soul's sake, and her intelligence:
She so degenerate, and grown depress'd,
Content to share affections with a beast;
The shape wherewith he should be now endued
Must bear no sign of man's similitude.
Therefore Promethean poets with the coals
Of their most genial, more-than-human souls
In living verse, created men like these,
With shapes of Centaurs, Harpies, Lapithes,
That they in prime of erudition,
When almost savage vulgar men were grown,
Seeing themselves in those Pierian founts,
Might mend their minds, ashamed of such ac-
    counts:
So when ye hear the sweetest Muse's son,
With heavenly rapture of his music won
Rocks, forests, floods, and winds to leave their
    course
In his attendance: it bewrays the force

His wisdom had, to draw men grown so rude
To civil love of art and fortitude,
And not for teaching others insolence
Had he his date-exceeding excellence
With sovereign poets, but for use applied,
And in his proper acts exemplified.

   And that in calming the infernal kind,
To wit, the perturbations of his mind,
And bringing his Eurydice from hell
(Which justice signifies) is proved well.
But if in right's observance any man
Look back, with boldness less than Orphean,
Soon falls he to the hell from whence he rose:
The fiction then would temperature dispose
In all the tender motives of the mind,
To make man worthy his hell-daunting kind.
The golden chain of Homer's high device
Ambition is, or cursed avarice,
Which all gods haling being tied to Jove,
Him from his settled height could never move:
Intending this, that though that powerful chain
Of most Herculean vigour to constrain
Men from true virtue, or their pristine states
Attempt a man that manless changes hates,
And is ennobled with a deathless love
Of things eternal, dignified above:
Nothing shall stir him from adorning still
This shape with virtue, and his power with will.

   But as rude painters that contend to show
Beasts, fowls, or fish, all artless to bestow

On every side his native counterfeit,
Above his head, his name had need to set:
So men that will be men, in more than face
(As in their foreheads), should in actions place
More perfect characters, to prove they be
No mockers of their first nobility,
Else may they easily pass for beasts or fowls:
Souls praise our shapes, and not our shapes our
      souls.

And as when Chloris paints th' enamell'd meads,
A flock of shepherds to the bagpipe treads
Rude rural dances with their country loves:
Some afar off observing their removes,
Turns, and returns, quick footing, sudden stands,
Reelings aside, odd actions with their hands;
Now back, now forwards, now lock'd arm in
      arm,
Not hearing music, think it is a charm,
That like loose froes at bacchanalian feasts,
Makes them seem frantic in their barren jests.
And being cluster'd in a shapeless crowd,
With much less admiration are allow'd;
So our first excellence, so much abused,
And we (without the harmony was used,
When Saturn's golden sceptre struck the strings
Of civil government) make all our doings
Savour of rudeness and obscurity,
And in our forms show more deformity,
Than if we still were wrapt and smothered
In that confusion out of which we fled.

And as when hosts of stars attend thy flight,
Day of deep students, most contentful night,
The morning (mounted on the Muses' steed)
Ushers the sun from Vulcan's golden bed,
And then from forth their sundry roofs of rest,
All sorts of men, to sorted tasks address'd,
Spread this inferior element, and yield
Labour his due: the soldier to the field,
Statesmen to council, judges to their pleas,
Merchants to commerce, mariners to seas:
All beasts, and birds, the groves and forests range,
To fill all corners of this round Exchange,
Till thou (dear Night, O goddess of most worth)
Lett'st thy sweet seas of golden humour forth;
And eagle-like dost with thy starry wings
Beat in the fowls and beasts to Somnus' lodgings
And haughty Day to the infernal deep,
Proclaiming silence, study, ease, and sleep.
All things before thy forces put in rout,
Retiring where the morning fired them out.

So to the chaos of our first descent
(All days of honour and of virtue spent)
We basely make retreat, and are no less
Than huge impolish'd heaps of filthiness.
Men's faces glitter, and their hearts are black,
But thou (great mistress of heaven's gloomy rack)
Art black in face, and glitter'st in thy heart.
There is thy glory, riches, force, and art;
Opposed earth beats black and blue thy face
And often doth thy heart itself deface,
For spite that to thy virtue-famed train,

All the choice worthies that did ever reign
In eldest age, were still preferr'd by Jove,
Esteeming that due honour to his love.
There shine they: not to seamen guides alone,
But sacred precedents to every one.
There fix'd for ever, when the day is driven,
Almost four hundred times a year from heaven.
In hell then let her sit, and never rise,
Till morns leave blushing at her cruelties.

Meanwhile, accept, as followers of thy train
(Our better parts aspiring to thy reign),
Virtues obscured and banished the day,
With all the glories of this spongy sway,
Prison'd in flesh, and that poor flesh in bands
Of stone and steel, chief flowers of virtue's gar-
    lands.

O then most tender fortress of our woes,
That bleeding lie in virtue's overthrows,
Hating the whoredom of this painted light:
Raise thy chaste daughters, ministers of right,
The dreadful and the just Eumenides,
And let them wreak the wrongs of our disease,
Drowning the world in blood, and stain the skies
With their spilt souls, made drunk with tyrannies.

Fall, Hercules, from heaven, in tempests hurl'd,
And cleanse this beastly stable of the world:
Or bend thy brazen bow against the sun,
As in Tartessus, when thou hadst begun
Thy task of oxen: heat in more extremes

Than thou wouldst suffer, with his envious beams.
Now make him leave the world to Night and
    dreams.
Never were virtue's labours so envied
As in this light: shoot, shoot, and stoop his
    pride.
Suffer no more his lustful rays to get
The earth with issue: let him still be set
In Somnus' thickets: bound about the brows,
With pitchy vapours, and with ebon boughs.

  Rich-taper'd sanctuary of the blest,
Palace of ruth, made all of tears, and rest,
To thy black shades and desolation
I consecrate my life; and living moan,
Where furies shall for ever fighting be,
And adders hiss the world for hating me,
Foxes shall bark, and night-ravens belch in groans,
And owls shall halloo my confusions:
There will I furnish up my funeral bed,
Strew'd with the bones and relics of the dead.
Atlas shall let th' Olympic burthen fall,
To cover my untombed face withal.
And when as well the matter of our kind,
As the material substance of the mind,
Shall cease their revolutions, in abode
Of such impure and ugly period,
As the old essence and insensive prime:
Then shall the 'ruins of the fourfold time,
Turn'd to that lump (as rapting torrents rise),
For ever murmur forth my miseries.

Ye living spirits then, if any live,
Whom like extremes do like affections give,
Shun, shun this cruel light, and end your thrall,
In these soft shades of sable funeral:
From whence with ghosts whom vengeance holds
      from rest,
Dog-fiends and monsters haunting the distress'd,
As men whose parents tyranny hath slain,
Whose sisters rape, and bondage do sustain.
But you that ne'er had birth, nor ever proved,
How dear a blessing 'tis to be beloved,
Whose friends' idolatrous desire of gold,
To scorn and ruin have your freedom sold:
Whose virtues feel all this, and show your eyes,
Men made of Tartar, and of villanies.
Aspire th' extraction, and the quintessence
Of all the joys in earth's circumference:
With ghosts, fiends, monsters: as men robb'd and
      rack'd,
Murther'd in life: from shades with shadows
      black'd:
Thunder your wrongs, your miseries and hells,
And with the dismal accents of your knells
Revive the dead, and make the living die
In ruth and terror of your tortury:
Still all the power of art into your groans,
Scorning your trivial and remissive moans,
Compact of fiction, and hyperboles
(Like wanton mourners cloy'd with too much ease),
Should leave the glasses of the hearers' eyes
Unbroken, counting all but vanities.
But paint, or else create in serious truth,

A body figured to your virtues' ruth,
That to the sense may show what damned sin,
For your extremes this chaos tumbles in.
But woe is wretched me, without a name:
Virtue feeds scorn, and noblest honour, shame:
Pride bathes in tears of poor submission,
And makes his soul the purple he puts on.

    Kneel then with me, fall worm-like on the
        ground,
And from th' infectious dunghill of this round,
From men's brass wits and golden foolery,
Weep, weep your souls, into felicity:
Come to this house of mourning, serve the Night,
To whom pale Day (with whoredom soaked quite)
Is but a drudge, selling her beauty's use
To rapes, adulteries, and to all abuse.
Her labours feast imperial Night with sports,
Where loves are Christmass'd, with all pleasure's
        sorts;
And whom her fugitive and far-shot rays
Disjoin, and drive into ten thousand ways,
Night's glorious mantle wraps in safe abodes,
And frees their necks from servile labour's loads:
Her trusty shadows succour men dismay'd,
Whom Day's deceitful malice hath betray'd:
From the silk vapours of her ivory port,
Sweet Protean dreams she sends of every sort:
Some taking forms of princes, to persuade
Of men deject, we are their equals made,
Some clad in habit of deceased friends,

For whom we mourn'd, and now have wish'd
    amends;
And some (dear favour) lady-like attired,
With pride of beauty's full meridian fired:
Who pity our contempts, revive our hearts;
For wisest ladies love the inward parts.

If these be dreams, even so are all things else,
That walk this round by heavenly sentinels:
But from Night's port of horn she greets our eyes
With graver dreams inspired with prophecies,
Which oft presage to us succeeding chances,
We proving that awake, they show in trances.
If these seem likewise vain, or nothing are,
Vain things, or nothing come to virtue's share;
For nothing more than dreams with us she finds:
Then since all pleasures vanish like the winds,
And that most serious actions not respecting
The second light, are worth but the neglecting,
Since day, or light, in any quality,
For earthly uses do but serve the eye;
And since the eye's most quick and dangerous use,
Enflames the heart, and learns the soul abuse,
Since mournings are preferr'd to banquetings,
And they reach heaven, bred under sorrow's wings;
Since Night brings terror to our frailties still,
And shameless Day, doth marble us in ill.

All you possess'd with indepressed spirits,
Endued with nimble, and aspiring wits,
Come consecrate with me, to sacred Night
Your whole endeavours, and detest the light.
Sweet Peace's richest crown is made of stars,

Most certain guides of honour'd mariners,
No pen can anything eternal write,
That is not steep'd in humour of the Night.

Hence beasts, and birds to caves and bushes then,
And welcome Night, ye noblest heirs of men,
Hence Phœbus to thy glassy strumpet's bed,
And never more let Themis' daughters spread
The golden harness on thy rosy horse,
But in close thickets run thy oblique course.

See now ascends, the glorious bride of brides,
Nuptials, and triumphs, glittering by her sides,
Juno and Hymen do her train adorn,
Ten thousand torches round about them borne:
Dumb silence mounted on the Cyprian star,
With becks rebukes the winds before his car,
Where she advanced; beats down with cloudy mace,
The feeble light to black Saturnius' palace:
Behind her, with a brace of silver hinds,
In ivory chariot, swifter than the winds,
Great Hyperion's horned daughter drawn.
Enchantress-like deck'd in disparent lawn,
Circled with charms and incantations,
That ride huge spirits, and outrageous passions:
Music, and mood, she loves, but love she hates
(As curious ladies do, their public cates).
This train, with meteors, comets, lightenings,
The dreadful presence of our empress sings:
Which grant for ever (O eternal Night)
Till virtue flourish in the light of light.
                    Explicit Hymnus.

HYMNUS IN CYNTHIAM.

NATURE's bright eyesight, and the Night's fair
    soul,
That with thy triple forehead dost control
Earth, seas, and hell; and art in dignity
The greatest and swiftest planet in the sky.

Peaceful and warlike, and the power of fate,
In perfect circle of whose sacred state
The circles of our hopes are compassed:
All wisdom, beauty, majesty, and dread,
Wrought in the speaking portrait of thy face.
Great Cynthia, rise out of thy Latmian palace,
Wash thy bright body in th' Atlantic streams,
Put on those robes that are most rich in beams;
And in thy all-ill-purging purity
(As if the shady Cytheron did fry
In sightful fury of a solemn fire),
Ascend thy chariot, and make earth admire
Thy old swift changes, made a young fix'd prime,
O let thy beauty scorch the wings of time,
That fluttering he may fall before thine eyes,
And beat himself to death before he rise:
And as heaven's genial parts were cut away
By Saturn's hands, with adamantine harpey,
Only to show that since it was composed
Of universal matter, it enclosed

No power to procreate another heaven,
So since that adamantine power is given
To thy chaste hands, to cut off all desire
Of fleshly sports, and quench to Cupid's fire:
Let it approve: no change shall take thee hence,
Nor thy throne bear another inference;
For if the envious forehead of the earth
Lour on thy age, and claim thee as her birth,
Tapers nor torches, nor the forests burning,
Soul-winging music, nor tear-stilling mourning
(Used of old Romans and rude Macedons
In thy most sad and black discessions),
We know can nothing further thy recall,
When Night's dark robes (whose objects blind us
    all)
Shall celebrate thy changes' funeral.
But as in that thrice dreadful foughten field
Of ruthless Cannas, when sweet rule did yield
Her beauties' strongest proofs, and hugest love:
When men as many as the lamps above,
Arm'd Earth in steel, and made her like the skies,
That two Auroras did in one day rise.
Thus with the terror of the trumpets' call,
The battles join'd as if the world did fall:
Continued long in life-disdaining fight,
Jove's thundering eagles feather'd like the night,
Hovering above them with indifferent wings,
Till Blood's stern daughter, cruel Tyche, flings
The chief of one side, to the blushing ground,
And then his men (whom griefs and fears con-
    found)
Turn'd all their cheerful hopes to grim despair,

Some casting off their souls into the air,
Some taken prisoners, some extremely maim'd,
And all (as men accursed) on fate exclaim'd.
So, gracious Cynthia, in that sable day,
When interposed earth takes thee away
(Our sacred chief and sovereign general),
As crimson a retreat, and steep a fall,
We fear to suffer from this peace and height,
Whose thankless sweet now cloys us with receipt.

The Romans set sweet music to her charms,
To raise thy stoopings, with her airy arms:
Used loud resoundings with auspicious brass:
Held torches up to heaven, and flaming glass,
Made a whole forest but a burning eye,
T' admire thy mournful partings with the sky.
The Macedonians were so stricken dead,
With skill-less horror of thy changes dread;
They wanted hearts, to lift-up sounds, or fires,
Or eyes to heaven; but used their funeral tyres,
Trembled, and wept; assured some mischief's fury
Would follow that afflicting augury.

Nor shall our wisdoms be more arrogant
(O sacred Cynthia), but believe thy want
Hath cause to make us now as much afraid:
Nor shall Democrates, who first is said,
To read in nature's brows thy changes' cause,
Persuade our sorrows to a vain applause.

Time's motion, being like the reeling sun's,
Or as the sea reciprocally runs,

..iath brought us now to their opinions;
As in our garments, ancient fashions
Are newly worn; and as sweet poesy
Will not be clad in her supremacy
With those strange garments (Rome's hexam-
    eters),
As she is English; but in right prefers
Our native robes (put on with skilful hands
English heroics) to those antic garlands,
Accounting it no meed, but mockery,
When her steep brows already prop the sky,
To put on start-ups, and yet let it fall.
No otherwise (O queen celestial)
Can we believe Ephesia's state will be
But spoil with foreign grace, and change with
    thee
The pureness of thy never-tainted life,
Scorning the subject title of a wife,
Thy body not composed in thy birth,
Of such condensed matter as the earth.
Thy shunning faithless men's society,
Betaking thee to hounds and archery,
To deserts, and inaccessible hills,
Abhorring pleasure in Earth's common ills,
Commit most willing rapes on all our hearts:
And make us tremble, lest thy sovereign parts
(The whole preservers of our happiness)
Should yield to change, eclipse, or heaviness.
And as thy changes happen by the site,
Near, or far distance, of thy father's light,
Who (set in absolute remotion) reaves
Thy face of light, and thee all darken'd leaves:

So for thy absence to the shade of death
Our souls fly mourning, winged with our breath.

Then set thy crystal and imperial throne,
Girt in thy chaste and never-loosing zone,
'Gainst Europe's Sun directly opposite,
And give him darkness that doth threat thy light.

O how accursed are they thy favour scorn!
Diseases pine their flocks, tares spoil their corn:
Old men are blind of issue, and young wives
Bring forth abortive fruit, that never thrives.

But then how bless'd are they thy favour graces,
Peace in their hearts, and youth reigns in their
      faces:
Health strengths their bodies, to subdue the seas,
And dare the Sun, like Theban Hercules,
To calm the furies, and to quench the fire:
As at thy altars, in thy Persic empire,
Thy holy women walk'd with naked soles
Harmless, and confident, on burning coals:
The virtue-temper'd mind, ever preserves,
Oils, and expulsatory balm that serves
To quench lust's fire in all things it anoints,
And steels our feet to march on needles' points:
And 'mongst her arms hath armour to repel
The cannon and the fiery darts of hell:
She is the great enchantress that commands
Spirits of every region, seas, and lands,
Round heaven itself, and all his sevenfold heights,
Are bound to serve the strength of her conceits.

A perfect type of thy Almighty state,
That hold'st the thread, and rulest the sword of
    fate.

    Then you that exercise the virgin court
Of peaceful Thespia, my muse consort,
Making her drunken with Gorgonean dews,
And therewith all your ecstasies infuse,
That she may reach the topless starry brows
Of steep Olympus, crown'd with freshest boughs
Of Daphnean laurel, and the praises sing
Of mighty Cynthia: truly figuring
(As she is Hecate) her sovereign kind,
And in her force, the forces of the mind:
An argument to ravish and refine
An earthly soul, and make it mere divine.
Sing then withal, her palace brightness bright,
The dazzle-sun perfections of her light;
Circling her face with glories, sing the walks,
Where in her heavenly magic mood she stalks.
Her arbours, thickets, and her wondrous game,
(A huntress, being never match'd in fame),
Presume not then ye flesh-confounded souls,
That cannot bear the full Castalian bowls,
Which sever mounting spirits from the senses,
To look in this deep fount for thy pretences:
The juice more clear than day, yet shadows
    night,
Where humour challengeth no drop of right:
But judgment shall display, to purest eyes
With ease, the bowels of these mysteries.

See then this planet of our lives descended
To rich Ortygia, gloriously attended,
Not with her fifty ocean nymphs; nor yet
Her twenty foresters: but doth beget
By powerful charms, delightsome servitors
Of flowers and shadows, mists and meteors:
Her rare Elysian palace she did build
With studied wishes, which sweet hope did gild
With sunny foil, that lasted but a day:
For night must needs importune her away.
The shapes of every wholesome flower and tree
She gave those types of her felicity.
And Form herself she mightily conjured
Their priceless values might not be obscured,
With disposition baser than divine,
But make that blissful court others to shine
With all accomplishment of architect,
That not the eye of Phœbus could detect.
Form then, 'twixt two superior pillars framed
This tender building, Pax Imperii named,
Which cast a shadow like a Pyramis.
Whose basis in the plain or back part is
Of that quaint work: the top so high extended,
That it the region of the moon transcended:
Without, within it, every corner fill'd
By beauteous form, as her great mistress will'd.
Here as she sits, the thunder-loving Jove
In honours past all others shows his love,
Proclaiming her in complete Empery,
Of whatsoever the Olympic sky
With tender circumvecture doth embrace,
The chiefest planet that doth heaven enchase.

Dear goddess, prompt, benign, and bounteous,
That hears all prayers, from the least of us
Large riches gives, since she is largely given,
And all that spring from seed of earth and heaven
She doth command: and rules the fates of all,
Old Hesiod sings her thus celestial.
And now to take the pleasures of the day,
Because her night-star soon will call away,
She frames of matter intimate before
(To wit, a white and dazzling meteor),
A goodly nymph, whose beauty, beauty stains
Heavens with her jewels; gives all the reins
Of wished pleasance; frames her golden wings,
But them she binds up close with purple strings,
Because she now will have her run alone,
And bid the base to all affection.
And Euthimya is her sacred name,
Since she the cares and toils of earth must tame:
Then straight the flowers, the shadows and the
          mists
(Fit matter for most pliant humourists),
She hunters makes: and of that substance hounds
Whose mouths deaf heaven, and furrow earth with
          wounds,
And marvel not a nymph so rich in grace
To hounds' rude pursuits should be given in chase.
For she could turn herself to every shape
Of swiftest beasts, and at her pleasure 'scape;
Wealth fawns on fools; virtues are meat for vices,
Wisdom conforms herself to all Earth's guises,
Good gifts are often given to men past good,
And Noblesse stoops sometimes beneath his blood.

The hounds that she created, vast, and fleet
Were grim Melampus, with th' Ethiop's feet,
White Leucon; all-eating Pamphagus,
Sharp-sighted Dorceus, wild Oribasus,
Storm-breathing Lelaps, and the savage Theron,
Wing-footed Pterelas, and hind-like Ladon,
Greedy Harpyia, and the painted Stycté,
Fierce Trigis, and the thicket-searcher Agre,
The black Melaneus, and the bristled Lachne,
Lean-lustful Cyprius, and big-chested Aloe.
These and such other now the forest ranged,
And Euthimya to a panther changed,
Holds them sweet chase; their mouths they freely
        spend,
As if the earth in sunder they would rend.
Which change of music liked the goddess so,
That she before her foremost nymph would go,
And not a huntsman there was eagerer seen
In that sport's love (yet all were wondrous keen)
Than was their swift and windy-footed queen.
But now this spotted game did thicket take,
Where not a hound could hunger'd passage make:
Such proof the covert was, all arm'd in thorn,
With which in their attempts the dogs were torn,
And fell to howling in their happiness:
As when a flock of school-boys, whom their mistress
Held closely to their books, gets leave to sport,
And then like toil-freed deer, in headlong sort,
With shouts, and shrieks, they hurry from the
        school.
Some strew the woods, some swim the silver pool:
All as they list to several pastimes fall,

To feed their famish'd wantonness withal.
When straight, within the woods some wolf or bear,
The heedless limbs of one doth piecemeal tear,
Affrighteth other, sends some bleeding back,
And some in greedy whirl-pits suffer wrack.
So did the bristled covert check with wounds
The licorous haste of these game-greedy hounds.

In this vast thicket (whose description's task
The pens of furies, and of fiends would ask:
So more than human-thoughted horrible)
The souls of such as lived implausible,
In happy empire of this goddess' glories,
And scorn'd to crown her fanes with sacrifice,
Did ceaseless walk; exspiring fearful groans,
Curses and threats for their confusions.
Her darts, and arrows, some of them had slain,
Others her dogs eat, painting her disdain,
After she had transformed them into beasts:
Others her monsters carried to their nests,
Rent them in pieces, and their spirits sent
To this blind shade, to wail their banishment.
The huntsmen hearing (since they could not hear)
Their hounds at fault; in eager chase drew near,
Mounted on lions, unicorns, and boars,
And saw their hounds lie licking of their sores,
Some yearning at the shroud, as if they chid
Her stinging tongues, that did their chase forbid:
By which they knew the game was that way gone.
Then each man forced the beast he rode upon,
T' assault the thicket; whose repulsive thorns
So gall'd the lions, boars, and unicorns,

Dragons, and wolves; that half their courages
Were spent in roars, and sounds of heaviness:
Yet being the princeliest, and hardiest beasts,
That gave chief fame to those Ortygian forests,
And all their riders furious of their sport,
A fresh assault they gave, in desperate sort:
And with their falchions made their ways in
       wounds,
The thicket open'd, and let in the hounds.
But from her bosom cast prodigious cries,
Wrapt in her Stygian fumes of miseries:
Which yet the breaths of these courageous steeds
Did still drink up, and clear'd their venturous heads:
As when the fiery coursers of the sun,
Up to the palace of the morning run,
And from their nostrils blow the spiteful day:
So yet those foggy vapours made them way.
But pressing further, saw such cursed sights,
Such Ætnas fill'd with strange tormented sprites,
That now the vaporous object of the eye
Out-pierced the intellect in faculty.
Baseness was nobler than Nobility:
For ruth (first shaken from the brain of Love,
And love the soul of virtue) now did move,
Not in their souls (spheres mean enough for such),
But in their eyes; and thence did conscience touch
Their hearts with pity, where her proper throne
Is in the mind, and there should first have shone:
Eyes should guide bodies, and our souls our eyes,
But now the world consists on contraries.
So sense brought terror, where the mind's presight
Had saved that fear, and done but pity right.

But servile fear, now forged a wood of darts
Within their eyes, and cast them through their
      hearts:
Then turn'd they bridle, then half slain with fear,
Each did the other backwards overbear,
As when th' Italian Duke, a troop of horse
Sent out in haste against some English force,
From stately-sighted sconce-torn Nimiguen,
Under whose walls the wall most Cynthian,
Stretcheth her silver limbs loaded with wealth,
Hearing our horse were marching down by stealth.
(Who looking for them) war's quick artisan,
Fame-thriving Vere, that in those countries wan
More fame than guerdon; ambuscadoes laid
Of certain foot, and made full well appaid
The hopeful enemy, in sending those
The long-expected subjects of their blows
To move their charge; which straight they give
      amain,
When we retiring to our strength again,
The foe pursues, assured of our lives,
And us within our ambuscado drives;
Who straight with thunder of the drums and shot,
Tempest their wraths on them that wist it not.
Then (turning headlong) some escaped us so,
Some left to ransom, so to overthrow,
In such confusion did this troop retire,
And thought them cursed in that game's desire:
Out flew the hounds, that there could nothing find,
Of the sly panther, that did beard the wind,
Running into it full, to clog the chase,
And tire her followers with too much solace.

And but the superficies of the shade,
Did only sprinkle with the scent she made,
As when the sunbeams on high billows fall,
And make their shadows dance upon a wall,
That is the subject of his fair reflectings.
Or else; as when a man in summer evenings,
Something before sunset, when shadows be
Rack'd with his stooping, to the highest degree,
His shadow climes the trees, and scales a hill,
While he goes on the beaten passage still:
So slightly touch'd the panther with her scent,
This irksome covert, and away she went,
Down to a fruitful island sited by,
Full of all wealth, delight, and empery,
Ever with child of curious architect,
Yet still deliver'd; paved with dames select,
On whom rich feet in foulest boots might tread,
And never found them: for kind Cupid spread
Such perfect colours on their pleasing faces,
That their reflects clad foulest weeds with graces.
Beauty strikes fancy blind; pied show deceives us,
Sweet banquets tempt our healths, when temper
     leaves us,
Inchastity is ever prostitute,
Whose trees we loathe, when we have pluck'd their
     fruit.

Hither this panther fled, now turn'd a boar,
More huge than that th' Ætolians plagued so sore,
And led the chase through noblest mansions,
Gardens and groves, exempt from paragons,
In all things ruinous, and slaughtersome,

As was that scourge to the Ætolian kingdom:
After as if a whirlwind drave them on,
Full cry, and close, as if they all were one
The hounds pursue, and fright the earth with
      sound,
Making her tremble; as when winds are bound
In her cold bosom, fighting for event:
With whose fierce ague all the world is rent.

  But Day's arm (tired to hold her torch to them)
Now let it fall within the Ocean stream,
The goddess blew retreat, and with her blast,
Her morn's creation did like vapours waste:
The winds made wing into the upper light,
And blew abroad the sparkles of the night.
Then (swift as thought) the bright Titanides,
Guide and great sovereign of the marble seas,
With milk-white heifers, mounts into her sphere,
And leaves us miserable creatures here.

   Thus nights, fair days, thus griefs do joys sup-
      plant:
Thus glories graven in steel and adamant
Never supposed to waste, but grow by wasting
(Like snow in rivers fall'n), consume by lasting.
O then thou great elixir of treasures,
From whom we multiply our world of pleasures,
Descend again, ah, never leave the earth,
But as thy plenteous humours gave us birth,
So let them drown the world in night and death
Before this air, leave breaking with thy breath.
Come, goddess, come; the double father'd son,

Shall dare no more amongst thy train to run,
Nor with polluted hands to touch thy veil:
His death was darted from the scorpion's tail,
For which her form to endless memory,
With other lamps, doth lend the heavens an eye,
And he that show'd such great presumption,
Is hidden now, beneath a little stone.

　If proud Alpheus offer force again,
Because he could not once thy love obtain,
Thou and thy nymphs shall stop his mouth with
　　mire,
And mock the fondling, for his mad aspire.
Thy glorious temple, great Lucifera,
That was the study of all Asia,
Two hundred twenty summers to erect,
Built by Chersiphrone thy architect,
In which two hundred twenty columns stood,
Built by two hundred twenty kings of blood,
Of curious beauty, and admired height,
Pictures and statues, of as praiseful sleight,
Convenient for so chaste a goddess' fane
(Burnt by Herostratus), shall now again
Be re-exstruct, and this Ephesia be
Thy country's happy name, come here with thee,
As it was there so shall it now be framed,
And thy fair virgin-chamber ever named.
And as in reconstruction of it there,
There ladies did no more their jewels wear,
But frankly contribute them all to raise
A work of such a chaste religious praise:
So will our ladies; for in them it lies,

To spare so much as would that work suffice.
Our dames well set their jewels in their minds,
Insight illustrates; outward bravery blinds,
The mind hath in herself a deity,
And in the stretching circle of her eye
All things are compass'd, all things present still,
Will framed to power, doth make us what we will.
But keep your jewels, make ye braver yet,
Elysian ladies; and (in riches set,
Upon your foreheads) let us see your hearts;
Build Cynthia's temple in your virtuous parts,
Let every jewel be a virtue's glass:
And no Herostratus shall ever rase
Those holy monuments: but pillars stand,
Where every Grace and Muse shall hang her gar-
  land.

The mind in that we like, rules every limb,
Gives hands to bodies, makes them make them trim;
Why then in that the body doth dislike,
Should not his sword as great a veney strike?
The bit and spur that monarch ruleth still,
To further good things and to curb the ill,
He is the Ganymede, the bird of Jove,
Rapt to her sovereign's bosom for his love,
His beauty was it, not the body's pride,
That made him great Aquarius stellified.
And that mind most is beautiful and high,
And nearest comes to a Divinity,
That furtherest is from spot of Earth's delight,
Pleasures that lose their substance with their
  sight,

Such one, Saturnius ravisheth to love,
And fills the cup of all content to Jove.

If wisdom be the mind's true beauty then,
And that such beauty shines in virtuous men,
If those sweet Ganymedes shall only find,

Love of Olympus, are those wizards wise,
That nought but gold, and his dejections prize?
This beauty hath a fire upon her brow,
That dims the sun of base desires in you,
And as the cloudy bosom of the tree,
Whose branches will not let the summer see
His solemn shadows; but do entertain
Eternal winter: so thy sacred train,
Thrice mighty Cynthia, should be frozen dead,
To all the lawless flames of Cupid's godhead.
To this end let thy beams' divinities
For ever shine upon their sparkling eyes,
And be as quench to those pestiferent fires,
That through their eyes impoison their desires.
Thou never yet wouldst stoop to base assault,
Therefore those poets did most highly fault,
That feign'd thee fifty children by Endymion,
And they that write thou hadst but three alone,
Thou never any hadst, but didst affect,
Endymion for his studious intellect.
Thy soul-chaste kisses were for virtue's sake,
And since his eyes were evermore awake,
To search for knowledge of thy excellence,
And all astrology: no negligence
Or female softness fed his learned trance,

Nor was thy veil once touch'd with dalliance.
Wise poets feign thy godhead properly
The thresholds of men's doors did fortify,
And therefore built they thankful altars there,
Serving thy power in most religious fear.
Dear precedent for us to imitate,
Whose doors thou guard'st against imperious fate,
Keeping our peaceful households safe from sack,
And free'st our ships when others suffer wrack.
Thy virgin chamber then that sacred is,
No more let hold an idle Salmacis,
Nor let more sleights Cydippe injury:
Nor let black Jove, possess'd in Sicily,
Ravish more maids, but maids subdue his might,
With well-steel'd lances of thy watchful sight.

Then in thy clear and icy pentacle,
Now execute a magic miracle:
Slip every sort of poison'd herbs and plants,
And bring thy rabid mastiffs to these haunts.
Look with thy fierce aspect, be terror-strong,
Assume thy wondrous shape of half a furlong:
Put on thy feet of serpents, viperous hairs,
And act the fearfull'st part of thy affairs:
Convert the violent courses of thy floods,
Remove whole fields of corn, and hugest woods,
Cast hills into the sea, and make the stars
Drop out of heaven, and lose thy mariners.
So shall the wonders of thy power be seen,
And thou for ever live the planets' queen.
Explicit Hymnus.
Omnis ut umbra.

OVID'S BANQUET OF SENSE.

[1595.]

TO

THE TRULY LEARNED AND MY WORTHY FRIEND,

MASTER MATTHEW ROYDON.

SUCH is the wilful poverty of judgments, sweet Matthew, wandering like passportless men, in contempt of the divine discipline of Poesy, that a man may well fear to frequent their walks. The profane multitude I hate, and only consecrate my strange poems to those searching spirits, whom learning hath made noble, and nobility sacred; endeavouring that material oration, which you call *Schema;* varying in some rare fiction, from popular custom, even for the pure sakes of ornament and utility; this of Euripides exceeding sweetly relishing with me; *Lentem coquens ne quicquam dentis addito.*

But that Poesy should be as pervial as oratory, and plainness her special ornament, were the plain way to barbarism, and to make the ass run proud of his ears, to take away strength from lions, and give camels horns.

That *Energia,* or clearness of representation, required in absolute poems, is not the perspicuous delivery of a low invention; but high and hearty invention expressed in most significant and unaffected phrase. It serves not a skilful painter's turn to draw the figure of a face only to make known who it represents; but he must limn, give lustre, shadow, and heightening; which though ignorants will esteem spiced, and too curious, yet such as have the judicial perspective will see it hath motion, spirit, and life.

There is no confection made to•last, but it is admitted more cost and skill than presently-to-be-used simples; and in my opinion, that which being with a little endeavour searched, adds a kind of majesty to Poesy, is better than that which every cobbler may sing to his patch.

Obscurity in affection of words and indigested conceits, is pedantical and childish; but where it shroudeth itself in the.heart of his subject, uttered with fitness of figure and expressive epithets, with that darkness will I still labour to be shadowed. Rich minerals are digged out of the bowels of the earth, not found in the superficies and dust of it; charms made of unlearned characters are not consecrate by the Muses, which are divine artists, but by Euippe's daughters, that challenged them with mere nature, whose breasts I doubt not had been well worthy commendation, if their comparison had not turned them into pyes.

Thus (not affecting glory for mine own slight labours, but desirous others should be more worthily glorious, nor professing sacred Poesy in any degree), I thought good to submit to your apt judgment, acquainted long since with the true habit of Poesy; and now, since your labouring wits endeavour heaven-high thoughts of Nature, you have actual means to sound the philosophical conceits, that my new pen so seriously courteth. I know that empty and dark spirits will complain of palpable night; but those that beforehand have a radiant and light-bearing intellect, will say they can pass through Corinna's garden without the help of a lantern.

His ref. to Ovid

> Your own most worthily
> and sincerely affected,
> GEORGE CHAPMAN.

NARRATIO.

THE earth from heavenly light conceived heat,
　　Which mixed all her moist parts with her dry,
When with right beams the Sun her bosom beat,
　　And with fit food her plants did nutrify.
They which to Earth as to their mother cling,
　　In forked roots now sprinkled plenteously
With her warm breath, did hasten to the spring,
Gather their proper forces and extrude
All power but that with which they stood endued.

Then did Cyrrhus fill his eyes with fire,
Whose ardour curl'd the foreheads of the trees,
And made his green-love burn in his desire;
When youth and ease, collectors of love's fees,
　　Enticed Corinna to a silver spring,
Enchasing a round bower which with it sees,
　　As with a diamant doth an amell'd ring,
Into which eye most pitifully stood,
Niobe shedding tears that were her blood.

Stone Niobe, whose statue to this fountain,
In great Augustus Cæsar's grace was brought
From Sypilus, the steep Mygdonian mountain;
That statue 'tis, still weeps for former thought,
　　Into this spring Corinna's bathing place,
So cunningly to optic reason wrought

That afar off it show'd a woman's face,
Heavy and weeping; but more nearly view'd
Nor weeping, heavy, nor a woman show'd.

In summer only wrought her ecstasy,
And that her story might be still observed,
Octavius caused in curious imagery
Her fourteen children should at large be carved,
  Their fourteen breasts with fourteen arrows
      gored;
And set by her, that for her seed so starved,
  To a stone sepulchre herself deplored;
In ivory were they cut, and on each breast,
In golden elements their names imprest.

Her sons were Sypilus, Agenor, Phœdimus,
Ismenus, Argus, and Damasicthen,
The seventh call'd, like his grandsire, Tantalus.
Her daughters were the fair Astiochen,
  Chloris, Næera, and Pelopie,
Phaeta, proud Phthia, and Eugigen;
  All these apposed to violent Niobe,
Had looks so deadly sad, so lively done,
As if Death lived in their confusion.

Behind their mother two pyramides,
Of freckled marble, through the arbour view'd,
On whose sharp brows, Sol and Tytanides,
In purple and transparent glass were hew'd,
  Through which the sunbeams on the statues
      staying,
Made their pale bosoms seem with blood imbrued,

Those two stern planets' rigours still bewraying
To these dead forms came living beauty's essence,
Able to make them startle with her presence.

In a loose robe of tinsel forth she came,
Nothing but it betwixt her nakedness
And envious light. The downward-burning flame
Of her rich hair did threaten new access
    Of venturous Phaeton to scorch the fields;
And thus to bathing came our poet's goddess,
    Her handmaids bearing all things pleasure
        yields
To such a service; odours most delighted,
And purest linen which her looks had whited.
Then cast she off her robe and stood upright,
As lightning breaks out of a labouring cloud;
Or as the morning heaven casts off the night,
Or as that heaven cast off itself, and show'd
    Heaven's upper light, to which the brightest
        day
Is but a black and melancholy shroud;
    Or as when Venus strived for sovereign sway
Of charmful beauty in young Troy's desire,
So stood Corinna, vanishing her 'tire.

A soft enflower'd bank embraced the fount;
Of Chloris' ensigns, an abstracted field
Where grew melanthy, great in bees' account,
Amareus, that precious balm doth yield,
    Enamell'd pansies, used at nuptials still,
Diana's arrow, Cupid's crimson shield,
    Ope-morn, night-shade, and Venus' navil,

Solemn violets, hanging head as shamed,
And verdant calaminth, for odour famed.

Sacred nepenthe, purgative of care,
And sovereign rumex, that doth rancour kill,
Sya and hyacinth, that furies wear,
White and red jasmines, merry, meliphil,
　Fair crown-imperial, emperor of flowers,
Immortal amaranth, white aphrodil,
　　And cup-like twillpants, strow'd in Bacchus'
　　　bowers.
These cling about this nature's naked gem,
To taste her sweets, as bees do swarm on them.

And now she used the fount where Niobe,
Tomb'd in herself, pour'd her lost soul in tears
Upon the bosom of this Roman Phœbe;
Who, bathed and odour'd, her bright limbs she
　　rears,
　And drying her on that disparent round,
Her lute she takes to enamour heavenly ears,
　And try, if with her voice's vital sound,
She could warm life through those cold statues
　　spread,
And cheer the dame that wept when she was dead.

And thus she sung, all naked as she sat,
Laying the happy lute upon her thigh,
Not thinking any near to wonder at
The bliss of her sweet breast's divinity.

THE SONG OF CORINNA.

'Tis better to contemn than love,
And to be fair than wise,
For souls are ruled by eyes:
And *Jove's* bird seized by *Cypris'* dove
It is our grace and sport to see,
Our beauty's sorcery,
That makes, like destiny,
Men follow us the more we flee;
That sets wise glosses on the fool,
And turns her cheeks to books,
Where wisdom sees in looks,
Derision, laughing at his school,
    Who, loving, proves profaneness holy,
    Nature our fate, our wisdom folly.

While this was singing, Ovid young in love
With her perfections, never proving yet
How merciful a mistress she would prove,
Boldly embraced the power he could not let,
    And, like a fiery exhalation,
Follow'd the sun he wish'd might never set;
    Trusting herein his constellation,
Ruled by love's beams, which Julia's eyes erected,
Whose beauty was the star his life directed.

And having drench'd his ancles in those seas,
He needs would swim, and cared not if he drown'd,
Love's feet are in his eyes; for if he please
The depth of beauty's gulfy flood to sound,
    He goes upon his eyes, and up to them
At the first step he is; no shadier ground

Could Ovid find; but in love's holy stream
Was past his eyes, and now did wet his ears,
For his high sovereign's silver voice he hears.

Whereat his wit assumed fiery wings,
Soaring above the temper of his soul;
And he the purifying rapture sings
Of his ears' sense, takes full the Thespian bowl,
 And it carouseth to his mistress' health,
Whose sprightful verdure did dull flesh control;
 And his conceit he crowneth with the wealth
Of all the muses in his pleased senses,
When with the ears' delight he thus commences:—

"Now, Muses, come, repair your broken wings,
Pluck'd and profaned by rustic ignorance,
With feathers of these notes my mistress sings;
And let quick verse her drooping head advance
 From dungeons of contempt to smite the stars;
In Julia's tunes, led forth by furious trance,
 A thousand muses come to bid you wars.
Dive to your spring, and hide you from the stroke,
All poets' furies will her tunes invoke.

"Never was any sense so set on fire
With an immortal ardour, as mine ears;
Her fingers to the strings doth speech inspire
And number'd laughter, that the descant bears
 To her sweet voice, whose species through my
  sense,
My spirits to their highest function rears;
 To which impress'd with ceaseless confluence,

It useth them, as proper to her power,
Marries my soul, and makes itself her dower.

" Methinks her tunes fly guilt, like Attic bees,
To my ears' hives with honey tried to air;
My brain is but the comb, the wax, the lees,
My soul the drone that lives by their affair.
　O so it sweets, refines and ravisheth.
And with what sport they sting in their repair:
　Rise then in swarms and sting me thus to death,
Or turn me into swound, possess me whole
Soul to my life, and essence to my soul.

" Say, gentle Air, O does it not thee good,
Thus to be smit with her correcting voice?
Why dance ye not, ye daughters of the wood?
Wither for ever, if not now rejoice.
　Rise stones, and build a city with her notes,
And notes infuse with your most Cynthian noise,
　To all the trees, sweet flowers, and crystal floats,
That crown and make this cheerful garden quick,
Virtue, that every touch may make such music.

" O that as man is call'd a little world,
The world might shrink into a little man,
To hear the notes about this garden hurl'd,
That skill dispersed in tunes so Orphean
　Might not be lost in smiting stocks and trees,
That have no ears, but grown as it began
　Spread their renowns as far as Phœbus sees
Through earth's dull veins; that she like heaven
　　　might move
In ceaseless music, and be fill'd with love.

"In precious incense of her holy breath,
My love doth offer hecatombs of notes
To all the gods, who now despise the death
Of oxen, heifers, wethers, swine, and goats.
   A sonnet in her breathing sacrificed,
Delights them more than all beasts' bellowing
      throats,
   As much with heaven as with my hearing prized,
And as guilt atoms in the sun appear,
So greet these sounds the grissels of mine ear.

"Whose pores do open wide to their regreet,
And my implanted air, that air embraceth,
Which they impress; I feel their nimble feet.
Tread my ear's labyrinth; their sport amazeth,
   They keep such measure; play themselves and
      dance,
And now my soul in Cupid's furnace blazeth,
   Wrought into fury with their dalliance:
And as the fire the parched stubble burns,
So fades my flesh and into spirit turns.

"Sweet tunes, brave issue, that from Julia come,
Shook from her brain, arm'd like the queen of Ire,
For first conceived in her mental womb,
And nourish'd with her soul's discursive fire,
   They grew into the power of her thought;
She gave them downy plumes from her attire,
   And then to strong imagination brought,
That to her voice; wherein most movingly
She, blessing them with kisses, lets them fly;

" Who fly rejoicing; but, like noblest minds,
In giving others life, themselves do die,
Not able to endure earth's rude unkinds
Bred in my sovereign's parts too tenderly.
    O that as intellects themselves transite,
To each intelligible quality,
    My life might pass into my love's conceit,
Thus to be form'd in words, her tunes, and breath,
And with her kisses sing itself to death.

" This life were wholly sweet, this only bliss,
Thus would I live to die, thus sense were feasted,
My life that in my flesh a chaos is
Should to a golden world be thus digested;
    Thus should I rule her face's monarchy
Whose looks in several empires are invested,
    Crown'd now with smiles, and then with modesty,
Thus in her tunes' division I should reign,
For her conceit does all, in every vein.

" My life then turn'd to that, t' each note and word,
Should I consort her look, which sweeter sings,
Where songs of solid harmony accord,
Ruled with love's rule, and prick'd with all his
            stings;
    Thus should I be her notes before they be,
While in her blood they sit with fiery wings,
    Not vapour'd in her voice's 'stillery.
Nought are these notes, her breast so sweetly
            frames,
But motions, fled out of her spirit's flames.

" For as when steel and flint together smit,
With violent action spit forth sparks of fire,
And make the tender tinder burn with it;
So my love's soul doth lighten her desire
  Upon her spirits in her notes' pretence,
And they convey them, for distinct attire,
  To use the wardrobe of the common sense;
From whence in veils of her rich breath they fly,
And feast the ear with this felicity.

" Methinks they raise me from the heavy ground,
And move me swimming in the yielding air;
As Zephyr's flowery blasts do toss a sound,
Upon their wings will I to heaven repair,
  And sing them so, gods shall descend and hear,
Ladies must be adored that are but fair,
  But apt besides with art to tempt the ear
In notes of nature, is a goddess' part,
Though oft men's nature's notes please more than
        Art.

" But here are Art and Nature both confined,
Art casting Nature in so deep a trance
That both seem dead because they be divined.
Buried is heaven in earthly ignorance,
  Why break not men then strumpet Folly's bounds,
To learn at this pure virgin utterance?
  No, none but Ovid's ears can sound these sounds,
Where sing the hearts of Love and Poesy;
Which make my muse so strong, she works too
        high."

Now in his glowing ears her tunes did sleep,
And as a silver bell, with violent blow
Of steel or iron, when his sounds most deep
Go from his sides and air's soft bosom flow,
   A great while after murmurs at the stroke,
Letting the hearer's ears his hardness know,
   So chid the air to be no longer broke;
And left the accents panting in his ear,
Which in this banquet his first service were.

Olfactus.   Herewith, as Ovid something nearer
        drew
Her odours, odour'd with her breath and breast
Into the censer of his savour flew,
As if the phœnix hasting to her rest
   Had gather'd all th' Arabian spicery
T' embalm her body in her tomb, her nest,
   And there lay burning 'gainst Apollo's eye;
Whose fiery air straight piercing Ovid's brain,
Inflamed his muse with a more odorous vein.

And thus he sung, " Come, sovereign odours, come
Restore my spirits now in love consuming,
Wax hotter, air, make them more favoursome,
My fainting life with fresh-breathed soul per-
      fuming.
   The flames of my disease are violent,
And many perish on late helps presuming,
   With which hard fate must I yet stand content,
As odours put in fire most richly smell,
So men must burn in love that will excel.

" And as the air is rarefied with heat,
But thick and gross with summer-killing cold,
So men in love aspire perfection's seat,
When others, slaves to base desires, are sold.
    And if that men near Ganges lived by scent
Of flowers and trees, more I a thousand-fold
    May live by these pure fumes that do present
My mistress' quickening and consuming breath
Where her wish flies with power of life and death.

" Methinks, as in these liberal fumes I burn,
My mistress' lips be near with kiss-entices,
And that which way soever I can turn,
She turns withal, and breathes on me her spices,
    As if too pure for search of human eyes,
She flew in air disburthening Indian prizes,
    And made each earthly fume to sacrifice.
With her choice breath fell Cupid blows his fire,
And after, burns himself in her desire.

" Gentle and noble are their tempers framed,
That can be quicken'd with perfumes and sounds,
And they are cripple-minded, gout-wit lamed,
That lie like fire-fit blocks, dead without wounds,
    Stirr'd up with nought but hell-descending
      gain,
The soul of fools that all their soul confounds,
    The art of peasants and our nobles' stain,
The bane of virtue and the bliss of sin,
Which none but fools and peasants glory in.

" Sweet sounds and odours are the heavens on
    earth
Where virtues live, of virtuous men deceased,
Which in such like receive their second birth
By smell and hearing endlessly increased.
    They were mere flesh were not with them de-
      lighted,
And every such is perish'd like a beast,
    As all they shall that are so foggy-sprighted:
Odours feed love, and love clear heaven discovers,
Lovers wear sweets then—sweetest minds be lovers.

" Odour in heat and dryness is consite;
Love, then a fire, is much thereto affected;
And as ill smells do kill his appetite,
With thankful savours it is still protected.
    Love lives in spirits; and our spirits be
Nourish'd with odours, therefore love refected;
    And air, less corpulent in quality
Than odours are, doth nourish vital spirits,
Therefore may they be proved of equal merits.

" O sovereign odours; not of force to give
Food to a thing that lives nor let it die,
But to add life to that did never live;
Nor to add life, but immortality.
    Since they partake her heat that like the fire
Stolen from the wheels of Phœbus' waggonry,
    To lumps of earth can manly life inspire,
Else be these fumes the lives of sweetest dames
That, dead, attend on her for novel frames.

" Rejoice, blest clime, thy air is so refined,
That while she lives no hungry pestilence
Can feed her poison'd stomach with thy kind;
But as the unicorn's pregredience
   To venom'd pools doth purge them with his
      horn,
And after him the desert's residence
   May safely drink, so in the wholesome morn
After her walk, who there attends her eye,
Is sure that day to taste no malady."

Thus was his course of odours sweet and slight,
Because he long'd to give his sight assay,
And as in fervour of the summer's height,
The sun is so ambitious in his sway;
   He will not let the night an hour be placed,
So in this Cupid's night—oft seen in day,
   Now spread with tender clouds these odours
      cast—
Her sight, his sun so wrought in his desires,
His savour vanish'd in his visual fires.

So vulture love on his increasing liver,
And fruitful entrails eagerly did feed,
And with the golden'st arrow in his quiver,
Wounds him with longings that like torrents bleed.
   To see the mine of knowledge that enrich'd
His mind with poverty, and desperate need.
   A sight that with the thought of sight bewitch'd;
A sight taught magic his deep mystery
Quicker in danger than Diana's eye.

Stay, therefore, Ovid; venture not; a sight
May prove thy rudeness more than show thee lov-
    ing;
And make my mistress think thou think'st her
    light,
Which thought with lightest dames is nothing
    moving.
  The slender hope of favour thou hast yet,
Should make thee fear, such gross conclusions
    proving:
  Besides, the thicket Flora's hands hath set
To hide thy theft, is thin and hollow-hearted;
Not meet to have so high a charge imparted.

And should it keep thy secrets, thine own eye
Would fill thy thoughts so full of lightenings
That thou must pass through more extremity,
Or stand content to burn beneath their wings.
  Her honour 'gainst thy love in wager laid,
Thou would'st be prick'd with other senses' stings,
  To taste, and feel, and yet not there be stay'd:
These casts he cast and more, his wits more quick
Than can be cast by wit's arithmetic.

Forward and back and forward went he thus,
Like wanton Thamysis that hastes to greet
The brackish court of old Oceanus;
And as by London's bosom she doth fleet,
  Casts herself proudly through the bridge's twists,
Where, as she takes again her crystal feet,
  She curls her silver hair like amourists,

Smoothes her bright cheeks, adorns her brow with
    ships,
And, empress-like, along the coast she trips.

Till coming near the sea, she hears him roar,
Tumbling her churlish billows in her face,
Then, more dismay'd than insolent before,
Charged to rough battle for his smooth embrace,
  She croucheth close within her winding banks,
And creeps retreat into her peaceful palace;
  Yet straight high-flowing in her female pranks
Again she will be wanton, and again,
By no means staid, nor able to contain.

So Ovid with his strong affections striving,
Mask'd in a friendly thicket near her bower,
Rubbing his temples, fainting and reviving,
Fitting his garments, praying to the hour,
  Backwards and forwards went, and durst not
    venture
To tempt the tempest of his mistress' lour,
  Or let his eyes her beauty's ocean enter,
At last with prayer he pierceth Juno's ear,
Great goddess of audacity and fear.

"Great goddess of audacity and fear,
Queen of Olympus, Saturn's eldest seed,
That dost the sceptre over Samos bear,
And rulest all nuptial rites with power and meed,
  Since thou in nature art the mean to mix
Still sulphur humours, and canst therefore speed
  Such as in Cyprian sports their pleasures fix,

Venus herself, and Mars by thee embracing,
Assist my hopes, me and my purpose gracing.

" Make love within me not too kind but, pleasing,
Exiling aspen fear out of his forces,
My inward sight with outward seeing, easing,
And if he please further to stretch his courses,
 Arm me with courage to make good his charges;
Too much desire to please, pleasure divorces,
 Attempts, and not entreats, get ladies' largess.
Wit is with boldness prompt, with terror daunted,
And grace is sooner got of dames than granted."

Visus. This said, he charged the arbour with
  his eye,
 Which pierced it through, and at her breasts re-
  flected,
Striking him to the heart with ecstasy;
As do the sunbeams 'gainst the earth prorected,
 With their reverberate vigour mount in flames,
And burn much more than where they were di-
  rected,
 He saw th' extraction of all fairest dames:
The fair of beauty, as whole countries come
And show their riches in a little room.

Here Ovid sold his freedom for a look,
And with that look was ten times more enthrall'd,
He blush'd, look'd pale, and like a fever shook,
And as a burning vapour being exhaled,
 Promised by Phœbus' eye to be a star,
Heaven's walls denying to be further scaled,

The force dissolves that drew it up so far:
And then it lightens 'gainst his death and falls,
So Ovid's power, this powerful sight appals.

This beauty's fair is an enchantment made
By Nature's witchcraft, tempting men to buy,
With endless shows, what endlessly will fade,
Yet promise chapmen all eternity;
   But like to goods ill got, a fate it hath,
Brings men enrich'd therewith to beggary,
   Unless th' enricher be as rich in faith,
Enamour'd, like good self-love, with her own,
Seen in another, then 'tis heaven alone.

For sacred beauty is the fruit of sight,
The courtesy that speaks before the tongue,
The feast of souls, the glory of the light,
Envy of age, and everlasting young,
   Pity's commander, Cupid's richest throne,
Music entranced, never duly sung,
   The sum and court of all proportion;
And that I may dull speeches best afford
All rhetoric's flowers in less than in a word.

Then in the truest wisdom can be thought
Spite of the public axiom worldings hold,
That nothing wisdom is that getteth nought,
This all-things-nothing, since it is no gold.
   Beauty enchasing love, love gracing beauty,
To such as constant sympathies enfold,
   To perfect riches doth a sounder duty
Than all endeavours, for by all consent,
All wealth and wisdom rests in true content.

Contentment is our heaven, and all our deeds
Bend in that circle, seld' or never closed,
More than the letter in the word precedes,
And to conduce that compass is reposed.
　More force and art in beauty join'd with love
Than thorns with wisdom, joys of them composed
　Are arms more proof 'gainst any grief we prove
Than all their virtue-scorning misery,
Or judgments graven in stoic gravity.

But as weak colour always is allow'd
The proper object of a human eye,
Though light be with a far more force endow'd
In stirring up the visual faculty,
　This colour being but of virtuous light
A feeble image; and the cause doth lie
　In th' imperfection of a human sight,
So this for love and beauty, love's cold fire
May serve for my praise, though it merit higher.

With this digression we will now return
To Ovid's prospects in his fancy's storm.
He thought he saw the arbour's bosom burn,
Blazed with a fire wrought in a lady's form;
　Where silver pass'd the least; and Nature's vaunt
Did such a precious miracle perform,
　She lay, and seem'd a flood of diamant
Bounded in flesh; as still as Vesper's hair,
When not an aspen-leaf is stirr'd with air.

She lay at length, like an immortal soul
At endless rest in blest Elysium;

And then did true felicity enrol
So fair a lady figure of her kingdom.
  Now Ovid's muse as in her tropic shined,
And he, struck dead, was mere heaven-born be-
     come,
  So his quick verse in equal height was shrined;
Or else blame me as his submitted debtor,
That never mistress had to make me better.

Now as she lay attired in nakedness,
His eye did carve him on that feast of feasts;
" Sweet fields of life which Death's foot dare not
     press,
Flower'd with th' unbroken waves of my love's
     breasts,
  Unbroke by depth of those her beauty's floods;
See where, with bent of gold curl'd into nests
   In her head's grove, the spring-bird lameat
     broods;
Her body doth present those fields of peace,
Where souls are feasted with the soul of ease.

" To prove which paradise that nurseth these,
See, see the golden rivers that renew it;
Rich Gehon, Tigris, Phison, Euphrates,
Two from her bright Pelopian shoulders crown it.
  And two out of her snowy hills do glide,
That with a deluge of delights do drown it;
  The highest two their precious streams divide
To ten pure floods that do the body duty,
Bounding themselves in length but not in beauty.

" These wind their courses through the painted
     bowers,
And raise such sounds in their inflection
As ceaseless start from Earth fresh sorts of flowers,
And bound that book of life with every section.

    In these the muses dare not swim for drowning,
Their sweetness poisons with such blest infection,
    And leaves the only lookers on them swooning,
These forms so decks, and colour makes so shine
That gods for them would cease to be divine.

" Thus though my love be no Elysium
That cannot move from her prefixed place;
Yet have her feet no power from thence to come,
For where she is, is all Elysian grace.

    And as those happy men are sure of bliss,
That can perform so excellent a race,
    As that Olympiad where her favour is,
So she can meet them, blessing them the rather,
And give her sweets, as well as let men gather.

" Ah! how should I be so most happy then
T' aspire that place, or make it come to me?
To gather, or be given, the flower of women?
Elysium must with virtue gotten be,

    With labours of the soul and continence,
And these can yield no joy with such as she,
    She is a sweet Elysium, for the sense,
And nature doth not sensual gifts infuse
But that with sense she still intends their use.

" The sense is given us to excite the mind,
And that can never be by sense excited,
But first the sense must her contentment mind,
We therefore must procure the sense delighted,
　　That so the soul may use her faculty ;
Mine eye then to this feast hath her invited,
　　That she might serve the sovereign of mine eye,
She shall bid Time, and Time so feasted never
Shall grow in strength of her renown for ever.

" Betwixt mine eye and object, certain lines
Move in the figure of a pyramis,
Whose chapter in mine eye's gray apple shines
The base within my sacred object is ;
　　On this will I inscribe in golden verse
The marvels reigning in my sovereign's bliss,
　　The arcs of sight and how her arrows pierce :
This in the region of the air shall stand
In Fame's brass court, and all her trumps command.

" Rich Beauty, that each lover labours for,
Tempting as heaps of new-coin'd glowing gold—
Rack'd of some miserable treasurer—
Draw his desires, and them in chains enfold,
　　Urging him still to tell it, and conceal it,
But beauty's treasure never can be told,
　　None can peculiar joy, yet all must steal it.
O Beauty! this same bloody siege of thine
Starves me that yield, and feeds me till I pine.

" And as a taper burning in the dark—
As if it threaten'd every watchful eye
That viewing burns it—makes that eye his mark

And hurls gilt darts at it continually,
　Or as it envied, any eye but it
Should see in darkness, so my mistress' beauty
　From forth her secret stand, my heart doth hit;
And like the dart of Cephalus doth kill
Her perfect lover, though she mean no ill.

" Thus, as the innocence of one betray'd
Carries an Argus with it, though unknown,
And fate to wreak the treachery bewray'd;
Such vengeance hath my mistress' beauty shown
　On me, the traitor to her modesty,
So unassail'd, I quite am overthrown,
　And in my triumph bound in slavery.
O Beauty! still thy Empire swims in blood,
And in thy peace war stores himself with food.

" O Beauty, how attractive is thy power!
For as the life's heat clings about the heart,
So all men's hungry eyes do haunt thy bower.
Reigning in Greece, Troy swam to thee in Art,
　Removed to Troy, Greece follow'd thee in fears;
Thou drew'st each sireless sword, each childless
　　dart,
　And pull'd'st the towers of Troy about thine
　　ears;
Shall I then muse that thus thou drawest me?
No, but admire, I stand thus far from thee."

Herewith she rose like the autumnal star,
Fresh burnish'd in the lofty ocean flood,
That darts his glorious influence more **far**
Than any lamp of bright Olympus' brood;

She lifts her lightning arms above her head,
And stretcheth a meridian from her blood,
 That slept awake in her Elysian bed:
Then knit she up, lest loose, her glowing hair
Should scorch the centre and incense the air.

Thus when her fair heart-binding hands had tied
Those liberal tresses, her high frontier part
She shrunk in curls, and curiously plied
Into the figure of a swelling heart;
 And then with jewels of device, it graced:
One was a sun graven at his even's depart,
 And under that a man's huge shadow placed,
Wherein was writ, in sable charactery,
Decrescente nobilitate, crescunt obscuri.

Another was an eye in sapphire set,
And close upon it, a fresh laurel spray,
The skilful poise was: *Medio caret,*
To show not eyes but means must truth display.
 The third was an Apollo with his team
About a dial and a world in way.
 The motto was, *Teipsum et orbem,*
Graven in the dial; these exceeding rare
And other like accomplements she ware.

Not Tigris, Nilus, nor swift Euphrates,
Quoth Ovid now, can more subdue my flame,
I must through hell adventure to displease,
To taste and touch, one kiss may work the same:
 If more will come, more then much more I will;
Each natural agent doth his action frame,
 To render that he works on like him still;

The fire on water working doth induce
Like quality unto his own in use.
But heaven in her a sparkling temper blew—
As love in me—and so will soon be wrought.
Good wits will bite at baits most strange and new,
And words well placed, move things were never
   thought;
 What goddess is it Ovid's wits shall dare,
And he disgrace them with attempting nought?
 My words shall carry spirits to ensnare,
The subtlest hearts affecting suits importune,
" Best loves are lost for wit when men blame for-
  tune."

Narratio. With this, as she was looking in her
   glass,
 She saw therein a man's face looking on her;
Whereat she started from the frighted grass
 As if some monstrous serpent had been shown
  her:
 Rising as when, the sun in Leo's sign,
Auriga with the heavenly goat upon her,
 Shows her horn'd forehead with her kids divine,
Whose rise kills vines, heaven's face with storms
  disguising
No man is safe at sea, the Hædy rising.

So straight wrapt she her body in a cloud
And threaten'd tempests for her high disgrace,
Shame from a bower of roses did unshroud
And spread her crimson wings upon her face;
 When running out poor Ovid humbly kneeling

Full in the arbour's mouth, did stay her race
  And said, " Fair nymph, great goddess, have
      some feeling
Of Ovid's pains ; but hear, and your dishonour
Vainly surmised, shall vanish with my horror."

" Traitor to ladies' modesties," said she,
" What savage boldness harden'd thee to this?
Or what base reckoning of my modesty?
What should I think thy facts' proud reason is? "
  " Love, sacred madam, love exhaling me—
Wrapt in his sulphur, to this cloud of his
  Made my affections his artillery,
Shot me at you his proper citadel
And losing all my forces, here I fell."

" This gloss is common, as thy rudeness strange
Not to forbear these private times," quoth she,
" Whose fixed rites none should presume to change,
Not where there is adjudged inchastity ;
  Our nakedness should be as much conceal'd
As our accomplishments desire the eye :
  It is a secret not to be reveal'd,
But as virginity, and nuptials clothed,
And to our honour all to be betrothed.

" It is a want, where our abundance lies,
Given a sole dower t' enrich chaste Hymen's bed,
A perfect image of our purities
And glass by which our actions should be dress'd.
  That tells us honour is as soon defiled,
And should be kept as pure, and incompress'd.
  But sight attainteth it : for Thought, Sight's child,

Begetteth sin; and Nature bides defame,
When light and lawless eyes bewray our shame."

" Dear mistress," answer'd Ovid, " to direct
Our actions, by the straitest rule that is,
We must in matters moral quite reject
Vulgar opinion, ever led amiss,
    And let authentic Reason be our guide,
The wife of Truth, and Wisdom's governess:
    The nature of all actions must be weigh'd,
And as they then appear, breed love or loathing:
Use makes things nothing huge, and huge things
       nothing.

" As in your sight, how can sight simply being
A sense receiving essence to his flame,
Sent from his object, give it harm by seeing
Whose action in the seer hath his frame?
    All excellence of shape is made for sight.
Else, to be like a beast were no defame;
    Hid beauties lose their ends, and wrong their
       right.
And can kind love, where no harm's kind can be,
Disgrace with seeing that is given to see?

" 'Tis I, alas! and my heart-burning eye
Do all the harm, and feel the harm we do:
I am no basilisk, yet harmless I
Poison with sight, and mine own bosom too;
    So am I to myself a sorceress
Bewitch'd with my conceits in her I woo:
    But you unwrong'd and all dishonourless,

No ill dares touch, affliction, sorcery,
One kiss of yours can quickly remedy.

" I could not times observe, as others might,
Of cold affects and watery tempers framed,
Yet well assured the wonder of your sight
Was so far off from seeing you defamed
   That ever in the fane of memory
Your love shall shine by it, in me inflamed.
   Then let your power be clad in lenity,
Do not, as others would, of custom storm,
But prove your wit as pregnant as your form.

" Nor is my love so sudden since my heart
Was long love's Vulcan, with his pants' unrest,
Hammering the shafts bred this delightsome smart:
And as when Jove at once from east and west,
   Cast off two eagles, to discern the sight
Of this world's centre, both his birds join'd breast
   In Cynthian Delphos, since Earth's navel hight:
So casting off my ceaseless thoughts to see
My heart's true centre, all do meet in thee.

" Cupid that acts in you, suffers in me
To make himself one triumph-place of twain,
Into your tunes and odours turned he,
And through my senses flew into my brain
   Where rules the Prince of sense whose throne he
      takes,
And of my motions' engines framed a chain
   To lead me where he list; and here he makes
Nature, my fate, enforce me; and resigns
The reins of all to you in whom he shines,

" For yielding love then, do not hate impart,
Nor let mine eye, your careful harbinger
That hath purvey'd your chamber in my heart,
Be blamed for seeing who it lodged there;
 The freër service merits greater meed,
Princes are served with unexpected cheer,
 And must have things in store before they need:
Thus should fair dames be wise and confident,
Not blushing to be noted excellent."

Now, as when Heaven is muffled with the vapours,
His long since just divorced wife the Earth,
In Envy's breaths, to mask his spurry tapers
From the unrich abundance of her birth,
 When straight the western issue of the air
Beats with his flowery wings those brats of dearth,
 And gives Olympus leave to show his fair,
So fled th' offended shadows of her cheer,
And show'd her pleased countenance full as clear.

Which for his fourth course made our Poet court
  her, etc.

Gustus. " This motion of my soul, my fantasy
Created by three senses put in act.
Let justice nourish with thy sympathy,
 Alterationem Putting my other senses into fact,
 pati est
 sentire. If now thou grant not, now
  changed that offence;
To suffer change doth perfect sense compact:
 Change then, and suffer for the use of sense,
We live not for ourselves, the ear, and eye,
And every sense must serve society.

" To furnish then this banquet where the taste
Is never used, and yet the cheer divine
The nearest mean, dear mistress, that thou hast
To bless me with it, is a kiss of thine,
Which grace shall borrow organs of my touch
T'advance it to that inward taste of mine,
  Which makes all sense, and shall delight as much.
Then with a kiss, dear life, adorn thy feast,
And let, as banquets should, the last be best."

Corinna. I see unbidden guests are boldest still,
And well you show how weak in soul you are,
That let rude sense subdue your reason's skill,
And feed so spoilfully on sacred fare:
  In temper of such needless feasts as this,
We show more bounty still the more we spare,
  Chiefly where birth and state so different is:
Air too much rarefied breaks forth in fire,
And favours too far urged do end in ire.

Ovid. The difference of our births, imperial
    dame,
Is herein noted with too trivial eyes
For your rare wits; that should your choices frame
To state of parts, that most doth royalize,
  Not to commend mine own; but that in yours
Beyond your birth, are peril's sovereignties
  Which, urged, your words had struck with
      sharper powers;
'Tis for mere look-like-ladies, and for men
To boast of birth that still be childeren,

" Running to father straight to help their needs;
True dignities and rites of reverence,
Are sown in minds, and reap'd in lively deeds,
And only policy makes difference
   'Twixt states, since virtue wants due imperance
Virtue makes honour, as the soul doth sense,
   And merit far exceeds inheritance,
The Graces fill love's cup, his feasts adorning
Who seeks your service now, the Graces scorning."

" Pure love," said she, " the purest grace sues,
And there is contact not by application
Of lips or bodies, but of bodies' virtues,
As in our elemental nation
   Stars by their powers, which are their heat and
      light,
Do heavenly works, and that which hath proba-
      tion
   By virtual contact hath the noblest plight,
Both for the lasting and affinity
It hath with natural divinity."

Ovid replied: " In this thy virtual presence,
Most fair Corinna, thou canst not effuse
The true and solid parts of thy pure essence,
But dost thy superficial beams produce
   Of thy rich substance; which because they flow
Rather from form than from the matter's use,
   Resemblance only of thy body show
Whereof they are thy wondrous species,
And 'tis thy substance must my longings ease.

" Speak then, sweet air, that givest our speech
   event,
And teach my mistress tractability,
That art to motion most obedient,
And though thy nature swelling be and high,
  And occupiest so infinite a space,
Yet yield'st to words, and art condensed thereby
  Past nature press'd into a little place;
Dear sovereign, then, make air thy rule in this,
And me thy worthy servant with a kiss."

" Ovid," said she, " I am well pleased to yield:
Bounty by virtue cannot be abused:
Nor will I coyly lift Minerva's shield
Against Minerva, honour is not bruised
  With such a tender pressure as a kiss,
Nor yielding soon to words, though seldom used,
  Niceness in civil favours folly is:
Long suits make never good a bad detection,
Nor yielding soon makes bad a good affection.

" To some, I know, and know it for a fault,
Order and reverence are repulsed in scaling,
When pride and rudeness enter with assault,
Consents to fall are worse to get than falling;
  Willing resistance takes away the will,
And too much weakness 'tis to come with calling;
  Force, in these frays, is better man than skill,
Yet I like skill, and, Ovid, if a kiss
May do thee so much pleasure, here it is."

Her moving towards him made Ovid's eye
Believe the firmament was coming down

To take him quick to immortality,
And that th' Ambrosian kiss set on the crown;
  She spake in kissing, and her breath infused
Restoring syrup to his taste, in swoon:
  And he imagined Hebe's hands had bruised
A banquet of the gods into his sense,
Which fill'd him with this furious influence.

" The motion of the heavens that did beget
The golden age, and by whose harmony
Heaven is preserved, in me on work is set;
All instruments of deepest melody,
  Set sweet in my desires to my love's liking;
With this sweet kiss in me, their tunes apply
  As if the best musician's hands were striking;
This kiss in me hath endless music closed,
Like Phœbus' lute on Nisus' towers imposed.

" And as a pebble cast into a spring,
We see a sort of trembling circles rise,
One forming other in their issuing,
Till over all the fount they circulize;
  So this perpetual-motion-making kiss
Is propagate through all my faculties,
  And makes my breast an endless fount of bliss,
Of which, if gods could drink, their matchless fare
Would make them much more blessed than they are.

" But as when sounds do hollow bodies beat,
Air gather'd there, compress'd and thickened,
The self-same way she came doth make retreat,
And so effects the sound re-echoed,
  Only in part because she weaker is

In that reddition, than when first she fled;
  So I, alas! faint echo of this kiss,
Only reiterate a slender part
Of that high joy it worketh in my heart.

" And thus with feasting, love is famish'd more,
Without my touch are all things turned to gold,
And till I touch I cannot joy my store;
To purchase others, I myself have sold;
  Love is a wanton famine, rich in food,
But with a richer appetite controll'd;
  An argument in figure and in mood,
Yet hates all arguments; disputing still
For sense 'gainst reason with a senseless will.

" Then, sacred madam, since **my**   Tactus.
        other senses
Have in your graces tasted such content,
Let wealth not to be spent fear no expenses,
But give thy bounty true eternizement;
  Making my sense's ground-work, which is feel-
        ing,
Effect the other, endless, excellent,
  Their substance with flint-softening softness
        stealing;
Then let me feel, for know, sweet beauty's queen,
Dames may be felt, as well as heard or seen.

" For if we be allow'd to serve the Ear
With pleasing tunes, and to delight the Eye
With gracious shows, the Taste with dainty cheer,
The Smell with odours, is't immodesty

To serve the senses' Emperor, sweet Feeling,
With those delights that fit his empery?
  Shall subjects free themselves and bind their
      king?
Minds taint no more with bodies' touch or tire,
Than bodies nourish with the mind's desire.

" The mind then clear, the body may be used,
Which perfectly your touch can spiritualize;
As by the great elixir is transfused
Copper to gold, then that deed of prize:
  Such as transform into corrupt effects
What they receive from nature's purities,
    Should not wrong them that hold her due re-
      spects;
To touch your quickening side then give me leave,
Th' abuse of things must not the use bereave."

Herewith, even glad his arguments to hear,
Worthily willing to have lawful grounds
To make the wondrous power of heaven appear
In nothing more than her perfections found,
  Close to her navel she her mantle wrests,
Slacking it upwards, and the folds unwound,
    Showing Latona's twins, her plenteous breasts,
The sun and Cynthia in their triumph-robes
Of lady-skin, more rich than both their globes.

Whereto she bade blest Ovid put his hand;
He, well acknowledging it much too base
For such an action, did a little stand,
Ennobling it with titles full of grace,

And conjures it with charge of reverend verse
To use with piety that sacred place,
  And through his Feeling's organ to disperse
Worth to his spirits, amply to supply
The pureness of his flesh's faculty.

And thus he said: " King of the king of senses,
Engine of all the engines under heaven,
To health and life defence of all defences,
Bounty by which our nourishment is given,
  Beauty's beautifier, kind acquaintance-maker,
Proportion's oddness that makes all things even,
    Wealth of the labourer, wrong's revengement
        taker,
Pattern of concord, lord of exercise,
And figure of that power the world did guise:

" Dear hand, most duly honoured in this,
And therefore worthy to be well employ'd,
Yet know that all that honour nothing is,
Compared with that which now must be enjoy'd;
  So think in all the pleasures these have shown
Liken'd to this, thou wert but mere annoy'd,
    That all hands' merits in thyself alone
With this one touch, have more than recompence,
And therefore feel with fear and reverence.

" See Cupid's Alps, which now thou must go over,
Where snow that thaws the sun doth ever lie,
Where thou may'st plain and feelingly discover
The world's fore-past, that flow'd with milk and
        honey;
    Where—like an empress seeing nothing wanting

That may her glorious child-bed beautify—
   Pleasure herself lies big with issue panting;
Ever deliver'd, yet with child still growing,
Full of all blessing, yet all bliss bestowing."

This said, he laid his hand upon her side,
Which made her start like sparkles from a fire,
Or like Saturnia from th' Ambrosian pride
Of her morn's slumber, frighted with admire,
   When Jove laid young Alcides to her breast,
So startled she, not with a coy retire,
   But with the tender temper she was blest,
Proving her sharp, undull'd with handling yet,
Which keener edge on Ovid's longings set.

And feeling still he sigh'd out this effect:
" Alas! why lent not heaven the soul a tongue?
Nor language, nor peculiar dialect,
To make her high conceits as highly sung?
   But that a fleshly engine must unfold
A spiritual notion: birth from princes sprung,
   Peasants must nurse, free virtue wait on gold,
And a profess'd, though flattering enemy,
Must plead my honour and my liberty.

" O, nature! how dost thou defame in this
Our human honours, yoking men with beasts,
And noblest minds with slaves; thus beauty's bliss,
Love and all virtues that quick spirit feasts
   Surfeit on flesh; and thou that banquet'st minds,
Most bounteous mistress, of thy dull-tongued guests
   Reap'st not due thanks; thus rude frailty binds

What thou givest wings; thus joys I feel in thee
Hang on my lips and will not utter'd be.

" Sweet touch, the engine that love's bow doth bend,
The sense wherewith he feels him deified,
The object whereto all his actions tend,
In all his blindness his most pleasing guide,
  For thy sake will I write the Art of Love,
Since thou dost blow his fire and feed his pride,
  Since in thy sphere his health and life doth move,
For thee I hate who hate society,
And such as self-love makes his slavery.

" In these dog-days how this contagion smothers
The purest blood with virtue's diet fined,
Nothing their own, unless they be some other's
Spite of themselves, are in themselves confined,
  And live so poor they are of all despised,
Their gifts held down with scorn should be divined,
  And they like mummers mask, unknown, un-
    prized:
A thousand marvels mourn in some such breast,
Would make a kind and worthy patron blest.

" To me, dear sovereign, thou art patroness,
And I, with that thy graces have infused,
Will make all fat and foggy brains confess
Riches may from a poor verse be deduced:
  And that gold's love shall leave them grovelling
    here,
When thy perfections shall to heaven be mused,
  Deck'd in bright verse, where angels shall appear,

His verse to the Queen

The praise of virtue, love, and beauty singing,
Honour to noblesse, shame to avarice bringing."

Here Ovid, interrupted with the view
Of other dames, who then the garden painted,
Shrouded himself, and did as death eschew
All note by which his love's fame might be tainted:
    And as when mighty Macedon had won
The monarchy of earth, yet when he fainted,
    Grieved that no greater action could be done,
And that there were no more worlds to subdue.
So love's defects, love's conqueror did rue.

But as when expert painters have display'd
To quickest life a monarch's royal hand,
Holding a sceptre, there is yet bewray'd
But half his fingers; when we understand
    The rest not to be seen; and never blame
The painter's art, in nicest censures scann'd.
    So in the compass of this curious frame
Ovid well knew there was much more intended,
With whose omission none must be offended.
                    Intentio, animi actio.
                        Explicit convivium.

A CORONET FOR HIS MISTRESS
PHILOSOPHY.

I.

MUSES that sing Love's sensual empery,
  And lovers kindling your enraged fires
At Cupid's bonfires burning in the eye,
  Blown with the empty breath of vain desires,
You that prefer the painted cabinet
  Before the wealthy jewels it doth store yee,
  That all your joys in dying figures set,
  And stain the living substance of your glory,
Abjure those joys, abhor their memory,
  And let my love the honour'd subject be
  Of love, and honour's complete history;
  Your eyes were never yet let in to see
The majesty and riches of the mind,
But dwell in darkness; for your God is blind.

II.

But dwell in darkness, for your God is blind,
  Humour pours down such torrents on his eyes;
  Which, as from mountains, fall on his base kind,
  And eat your entrails out with ecstasies.
Colour, whose hands for faintness are not felt,
  Can bind your waxen thoughts in adamant;
  And with her painted fires your heart doth melt,

See Son 153
£ H & L
line 153

*He has linked his sonnets to protect
them from being extracted to other poets.*

Which beat your souls in pieces with a pant.
But my love is the cordial of souls,
  Teaching by passion what perfection is,
  In whose fix'd beauties shine the sacred scroll,
  And long-lost records of your human bliss,
Spirit to flesh, and soul to spirit giving,
Love flows not from my liver but her living.

III.

Love flows not from my liver but her living,
  From whence all stings to perfect love are darted
  All power, and thought of prideful lust depriving
  Her life so pure and she so spotless-hearted.
In whom sits beauty with so firm a brow,
  That age, nor care, nor torment can contract it;
  Heaven's glories shining there, do stuff allow,
  And virtue's constant graces do compact it.
Her mind—the beam of God—draws in the fires
  Of her chaste eyes, from all earth's tempting
    fuel;
  Which upward lifts the looks of her desires,
  And makes each precious thought in her a jewel.
And as huge fires compress'd more proudly flame,
So her close beauties further blaze her fame.

IV.

So her close beauties further blaze her fame;
  When from the world, into herself reflected;
  She lets her shameless glory in her shame,
  Content for heaven to be of earth rejected.
She thus depress'd, knocks at Olympus' gate,
  And in th' untainted temple of her heart

Doth the divorceless nuptials celebrate
'Twixt God and her; where love's profaned dart
Feeds the chaste flames of Hymen's firmament,
    Wherein she sacrificeth, for her part;
    The robes, looks, deeds, desires and whole de-
        scent
Of female natures, built in shops of art,
Virtue is both the merit and reward
Of her removed and soul-infused regard.

V.

Of her removed and soul-infused regard,
    With whose firm species, as with golden lances,
    She points her life's field, for all wars prepared,
    And bears one chanceless mind, in all mischances;
Th' inverted world that goes upon her head,
    And with her wanton heels doth kick the sky,
    My love disdains, though she be honoured,
    And without envy sees her empery
Loathes all her toys, and thoughts cupidinine,
    Arranging in the army of her face
    All virtue's forces, to dismay loose eyne,
    That hold no quarter with renown or grace.
War to all frailty; peace of all things pure,
Her look doth promise and her life assure.

VI.

Her look doth promise and her life assure;
    A right line forcing a rebateless point,
    In her high deeds, through everything obscure,
    To full perfection; not the weak disjoint

Of female humours; nor the Protean rages
  Of pied-faced fashion, that doth shrink and swell,
  Working poor men like waxen images,
  And makes them apish strangers where they
    dwell,
Can alter her, titles of primacy,
Courtship of antic gestures, brainless jests,
  Blood without soul of false nobility,
  Nor any folly that the world infests
Can alter her who with her constant guises
To living virtues turns the deadly vices.

VII.

To living virtues turns the deadly vices;
  For covetous she is of all good parts,
  Incontinent, for still she shows entices
  To consort with them sucking out their hearts,
Proud, for she scorns prostrate humility,
  And gluttonous in store of abstinence,
  Drunk with extractions still'd in fervency
  From contemplation, and true continence,
Burning in wrath against impatience,
  And sloth itself, for she will never rise
  From that all-seeing trance, the band of sense,
  Wherein in view of all souls' skill she lies.
No constancy to that her mind doth move,
Nor riches to the virtues of my love.

VIII.

Nor riches to the virtues of my love,
  Nor empire to her mighty government;
  Which fair analysed in her beauties' grove,

Shows Laws for care, and Canons for content;
And as a purple tincture given to glass,
  By clear transmission of the sun doth taint
  Opposed subjects; so my mistress' face
Doth reverence in her viewers' brows depaint,
And like the pansy, with a little veil,
  She gives her inward work the greater grace;
  Which my lines imitate, though much they fail
Her gifts so high, and times' conceit so base;
Her virtues then above my verse must raise her,
For words want art, and Art wants words to praise
    her.

IX.

For words want art, and Art wants words to praise
    her;
  Yet shall my active and industrious pen
  Wind his sharp forehead through those parts that
    raise her,
And register her worth past rarest women.
Herself shall be my Muse; that well will know
  Her proper inspirations; and assuage—
  With her dear love—the wrongs my fortunes
    show,
Which to my youth bind heartless grief in age.
Herself shall be my comfort and my riches,
  And all my thoughts I will on her convert;
  Honour, and error, which the world bewitches,
  Shall still crown fools, and tread upon desert,
And never shall my friendless verse envy
Muses that Fame's loose feathers beautify.

X.

Muses that Fame's loose feathers beautify,
    And such as scorn to tread the theatre,
    As ignorant: the seed of memory
    Have most inspired, and shown their glories there
To noblest wits, and men of highest doom,
    That for the kingly laurel bent affair
    The theatres of Athens and of Rome,
    Have been the crowns, and not the base impair.
Far, then, be this foul cloudy-brow'd contempt
    From like-plumed birds: and let your sacred
        rhymes
    From honour's court their servile feet exempt,
    That live by soothing moods, and serving times:
And let my love adorn with modest eyes,
Muses that sing Love's sensual emperies.
                    Lucidius olim.

Lucidius ; light, bright, glittering
olim ; in time past, formerly

THE AMOROUS ZODIAC.

I.

I never see the sun, but suddenly
My soul is moved with spite and jealousy
   Of his high bliss, in his sweet course discern'd:
And am displeased to see so many signs,
As the bright sky unworthily divines,
   Enjoy an honour they have never earn'd.

II.

To think heaven decks with such a beauteous show,
A harp, a ship, a serpent, or a crow;
   And such a crew of creatures of no prices,
But to excite in us th' unshamefaced flames,
With which, long since, Jove wrong'd so many
     dames,
   Reviving in his rule their names and vices.

III.

Dear mistress, whom the Gods bred here below,
T' express their wondrous power, and let us know
   That before thee they nought did perfect make;
Why may not I—as in those signs, the sun—
Shine in thy beauties, and as roundly run,
   To frame, like him, an endless Zodiac.

IV.

With thee I'll furnish both the year and sky,
Running in thee my course of destiny:
  And thou shalt be the rest of all my moving,
But of thy numberless and perfect graces,
To give my moons their full in twelve months'
    spaces,
  I choose but twelve in guerdon of my loving.

V.

Keeping even way through every excellence,
I'll make in all an equal residence
  Of a new Zodiac; a new Phœbus guising,
When, without altering the course of nature,
I'll make the seasons good, and every creature
  Shall henceforth reckon day, from my first rising.

VI.

To open then the spring-time's golden gate,
And flower my race with ardour temperate,
  I'll enter by thy head, and have for house
In my first month, this heaven Ram-curled tress,
Of which Love all his charm-chains doth address,
  A sign fit for a spring so beauteous.

VII.

Lodged in that fleece of hair, yellow and curl'd,
I'll take high pleasure to enlight the world,
  And fetter me in gold, thy crisps implies

Earth, at this spring, spongy and languorsome
With envy of our joys in love become,
  Shall swarm with flowers, and air with painted
    flies.

VIII.

Thy smooth embow'd brow, where all grace I see,
My second month, and second house shall be;
  Which brow, with her clear beauties shall delight
The Earth, yet sad, and overture confer
To herbs, buds, flowers, and verdure-gracing Ver,
  Rendering her more than Summer exquisite.

IX.

All this fresh April, this sweet month of Venus,
I will admire this brow so bounteous;
  This brow, brave court of love and virtue builded;
This brow, where Chastity holds garrison;
This brow, that blushless none can look upon,
  This brow, with every grace and honour gilded.

X.

Resigning that, to perfect this my year,
I'll come to see thine eyes, that now I fear;
  Thine eyes, that, sparkling like two twinborn
    fires,
Whose looks benign, and shining sweets do grace
May's youthful month with a more pleasing face;
  Justly the Twins'-sign hold in my desires.

XI.

Scorch'd with the beams these sister-flames eject,
The living sparks thereof, Earth shall effect;
  The shock of our join'd fires the summer starting:
The season by degrees shall change again,
The days their longest durance shall retain;
  The stars their amplest light and ardour darting.

XII.

But now, I fear, that throned in such a shrine,
Playing with objects, pleasant and divine,
  I should be moved to dwell there thirty days.
O no, I could not in so little space
With joy admire enough their plenteous grace,
  But ever live in sunshine of their rays.

XIII.

Yet this should be in vain, my forced will
My course design'd, begun, shall follow still;
  So forth I must, when forth this month is wore,
And of the neighbour signs be born anew,
Which sign, perhaps, may stay me with the view,
  More to conceive, and so desire the more.

XIV.

It is thy nose, stern to thy bark of love,
Or which, pine-like, doth crown a flowery grove,
  Which nature strived to fashion with her best,
That she might never turn to show more skill,
And that the envious fool, used to speak ill,
  Might feel pretended fault choked in his breast.

XV.

The violent season in a sign so bright,
Still more and more, become more proud of light,
    Should still incense me in the following sign;
A sign, whose sight desires a gracious kiss,
And the red confines of thy tongue it is,
    Where, hotter than before, mine eyes would shine.

XVI.

So glow those corals, nought but fire respiring,
With smiles or words, or sighs her thoughts at-
        tiring;
    Or, be it she a kiss divinely frameth;
Or that her tongue shoots forward, and retires,
Doubling, like fervent Sirius, summer's fires,
    In Leo's month, which all the world enflameth.

XVII.

And now to bid the Boreal signs adieu,
I come to give thy virgin-cheeks the view
    To temper all my fire, and tame my heat,
Which soon will feel itself extinct and dead,
In those fair courts with modesty dispread,
    With holy, humble, and chaste thoughts replete.

XVIII.

The purple tinct thy marble cheeks retain,
The marble tinct thy purple cheeks doth stain.
    The lilies duly equall'd with thine eyes,
The tinct that dyes the morn with deeper red
Shall hold my course a month if, as I dread,
    My fires to issue want not faculties.

XIX.

To balance now thy more obscured graces,
'Gainst them the circle of thy head enchases—
   Twice three months used, to run through twice
      three houses—
To render in this heaven my labour lasting,
I haste to see the rest, and with one hasting,
   The dripping time shall fill the Earth carouses.

XX.

Then by the neck my autumn I'll commence,
Thy neck, that merits place of excellence
   Such as this is, where with a certain sphere,
In balancing the darkness with the light,
It might so weigh with scales of equal weight,
   Thy beauties seen with those do not appear.

XXI.

Now past my month t' admire for built most pure
This marble pillar and her lineature,
   I come t' inhabit thy most gracious teats—
Teats that feed Love upon the white <u>rhiphees</u>,
Teats where he hangs his glory and his trophies,
   When victor from the gods' war he retreats.

XXII.

Hid in the vale 'twixt these two hills confined,
This vale the nest of loves, and joys divined,
   Shall I enjoy mine ease; and fair be pass'd
Beneath these parching Alps; and this sweet cold
Is first, this month, heaven doth to us unfold;
   But there shall I still grieve to be displaced.

XXIII.

To sort from this most brave and pompous sign,
Leaving a little my ecliptic line
 (Less superstitious than the other sun),
The rest of my autumnal race I'll end
To see thy hand, whence I the crown attend,
 Since in thy past parts I have slightly run.

XXIV.

Thy hand, a lily gender'd of a rose
That wakes the morning, hid in night's repose:
 And from Apollo's bed the veil doth twine,
That each where doth th' Idalian minion guide
That bends his bow; that ties, and leaves untied
 The silver ribands of his little ensign.

XXV.

In fine, still drawing to th' Antarctic pole,
The tropic sign I'll run at for my goal;
 Which I can scarce express with chastity,
I know in heaven 'tis called Capricorn;
And with the sudden thought my case takes horn,
 So, heaven-like, Capricorn the name shall be.

XXVI.

This, wondrous fit, the wintry solstice seazeth,
Where darkness greater grows and day decreaseth,
 Where rather I would be in night than day;
But when I see my journeys do increase,
I'll straight despatch me thence, and go in peace
 To my next house, where I may safer stay.

XXVII.

This house alongst thy naked thighs is found,
Naked of spot; made fleshy, firm, and round,
    To entertain love's friends with feeling sport;
These Cupid's secret mysteries enfold,
And pillars are that Venus' fane uphold,
    Of her dear joys the glory and support.

XXVIII.

Sliding on thy smooth thighs to this month's end;
To thy well-fashion'd calves I will descend,
    That soon the last house I may apprehend,
Thy slender feet, fine slender feet that shame
Thetis' sheen feet, which poets so much fame;
    And here my latest season I will end.

L'ENVOY.

XXIX.

Dear mistress, if poor wishes heaven would hear,
I would not choose the empire of the water;
    The empire of the air, nor of the earth,
But endlessly my course of life confining,
In this fair Zodiac for ever shining,
    And with thy beauties make me endless mirth.

XXX.

But gracious love, if jealous heaven deny
My life this truly-blest variety,

Yet will I thee through all the world disperse;
If not in heaven, amongst those braving fires,
Yet here thy beauties, which the world admires,
Bright as those flames shall glister in my verse.

TO

MY ADMIRED AND SOUL-LOVED FRIEND, MASTER OF ALL
ESSENTIAL AND TRUE KNOWLEDGE,

M. HARRIOTS.

To you, whose depth of soul measures the height
And all dimensions of all works of weight,
Reason being ground, structure and ornament,
To all inventions grave and permanent,
And your clear eyes, the spheres where reason
     moves;
This artizan, this God of rational loves,
Blind Homer, in this Shield, and in the rest
Of his seven books, which my hard hand hath
     dress'd
In rough integuments, I send for censure,
That my long time and labours' deep extensure,
Spent to conduct him to our envious light,
In your allowance may receive some right
To their endeavours; and take virtuous heart,
From your applause, crown'd with their own desert.
Such crowns suffice the free and royal mind,
But these subjected hang-byes of our kind,
These children that will never stand alone,
But must be nourish'd with corruption,
Which are our bodies: that are traitors born
To their own crowns, their souls; betray'd to scorn,
To gaudy insolence and ignorance,

By their base flesh's frailties, that must dance
Profane attendance at their states and birth,
That are mere servants to this servile earth;
These must have other crowns for meeds than
      merits,
Or starve themselves, and <u>quench their fiery spirits.</u>
Thus as the soul upon the flesh depends,
Virtue must wait on wealth; we must make friends
Of the unrighteous mammon, and our sleights
Must bear the forms of fools or parasites.
Rich mine of knowledge, O that my strange muse
Without this body's nourishment could use
Her zealous faculties, only t' aspire,
Instructive light from your whole sphere of fire;
But woe is me, what zeal or power so ever,
My free soul hath, my body will be never
Able t' attend; never shall I enjoy
The end of my hapless birth; never employ
That smother'd fervour that in loathed embers
Lies swept from light, and no clear hour remembers.
O, had your perfect eye organs to pierce
Into that chaos whence this stifled verse
By violence breaks; where, glowworm-like, doth
      shine
In nights of sorrow, this hid soul of mine;
And how her genuine forms struggle for birth,
Under the claws of this foul panther earth:
Then under all those forms you should discern
My love to you, in my desire to learn.
Skill and the love of skill, do ever kiss;
No band of love so strong as knowledge is;
Which who is he, that may not learn of you,

Whom learning doth with his light's throne endow?
What learned fields pay not their flowers t' adorn
Your odorous wreath?   Compact, put on, and worn
By apt and adamantine industry,
Proposing still demonstrate verity
For your great object, far from plodding gain,
Or thirst of glory; when, absurd and vain,
Most students in their whole instruction are,
But in traditions more particular;
Leaning like rotten houses, on out beams,
And with true light fade in themselves like dreams.
True learning hath a body absolute,
That in apparent sense itself can suit,
Not hid in airy terms, as if it were
Like spirits fantastic, that put men in fear,
And are but bugs form'd in their foul conceits,
Nor made for sale, glazed with sophistic sleights,
But wrought for all times proof, strong to bid
        prease
And shiver ignorants, like Hercules,
On their own dung-hills; but our formal clerks,
Blown for profession, spend their souls in sparks,
Framed of dismember'd parts that make most show,
And like to broken limbs of knowledge go,
When thy true wisdom by thy learning won,
Shall honour learning while there shines a sun;
And thine own name in merit, far above
Their tympanies of state, that arms of love,
Fortune, or blood shall lift to dignity;
Whom though you reverence and your empery
Of spirit and soul, be servitude they think
And but a beam of light broke through a chink

To all their waterish splendour; and much more
To the great sun, and all things they adore,
In staring ignorance; yet your self shall shine
Above all this in knowledge most divine,
And all shall homage to your true worth owe,
You comprehending all, that all, not you.
   And when thy writings that now Error's night
Chokes earth with mists, break forth like eastern
     light,
Showing to every comprehensive eye
High sectious brawls becalm'd by unity,
Nature made all transparent, and her heart
Gript in thy hand, crushing digested Art
In flames unmeasured, measured out of it,
On whose head for a crown thy soul shall sit,
Crown'd with heaven's inward brightness showing
     clear
What true man is, and how like gnats appear,
O fortune-glossed pompists, and proud misers,
That are of arts such impudent despisers;
Then past anticipating dooms and scorns,
Which for self-grace each ignorant suborns,
Their glowing and amazed eyes shall see
How short of thy soul's strength my weak words be;
And that I do not like our poets prefer
For profit, praise, and keep a squeaking stir
With call'd-on muses to unchild their brains
Of wind and vapour: lying still in pains
Of worthy issue; but as one profess'd
In nought but truth's dear love the soul's true
     rest.
   Continue then your sweet judicial kindness

To your true friend, that though this lump of blind-
      ness,
This scornful, this despised, inverted world,
Whose head is fury-like with adders curl'd
And all her bulk a poison'd porcupine,
Her stings and quills darting at worths divine,
Keep under my estate with all contempt,
And make me live even from myself exempt.
Yet if you see some gleams of wrestling fire
Break from my spirit's oppression, showing desire
To become worthy to partake your skill,—
Since virtue's first and chief step is to will,—
Comfort me with it, and prove you affect me,
Through all the rotten spawn of earth reject me.
For though I now consume in poesy,
Yet Homer being my root I cannot die.
But lest to use all poesy in the sight
Of grave philosophy show brains too light
To comprehend her depth of mystery,
I vow 'tis only strong necessity
Governs my pains herein, which yet may use
A man's whole life without the least abuse.
And though to rhyme and give a verse smooth feet,
Uttering to vulgar palates passions sweet
Chance often in such weak capricious spirits,
As in nought else have tolerable merits,
Yet where high Poesy's native habit shines,
From whose reflections flow eternal lines,
Philosophy retired to darkest caves
She can discover: and the proud world's braves
Answer in anything but impudence
With circle of her general excellence.

For ample instance Homer more than serveth,
And what his grave and learned Muse deserveth,
Since it is made a courtly question now,
His competent and partless judge be you;
If these vain lines and his deserts arise
To the high searches of your serious eyes
As he is English: and I could not choose
But to your name this short inscription use,
As well assured you would approve my pain
In my traduction; and besides this vein
Excuse my thoughts as bent to others' aims
Might my will rule me, and when any flames
Of my press'd soul break forth to their own show,
Think they must hold engraven regard of you.
Of you in whom the worth of all the graces
Due to the mind's gifts, might embrue the faces
Of such as scorn them, and with tyrannous eye
Contemn the sweat of virtuous industry.
But as ill lines new fill'd with ink undried
An empty pen with their own stuff applied
Can blot them out: so shall their wealth-burst
    wombs
Be made with empty pen their honours' tombs.

His former life and name

These are the lines Jonson remembered when he wrote of Shakespeare 1635?

Harriot must have had a great hold on Morley-Chapman possibly by having helped him through the difficulties of 1593 – 1595 Harriot's "sweet judicial kindness" See bottom page 315 guides him.

THE TEARS OF PEACE.*

[1609.]

TO THE HIGH-BORN PRINCE OF MEN,

HENRY,

THRICE-ROYAL INHERITOR TO THE UNITED KINGDOMS OF GREAT BRITAIN.

INDUCTIO.

Now that our sovereign, the great King of Peace,
Hath, in her grace, outlabour'd Hercules;
And past his pillars, stretch'd her victories;
Since (as he were sole soul t' all royalties)
He moves all kings in this vast universe
To cast chaste nets on th' impious lust of Mars;
See all and imitate his goodness still
That, having clear'd so well war's outward ill)
He, god-like, still employs his firm desires
To cast learn'd ink upon those inward fires,
That kindle worse war in the minds of men,
Like to incense the outward war again:
Self-love inflaming so men's sensual blood
That all good public drowns in private good;

---

* *" Euthymiæ Raptus; or the Teares of Peace: With Inter-locutions.* By Geo. Chapman. At London, Printed by *H. L.* for Rich. Bonian, and H. Walley: and are to be solde at the spread-eagle, neere the great North-door of St. Pauls Church. 1609."

And that sinks under his own overfreight;
Men's reasons and their learnings, shipwrack'd
    quite;
And their religion, that should still be one,
Takes shapes so many that most know't in none.
Which I admiring, since in each man shined
A light so clear that by it all might find,
Being well inform'd, their object, perfect peace,
Which keeps the narrow path to happiness,
In that discourse, I shunn'd, as is my use,
The jarring preace, and all their time's abuse,
T' enjoy least trodden fields, and freëst shades;
Wherein (of all the pleasure that invades
The life of man, and flies all vulgar feet,
Since silent meditation is most sweet)
I sat to it; discoursing what main want
So ransack'd man, that it did quite supplant
The inward peace I spake of, letting in
At his loose veins, sad war and all his sin.
When suddenly, a comfortable light
Brake through the shade; and, after it, the sight
Of a most grave and goodly person shined,
With eyes turn'd upwards, and was outward, blind;
But inward, past and future things he saw,
And was to both, and present times, their law.
His sacred bosom was so full of fire
That 'twas transparent, and made him expire
His breath in flames, that did instruct, methought,
And (as my soul were then at full) they wrought.
At which, I casting down my humble eyes,
Not daring to attempt their fervencies;
He thus bespake me: " Dear mind, do not fear

My strange appearance; now 'tis time t' outwear
Thy bashful disposition, and put on
As confident a countenance as the Sun.
For what hast thou to look on, more divine
And horrid, than man is; as he should shine,
And as he doth? what freed from this world's strife,
What he is entering and what ending life?
All which thou only studiest, and dost know;
And more than which is only sought for show.
Thou must not undervalue what thou hast,
In weighing it with that which more is graced;
The worth that weigheth inward should not long
For outward prices.   This should make thee strong
In thy close value; nought so good can be
As that which lasts good betwixt God and thee.
Remember thine own verse: ' Should heaven turn
        hell,
For deeds well done, I would do ever well.' "
  This heard, with joy enough, to break the twine
Of life and soul, so apt to break as mine;
I brake into a trance, and then remain'd,
Like him, an only soul; and so obtain'd
Such boldness by the sense he did control,
That I set look to look, and soul to soul.
I view'd him at his brightest; though, alas,
With all acknowledgment, of what he was
Beyond what I found habited in me;
And thus I spake: " O thou that, blind, dost see
My heart and soul, what may I reckon thee,
Whose heavenly look shows not, nor voice sounds
        man? "
" I am," said he, " that spirit Elysian,

That in thy native air, and on the hill
Next Hitchin's left hand, did thy bosom fill
With such a flood of soul, that thou wert fain,
With exclamations of her rapture then,
To vent it to the echoes of the vale;
When, meditating of me, a sweet gale
Brought me upon thee; and thou didst inherit
My true sense, for the time then, in my spirit;
And I, invisibly, went prompting thee
To those fair greens where thou didst English me.'

Scarce he had utter'd this, when well I knew
It was my Prince's Homer whose dear view
Renew'd my grateful memory of the grace
His Highness did me for him; which in face
Methought the Spirit show'd, was his delight,
And added glory to his heavenly plight:
Who told me, he brought stay to all my state;
That he was Angel to me, Star, and Fate;
Advancing colours of good hope to me;
And told me my retired age should see
Heaven's blessing in a free and harmless life,
Conduct me, thro' earth's peace-pretending strife,
To that true Peace, whose search I still intend,
And to the calm shore of a loved end.

But now, as I cast round my ravish'd eye,
To see if this free soul had company,
Or that, alone, he lovingly pursued
The hidden places of my solitude;
He rent a cloud down with his burning hand
That at his back hung, 'twixt me and a land
Never inhabited, and said: " Now, behold
What main defect it is that doth enfold

The world, in ominous flatteries of a Peace
So full of worse than war; whose stern increase
Devours her issue." With which words, I view'd
A lady, like a deity indued,
But weeping like a woman, and made way
Out of one thicket, that saw never day,
Towards another; bearing underneath
Her arm, a coffin, for some prize of death;
And after her, in funeral form, did go
The wood's four-footed beasts, by two and two:
A male and female match'd, of every kind;
And after them, with like instinct inclined,
The airy nation felt her sorrow's stings;
Fell on the earth, kept rank, and hung their wings.
Which sight I much did pity and admire,
And long'd to know the dame that could inspire
Those bestials with such humane form and ruth;
And how I now should know the hidden truth
(As Homer promised) of that main defect
That makes men all their inward peace reject
For name of outward; then he took my hand;
Led to her, and would make myself demand
(Though he could have resolved me) what she was,
And from what cause those strange effects had
        pass?
For whom she bore that coffin, and so mourn'd?
To all which, with all mildness, she return'd
Answer, that she was Peace, sent down from
        heaven
With charge from th' Almighty Deity given
T' attend on men, who now had banish'd her
From their societies, and made her err

In that wild desert; only human love,
Banish'd in like sort, did a long time prove
That life with her; but now, alas, was dead,
And lay in that wood to be buried;
For whom she bore that coffin and did mourn;
And that those beasts were so much humane born,
That they in nature felt a love to peace;
For which they follow'd her, when men did cease.
This went so near her heart, it left her tongue;
And, silent, she gave time to note whence sprung
Men's want of peace, which was from want of love;
And I observed now, what that peace did prove
That men made shift with and did so much please.
For now, the sun declining to the seas,
Made long misshapen shadows; and true Peace
(Here walking in his beams) cast such increase
Of shadow from her, that I saw it glide
Through cities, courts, and countries; and descried
How, in her shadow only, men there lived,
While she walk'd here i'th' sun; and all that thrived
Hid in that shade their thrift; nought but her shade
Was bulwark 'gainst all war that might invade
Their countries or their consciences; since Love
(That should give Peace, her substance) now they
          drove
Into the deserts; where he suffer'd Fate,
And whose sad funerals beasts must celebrate.
With whom I freely wish'd I had been nursed,
Because they follow nature, at their worst,
And at their best, did teach her. As we went
I felt a scruple, which I durst not vent,
No, not to Peace herself, whom it concern'd,

For fear to wrong her; so well I have learn'd
To shun injustice, even to doves or flies;
But to the Devil, or the Destinies,
Where I am just, and know I honour Truth,
I'll speak my thoughts, in scorn of what ensueth.
Yet, not resolved in th' other, there did shine
A beam of Homer's freër soul in mine,
That made me see, I might propose my doubt;
Which was: if this were true Peace I found out,
That felt such passion? I proved her sad part;
And pray'd her call her voice out of her heart
(There kept a wrongful prisoner to her woe),
To answer, why she was afflicted so.
Or how, in her, such contraries could fall,
That taught all joy and was the life of all?
She answer'd: " Homer told me that there are
Passions, in which corruption hath no share;
There is a joy of soul; and why not then
A grief of soul, that is no scathe to men?
For both are passions, though not such as reign
In blood and humour, that engender pain.
Free sufferance for the truth, makes sorrow sing,
And mourning far more sweet than banquetting.
Good, that deserveth joy, receiving ill,
Doth merit justly as much sorrow still:
And is it a corruption to do right?
Grief that dischargeth conscience, is delight;
One sets the other off.   To stand at gaze
In one position, is a stupid maze,
Fit for a statue.   This resolved me well
That grief in peace, and peace in grief might dwell.
        And now fell all things from their natural birth:

Passion in Heaven; Stupidity, in Earth,
Inverted all; the Muses, Virtues, Graces,
Now suffer'd rude and miserable chases
From men's societies to that desert heath;
And after them, Religion (chased by death)
Came weeping, bleeding to the funeral:
Sought her dear Mother Peace, and down did **fall**
Before her, fainting, on her horned knees;
Turn'd horn, with praying for the miseries
She left the world in; desperate in their sin;
Marble her knees pierced; but heaven could not **win**
To stay the weighty ruin of his glory
In her sad exile; all the memory
Of heaven and heavenly things, razed of all hands;
Heaven moves so far off that men say it stands;
And Earth is turn'd the true and moving Heaven;
And so 'tis left; and so is all Truth driven
From her false bosom; all is left alone,
Till all be order'd with confusion.

    Thus the poor brood of Peace, driven and dis-
        tress'd,
Lay brooded all beneath their mother's breast;
Who fell upon them weeping, as they fell:
All were so pined that she contain'd them well.
And in this Chaos, the digestion
And beauty of the world lay thrust and thrown.
In this dejection Peace pour'd out her tears,
Worded, with some pause, in my wounded ears.

INVOCATIO.

O ye three-times-thrice sacred Quiristers
Of God's great Temple, the small Universe
Of ruinous man (thus prostrate as ye lie
Brooded and loaded with calamity,
Contempt and shame in your true mother Peace)
As you make sad my soul with your misease,
So make her able fitly to disperse
Your sadness and her own in sadder verse.
Now, old, and freely banish'd with yourselves
From men's societies, as from rocks and shelves,
Help me to sing and die, on our Thames' shore;
And let her lend me her waves to deplore,
In yours, and your most holy Sisters' falls,
Heaven's fall, and human Love's last funerals.
    And thou, great Prince of men, let thy sweet
        graces
Shine on these tears; and dry at length the faces
Of Peace and all her heaven-allied brood;
From whose doves' eyes is shed the precious blood
Of heaven's dear Lamb, that freshly bleeds in them.
Make these no toys then; gird the diadem
Of thrice Great Britain with their palm and bays;
And with thy Eagle's feathers, deign to raise
The heavy body of my humble Muse;
That thy great Homer's spirit in her may use
Her topless flight, and bear thy fame above
The reach of mortals and their earthly love;
To that high honour his Achilles won,
And make thy glory far outshine the sun.

While this small time gave Peace, in her kind
    throes,
Vent for the violence of her sudden woes;
She turn'd on her right side, and (leaning on
Her tragic daughter's bosom) look'd upon
My heavy looks, drown'd in imploring tears
For her and that so wrong'd dear race of hers,
At which even Peace express'd a kind of spleen.
And, as a careful mother I have seen
Chide her loved child, snatch'd with some fear from
    danger:
So Peace chid me; and first shed tears of anger.

THE TEARS OF PEACE.

Peace. Thou wretched man, whom I discover,
  born
To want and sorrow, and the vulgar's scorn;
Why haunt'st thou freely these unhaunted places
Empty of pleasures? empty of all graces,
Fashions and riches; by the best pursued
With broken sleep, toil, love, zeal, servitude,
With fear and trembling, with whole lives and
  souls?
While thou break'st sleeps, digg'st under earth, like
  moles,
To live, to seek me out, whom all men fly;
And think'st to find light in obscurity,
Eternity in this deep vale of death;
Look'st ever upwards, and livest still beneath;
Fill'st all thy actions with strife what to think,
Thy brain with air, and scatter'st it in ink,
Of which thou makest weeds for thy soul to wear,
As out of fashion, as the body's are.
 Interlo. I grant their strangeness, and their too
  ill grace,
And too much wretchedness, to bear the face
Or any likeness of my soul in them:
Whose instruments I rue with many a stream
Of secret tears for their extreme defects,
In uttering her true forms; but their respects

Need not be lessen'd for their being strange
Or not so vulgar as the rest that range
With headlong raptures, through the multitude;
Of whom they get grace for their being rude.
Nought is so shunn'd by virtue, thrown from truth,
As that which draws the vulgar dames and youth.
   Pe. Truth must confess it; for where lives there
     one,
That Truth or Virtue, for themselves alone,
Or seeks or not contemns? All, all pursue
Wealth, Glory, Greatness, Pleasure, Fashions new.
Who studies, studies these; who studies not
And sees that study, lays the vulgar plot
That all the learning he gets living by
Men but for form or humour dignify
(As himself studies but for form and show,
And never makes his special end, to know)
And that an idle, airy man of news,
A standing face, a property to use
In all things vile, makes bookworms, creep to him;
How scorns he books and bookworms! O how
     dim
Burns a true soul's light in his bastard eyes!
And as a forest overgrown breeds flies,
Toads, adders, savages, that all men shun;
When on the south-side, in a fresh May sun,
In varied herds, the beasts lie out and sleep,
The busy gnats in swarms a buzzing keep,
And gild their empty bodies (lift aloft)
In beams, that though they see all, difference
     nought:
So in men's merely outward and false peace,

Instead of polish'd men, and true increase,
She brings forth men with vices overgrown:
Women, so light, and like, few know their own;
For mild and human tongues, tongues fork'd that
        sting:
And all these (while they may) take sun, and spring,
To help them sleep, and flourish; on whose beams
And branches, up they climb, in such extremes
Of proud confusion, from just laws so far,
That in their peace, the long robe sweeps like war.

  In. That robe serves great men: why are great
        so rude?

  Pe. Since great and mean are all but multitude.
For regular learning, that should difference set
'Twixt all men's worths, and make the mean or
        great,
As that is mean or great, or chief stroke strike,
Serves the plebeian and the lord alike.
Their objects show their learnings are all one;
Their lives, their objects, learning loved by none.

  In. You mean, for most part; nor would it dis-
        please
That most part if they heard: since they profess
Contempt of learning, nor esteem it fit
Noblesse should study, see, or countenance it.

  Pe. Can men in blood be noble, not in soul?
Reason abhors it; since what doth control
The rudeness of the blood and makes it noble,
Or hath chief means, high birthright to redouble
In making manners soft, and manlike mild,
Not suffering humanes to run proud or wild,
In soul and learning; (or in love, or act)

In blood where both fail, then lies noblesse
    wrack'd.
  In. It cannot be denied; but could you prove
As well that th' act of learning, or the love—
Love being the act in will—should difference set
'Twixt all men's worths, and make the mean or
    great
As learning is, or great or mean in them,
Then clear her right stood to man's diadem.
  Pe. To prove that learning—the soul's actual
    frame,
Without which 'tis a blank, a smoke-hid flame—
Should sit great arbitress of all things done,
And in your souls, like gnomons in the sun,
Give rules to all the circles of your lives;—
I prove it by the regiment God gives
To man, of all things; to the soul of man,
To learning, of the soul. If then it can
Rule, live; of all things best is it not best?
O who, what God makes greatest dares make least?
But to use their terms: Life is root and crest
To all man's coat of noblesse; his soul is
Field to that coat; and learning differences
All his degrees in honour, being the coat.
And as a statuary, having got
An alabaster big enough to cut
A human image in, till he hath put
His tools and art to it—hewn, form'd, **left none**
Of the redundant matter in the stone—
It bears the image of a man no more
Than of a wolf, a camel, or a boar:
So when the soul is to the body given—

Being substance of God's image sent from heaven—
It is not his true image till it take
Into the substance those fit forms that make
His perfect image; which are then impress'd
By learning and impulsion, that invest
Man with God's form in living holiness,
By cutting from his body the excess
Of humours, perturbations, and affects,
Which Nature, without Art, no more ejects
Than without tools a naked artisan
Can in rude stone cut th' image of a man.

    In. How then do ignorants, who, oft we try,
Rule perturbations, live more humanly
Than men held learn'd?

    Pe. Who are not learn'd indeed
More than a house framed loose, that still doth need
The haling up and joining, is a house.
Nor can you call men mere religious,
That have goodwills to knowledge, ignorant:
For virtuous knowledge hath two ways to plant—
By power infused, and acquisition:
The first of which those good men graft upon,
For good life is the effect of learning's act,
Which th' action of the mind did first compact,
By infused love to Learning 'gainst all ill
Conquest's first step is, to all good, the will.

    In. If learning then in love or act must be
Means to good life and true humanity,
Where are our scarecrows now, or men of rags,
Of titles merely, places, fortunes, brags,
That want and scorn both? those inverted men,
Those dungeons, whose souls no more contain

The actual light of Reason than dark beasts?
Those clouds, driven still 'twixt God's beam and
      their breasts?
Those giants, throwing golden hills 'gainst heaven,
To no one spice of one humanity given?
   Pe. Of men there are three sorts that most foes
      be
To Learning and her love, themselves and me.
Active, Passive, and Intellective men,
Whose self-loves learning and her love disdain.
Your Active men consume their whole life's fire
In thirst of State-height, higher still and higher,
Like seeled pigeons mounting to make sport
To lower lookers-on, in seeing how short
They come of that they seek, and with what trouble
Lamely, and far from Nature, they redouble
Their pains in flying more than humbler wits,
To reach death more direct. For death that sits
Upon the fist of Fate, past highest air,
Since she commands all lives within that sphere,
The higher men advance, the nearer finds
Her sealed quarries; when, in bitterest winds,
Lightnings and thunders, and in sharpest hails
Fate casts her off at States; when lower sails
Slide calmly to their ends. Your Passive men—
So call'd of only passing time in vain—
Pass it in no good exercise, but are
In meats and cups laborious, and take care
To lose without all care their soul-spent time.
And since they have no means nor spirits to climb,
Like fowls of prey, in any high affair,
See how like kites they bangle in the air

To stoop at scraps and garbage, in respect
Of that which men of true peace should select,
And how they trot out in their lives the ring
With idly iterating oft one thing—
A new-fought combat, an affair at sea,
A marriage, or a progress, or a plea.
No news but fits them as if made for them,
Though it be forged, but of a woman's dream;
And stuff with such stolen ends their manless
        breasts—
Sticks, rags, and mud—they seem mere puttocks'
        nests:
Curious in all men's actions but their own,
All men and all things censure, though know none.
Your Intellective men, they study hard
Not to get knowledge but for mere reward;
And therefore that true knowledge that should be
Their studies' end, and is in nature free,
Will not be made their broker: having power
With her sole self to bring both bride and dower.
They have some shadows of her, as of me
Adulterate outward peace, but never see
Her true and heavenly face. Yet those shades
        serve,
Like errant-knights that by enchantments swerve
From their true lady's being, and embrace
An ugly witch with her fantastic face,
To make them think Truth's substance in their
        arms;
Which that they have not, but her shadow's charms,
See if my proofs be like their arguments,
That leave Opinion still her free dissents.

They have not me with them; that all men know
The highest fruit that doth of knowledge grow;
The bound of all true forms, and only act;
If they be true they rest, nor can be rack'd
Out of their posture by Time's utmost strength,
But last the more of force the more of length;
For they become one substance with the soul,
Which Time with all his adjuncts shall control.
But since men wilful may perchance
In part of Error's twofold ignorance,
Ill disposition, their skills look as high,
And rest in that divine security,
See if their lives make proof of such a peace;
For learning's truth makes all life's vain war cease;
It making peace with God, and joins to God;
Whose information drives her period
Through all the body's passive instruments,
And by reflection gives them soul-contents.
Besides, from perfect Learning you can never
Wisdom with her fair reign of passions sever.
For Wisdom is nought else than Learning fined,
And with the understanding power combined;
That is, a habit of both habits standing,
The blood's vain humours ever countermanding.
But if these show more humour than th' unlearn'd—
If in them more vain passion be discern'd—
More mad ambition, more lust, more deceit,
More show of gold than gold, than dross less
        weight,
If flattery, avarice have their souls so given,
Headlong, and with such devilish furies driven,
That fools may laugh at their imprudency

And villains blush at their dishonesty;
Where is true Learning proved to separate these,
And seat all forms in her soul's height in peace?
Raging Euripus, that in all their pride
Drives ships 'gainst roughest winds with his fierce
     tide,
And ebbs and flows seven times in every day,
Toils not on Earth with more irregular sway,
Nor is more turbulent and mad than they.
And shine like gold-worms, whom you hardly find
By their own light, not seen, but heard, like wind.
But this is Learning; to have skill to throw
Reins on your body's powers that nothing know,
And fill the soul's powers so with act and art
That she can curb the body's angry part;
All perturbations; all affects that stray
From their one object, which is to obey
Her sovereign empire; as herself should force
Their functions only to serve her discourse;
And that, to beat the straight path of one end,
Which is to make her substance still contend
To be God's image; in informing it
With knowledge: holy thoughts, and all forms fit
For that eternity ye seek in way
Of his sole imitation; and to sway
Your life's love so that he may still be centre
To all your pleasures; and you here may enter
The next life's peace; in governing so well
Your sensual parts that you as free may dwell,
Of vulgar raptures here as when calm death
Dissolves that learned empire with your breath.
To teach and live thus is the onely use

And end of Learning. Skill that doth produce
But terms, and tongues, and parroting of art
Without that power to rule the errant part,
Is that which some call learned ignorance;
A serious trifle, error in a trance.
And let a scholar all Earth's volumes carry,
He will be but a walking dictionary,
A mere articulate clock that doth but speak
By others' arts; when wheels wear, or springs
     break,
Or any fault is in him, he can mend
No more than clocks; but at set hours must spend
His mouth as clocks do: if too fast speech go,
He cannot stay it, nor haste if too slow.
So that, as travellers seek their peace through
     storms,
In passing many seas for many forms
Of foreign government, endure the pain
Of many faces seeing, and the gain
That strangers make of their strange-loving hu-
     mours,
Learn tongues; keep note-books; all to feed the
     tumours
Of vain discourse at home, or serve the course
Of state employment, never having force
T' employ themselves; but idle compliments
Must pay their pains, costs, slaveries, all their rents;
And though they many men know, get few friends.
So covetous readers, setting many ends
To their much skill to talk; studiers of phrase;
Shifters in art; to flutter in the blaze
Of ignorant countenance; to obtain degrees

And lie in Learning's bottom, like the lees
To be accounted deep by shallow men;
And carve all language in one glorious pen;
May have much fame for learning, but th' effect
Proper to perfect Learning—to direct
Reason in such an art as that it can
Turn blood to soul, and make both one calm man;
So making peace with God, doth differ far
From clerks that go with God and man to war.
   In. But may this peace and man's true empire
     then
By Learning be obtain'd, and taught to men?
   Pe. Let all men judge; who is it can deny
That the rich crown of old Humanity
Is still your birthright? and was ne'er let down
From heaven for rule of beasts' lives, but your
     own?
You learn the depth of arts, and, curious, dare
By them, in nature's counterfeits, compare
Almost with God; to make perpetually
Motion like heaven's; to hang sad rivers by
The air, in air; and earth 'twixt earth and heaven
By his own poise. And are these virtues given
To powerful art, and virtue's self denied?
This proves the other vain and falsified.
Wealth, honour, and the rule of realms doth fall
In less than reason's compass; yet what all
Those things are given for (which is living well)
Wants discipline and reason to compel.
O foolish men! how many ways ye vex
Your lives with pleasing them, and still **perplex**
Your liberties with licence; every way

Casting your eyes and faculties astray
From their sole object.   If some few bring forth
In nature freely something of some worth,
Much rude and worthless humour runs betwixt,
Like fruit in deserts with vile matter mixt.
Nor since they flatter flesh so, they are bold
As a most noble spectacle to behold
Their own lives; and like sacred light to bear
Their reason inward; for the soul in fear
Of every sort of vice she there contains,
Flies out, and wanders about other men's,
Feeding and fatting her infirmities.
And as in ancient cities, 'twas the guise
To have some ports of sad and hapless vent,
Through which all executed men they sent,
All filth, all offal, cast from what purged sin,
Nought chaste or sacred there going out or in;
So through men's refuse ears will nothing pierce
That's good or elegant; but the sword, the hearse,
And all that doth abhor from man's pure use,
Is each man's only siren, only muse.
And thus for one God, one fit good, they prize
These idle, foolish, vile varieties.

In. Wretched estate of men by fortune blest,
That being ever idle never rest;
That have goods ere they earn them, and for that
Want art to use them.   To be wonder'd at
Is Justice; for proportion, ornament,
None of the graces is so excellent.
Vile things adorn her: methought once I saw
How by the sea's shore she sat giving law
Even to the streams, and fish most loose and wild,

And was, to my thoughts, wondrous sweet and
    mild;
Yet fire blew from her that dissolved rocks;
Her looks to pearl turn'd pebble; and her locks
The rough and sandy banks to burnish'd gold;
Her white left hand did golden bridles hold,
And with her right she wealthy gifts did give,
Which with their left hands men did still receive;
Upon a world in her chaste lap did lie
A little ivory book that show'd mine eye
But one page only—that one verse contain'd
Where all arts were contracted and explain'd—
All policies of princes, all their forces,
Rules for their fears, cares, dangers, pleasures,
    purses,
All the fair progress of their happiness here
Justice converted and composed there.
All which I thought on when I had express'd,
Why great men of the great states they possess'd
Enjoy'd so little; and I now must note
The large strain of a verse I long since wrote;
Which methought much joy to men poor presented,
" God hath made none (that all might be) con-
    tented."

  Pe. It might for the capacity it bears,
Be that concealed and expressive verse
That Justice in her ivory manual writ,
Since all lines to man's peace are drawn in it.
For great men, though such ample stuff they have
To shape contentment, yet since like a wave
It flits and takes all forms, retaining none
Not fitted to their pattern which is one;

They may content themselves: God hath not given
To men mere earthly the true joys of heaven.
And so their wild ambitions either stay,
Or turn their headstrong course the better way,
For poor men, their cares may be richly eased,
Since rich with all they have live as displeased.

   In. You teach me to be plain. But what's the
       cause
That great and rich, whose stars win such applause
With such enforced and vile varieties;
Spend time, nor give their lives glad sacrifice;
But when they eat and drink, with tales, jests,
       sounds
As if like frantic men that feel no wounds,
They would expire in laughters? and so err
From their right way; that like a traveller,
Weariest when nearest to his journey's end,
Time best spent ever with most pain they spend?

   Pe. The cause is want of learning, which, being
      right,
Makes idleness a pain, and pain delight.
It makes men know that they, of all things born
Beneath the silver moon and golden morn,
Being only forms of God, should only fix
One form of life to those forms; and not mix
With beasts in forms of their lives. It doth teach
To give the soul her empire, and so reach
To rule of all the body's mutinous realm,
In which, once seated, she then takes the helm
And governs freely, steering to one port.
Then like a man in health the whole consort
Of his tuned body sings, which otherwise

Is like one full of wayward maladies,
Still out of tune; and like to spirits raised
Without a circle never is appaised.
And then they have no strength but weakens them,
No greatness but doth crush them into stream,
No liberty but turns into their snare,
Their learnings then do light them but to err.
Their ornaments are burthens, their delights
Are mercenary servile parasites,
Betraying, laughing; fiends that raised in fears
At parting shake their roofs about their ears.
Th' imprison'd thirst the fortunes of the free;
The free, of rich; rich, of nobility;
Nobility, of kings; and kngs, gods' thrones—
Even to their lightning flames and thunder-stones.
O liberal learning, that well used gives use
To all things good, how bad is thy abuse!
When only thy divine reflection can,
That lights but to thy love, make good a man;
How can the regular body of thy light
Inform and deck him? the ills infinite,
That, like beheaded hydras in that fen
Of blood and flesh in lewd illiterate men,
Answer their amputations with supplies
That twist their heads, and ever double rise:
Herculean Learning conquers; and O see
How many and of what foul forms they be!
Unquiet, wicked thoughts, unnumber'd passions,
Poorness of counsels, hourly fluctuations,
In intercourse, of woes and false delights;
Impotent wills to goodness; appetites
That never will be bridled, satisfied,

Nor know how or with what to be supplied;
Fears and distractions mix'd with greediness;
Stupidities of those things ye possess;
Furies for what ye lose; wrongs done for nonce
For present, past and future things at once,
Cares vast and endless; miseries swoln with pride;
Virtues despised and vices glorified;
All these true learning calms and can subdue.
But who turns learning this way? All pursue
War with each other that exasperates these
For things without, whose ends are inward peace;
And yet those inward rebels they maintain.
And as your curious sort of Passive men
Thrust their heads through the roofs of rich and
   poor
Through all their lives and fortunes, and explore
Foreign and home-affairs, their princes' courts,
Their council and bedchambers for reports;
And, like freebooters, wander out to win
Matter to feed their mutinous rout within;
Which are the greedier still, and overshoot
Their true-sought inward peace for outward boot;
So learned men in controversies spend
Of tongues and terms, reading and labours penn'd,
Their whole lives' studies; glory, riches, place,
In full cry with the vulgar giving chase;
And never with their learning's true use strive
To bridle strifes within them, and to live
Like men of peace whom Art of peace begat:
But as their deeds are most adulterate,
And show them false sons to their peaceful mother
In those wars, so their arts are proved no other.

And let the best of them a search impose
Upon his art; for all the things she knows—
All being referr'd to all to her unknown—
They will obtain the same proportion
That doth a little brook that never ran
Through summer's sun, compared with th' ocean.
But could he oracles speak, and write to charm
A wild of savages, take nature's arm
And pluck into his search the circuit
Of earth and heaven, the sea's space, and the spirit
Of every star; the powers of herbs, and stones;
Yet touch not at his perturbations,
Nor give them rule and temper to obey
Imperial reason, in whose sovereign sway
Learning is wholly used and dignified,
To what end serves he? is his learning tried,
That comforting and that creating fire
That fashions men? or that which doth inspire
Cities with civil conflagrations,
Countries and kingdoms?   That art that atones
All opposition to good life, is all.
Live well, ye learn'd, and all men ye enthral.
    In. Alas! they are discouraged in their courses,
And, like surprised forts, beaten from their forces.
Bodies on rights of souls did never grow
With ruder rage, than barbarous torrents flow
Over their sacred pastures, bringing in
Weeds and all rapine; temples now begin
To suffer second deluge; sin-drown'd beasts
Making their altars crack; and the 'filed nests
Of vulturous fowls filling their holy places,
For wonted ornaments and religious graces.

Pe. The chief cause is, since they themselves be-
    tray,
Take their foes' baits for some particular sway
T' invert their universal; and this still
Is cause of all ills else, their living ill.

In. Alas! that men should strive for others' sway,
But first to rule themselves; and that being way
To all men's bliss, why is it trod by none?
And why are rules so dully look'd upon
That teach that lively rule?

Pe. O horrid thing!
'Tis custom pours into your common spring
Such poison of example in things vain
That reason nor religion can constrain
Men's sights of serious things; and th' only cause
That neither human nor celestial laws
Draw man more compass; is his own slack bent
T' intend no more his proper regiment,
Where, if your Active men, or men of action,
Their policy, avarice, ambition, faction,
Would turn to making strong their rule of passion,
To search and settle them in approbation
Of what they are and shall be, which may be
By reason in despight of policy,
And in one true course couch their whole affairs
To one true bliss worth all the spawn of theirs;
If half the idle speech men Passive spend
At sensual meetings, when they recommend
Their sanguine souls in laughters to their peace,
Were spent in counsels, how they might decrease
That frantic humour of ridiculous blood,
Which adds, they vainly think, to their lives' flood;

And so converted in true human mirth
To speech, what they shall be, dissolved from earth,
In bridling it in flesh, with all the scope
Of their own knowledge here, and future hope:
If, last of all, your Intellective men
Would mix the streams of every jarring pen
In one calm current, that like land-floods now
Make all zeal's bounded rivers overflow;
Firm Truth with question every hour pursue,
And yet will have no question, all is true.
Search in that troubled Ocean for a ford
That by itself runs, and must bear accord
In each man's self, by banishing falsehood there,
Wrath, lust, pride, earthy thoughts, before else-
        where.
(For as in one man is the world enclosed,
So to form one it should be all disposed:)
If all these would concur to this one end,
It would ask all their powers; and all would spend
Life with that real sweetness which they dream
Comes in with objects that are mere extreme;
And make them outward pleasures still apply,
Which never can come in but by that key;
Others' advancements, others' fames desiring,
Thirsting, exploring, praising, and admiring,
Like lewd adulterers that their own wives scorn,
And other men's with all their wealth adorn;
Why in all outraying, varied joys and courses,
That in these errant times tire all men's forces,
Is this so common wonder of our days,
That in poor fore-times such a few could raise
So many wealthy temples, and these none?

All were devout then; all devotions one,
And to one end converted; and when men
Give up themselves to God, all theirs goes then.
A few well-given are a worth a world of ill;
And worlds of power not worth one poor good-will.
And what's the cause that (being but one) Truth
      spreads
About the world so many thousand heads
Of false opinions, all self-loved as true?
Only affection to things more than due,
One error kiss'd begetteth infinite.
How can men find truth in ways opposite?
And with what force they must take opposite ways,
When all have opposite objects? Truth displays
One colour'd ensign, and the world pursues
Ten thousand colours: see—to judge, who use
Truth in their arts—what light their lives do give,
For wherefore do they study but to live?
See I Eternity's straight milk-white way,
And one in this life's crooked vanities stray;
And shall I think he knows Truth following error?
This, only this, is the infallible mirror
To show why ignorants with learn'd men vaunt,
And why your learn'd men are so ignorant.
Why every youth in one hour will be old
In every knowledge; and why age doth mould.
Then, as in rules of true philosophy
There must be ever due analogy
Betwixt the power that knows and that is known,
So surely join'd that they are ever one;
The understanding part transcending still
To that it understands; that to his skill;

All offering to the soul—the soul to God,
By which do all things make their period
In his high power, and make him All-in-All;
So to ascend the high heaven-reaching scale
Of man's true peace, and make his Art entire
By calming all his Errors in desire;
(Which must precede that higher happiness)
Proportion still must traverse her access
Betwixt his power and will, his sense and soul;
And evermore the exorbitance control
Of all forms, passing through the body's power,
Till in the soul they rest as in their tower.

In. But as Earth's gross and elemental fire
Cannot maintain itself, but doth require
Fresh matter still to give it heat and light;
And when it is enflamed mounts not upright,
But struggles in his lame impure ascent,
Now this way works, and then is that way bent,
Not able straight to aspire to his true sphere
Where burns the fire eternal and sincere;
So best souls here, with heartiest zeals inflamed
In their high flight for heaven, earth bruised and
    lamed,
Make many faint approaches, and are fain
With much unworthy matter to sustain
Their holiest fire; and with sick feathers, driven,
And broken pinions, flutter towards heaven.

Pe. The cause is that you never will bestow
Your best t' enclose your lives 'twixt God and you;
To count the world's Love, Fame, Joy, Honour,
    nothing;
But life, with all your love to it, betrothing

To his love, his recomfort, his reward;
Since no good thought calls to him but is heard.
Nor need you think this strange, since he is there
Present within you, ever everywhere
Where good thoughts are; for Good hath no estate
Without him, nor himself is without that.
If then this commerce stand 'twixt you entire,
Try if he either grant not each desire,
Or so conform it to his will in stay,
That you shall find him there in the delay,
As well as th' instant grant; and so prove right
How easy his dear yoke is, and how light
His equal burthen; whether this commerce
'Twixt God and man be so hard or perverse
In composition, as the rarity
Or no-where pattern of it doth imply?
Or if, in worthy contemplation,
It do not tempt beyond comparison
Of all things worldly? Sensuality,
Nothing so easy; all earth's company—
Like rhubarb, or the drugs of Thessaly—
Compared in taste with that sweet? O, try then
If that contraction by the God of men,
Of all the law and prophets, laid upon
The tempting lawyer, were a load that none
Had power to stand beneath? If God's dear love
Thy conscience do not at first sight approve
Dear above all things; and, so pass this shelf
To love withal thy neighbour as thyself.
Not love as much, but as thyself, in this,
To let it be as free as thine own is—
Without respect of profit or reward,

Deceit or flattery, politic regard,
Or anything but naked Charity.
    In. I call even God himself to testify—
For men I know but few—that far above
All to be here desired I rate his love.
Thanks to his still-kiss'd hand that so hath framed
My poor and abject life, and so inflamed
My soul with his sweet all-want-seasoning love ·
In studying to supply, though not remove,
My desert fortunes and unworthiness
With some wish'd grace from him, that might ex-
      press
His presence with me; and so dignify
My life to creep on earth; behold the sky;
And give it means enough for this low plight;
Though hitherto with no one hour's delight,
Hearty or worthy, but in him alone—
Who like a careful guide hath haled me on—
And, every minute sinking, made me swim
To this calm shore, hid with his Son in him.
And here, ay me! as trembling I look back,
I fall again, and in my haven wrack;
Still being persuaded by the shameless light
That these are dreams of my retired night,
That all my reading, writing, all my pains
Are serious trifles, and the idle veins
Of an unthrifty angel that deludes
My simple fancy, and by fate excludes
My birth-accursed life from the bliss of men;
And then my hands I wring, my bosom then
Beat and could break ope, fill th' enraged air,
And knock at heaven with sighs, invoke despair

At once, to free the tired earth of my load;
That these recoils—that reason doth explode,
Religion damns, and my arm'd soul defies—
Wrastles with angels, telling heaven it lies,
If it deny the truth his Spirit hath writ,
Graven in my soul and there eternized it—
Should beat me from that rest, and that is this,
That these prodigious securities
That all men snore-in—drowning in vile lives
The souls of men because the body thrives—
'Are witchcrafts damnable; that all learnings are
Foolish and false, that with those vile lives square;
That these sour wizards that so gravely scorn
Learning with good life, kind 'gainst kind suborn;
And are no more wise than their shades are men,
Which—as my finger can go to my pen—
I can demonstrate that our knowledges—
Which we must learn if ever we profess
Knowledge of God, or have one notion true—
Are those which first and most we should pursue;
That in their searches all men's active lives
Are so far short of their contemplatives,
As bodies are of souls, this life of next:
And so much doth the form and whole context
Of matter, serving one, exceed the other,
That Heaven our Father is, as Earth our Mother;
And therefore in resemblance to approve,
Who are the true-bred, father'd by his love—
As heaven itself doth only virtually
Mix with the earth, his course keeping high,
And substance undisparaged, though his beams
Are drown'd in many dunghills, and their steams

To us obscure him, yet he ever shines:
So though our souls' beams dig in bodies' mines
To find them rich discourses through their senses;
And meet with many middens of offences,
Whose vapours choke their organs—yet should they
Disperse them by degrees, because their sway,
In power, is absolute; and in that power shine
As firm as heaven, heaven nothing so divine.
All this I hold; and since that all truth else,
That all else know or can hold, stays and dwells
On these grounds' uses, and should all contend
(Knowing our birth here serves but for this end,
To make true means and ways to our second life),
To ply those studies, and hold every strife
To other ends—more than to amplify,
Adorn, and sweeten these, deservedly—
As balls cast in our race, and but grass-knit
From both sides of our path t' ensnare our wit;
And thus, because the gaudy vulgar light
Burns up my good thoughts, form'd in temperate
        night,
Rising to see the good moon oftentimes—
Like the poor virtues of these vicious times—
Labour as much to lose her light as when
She fills her waning horns; and how, like men
Raised to high places, exhalations fall
That would be thought stars; I'll retire from all
The hot glades of ambition, company,
That with their vainness make this vanity;
And cool to death in shadows of this vale,
To which end I will cast this serpent's scale—
This load of life in life, this fleshy stone—

This bond and bundle of corruption—
This breathing sepulchre—this sponge of grief—
This smiling enemy—this household thief—
This glass of air, broken with less than breath—
This slave bound face to face to death till death;
And consecrate my life to you and yours.
In which objection, if that Power of Powers
That hath relieved me thus far, with a hand
Direct and most immediate, still will stand
Betwixt me and the rapines of the Earth;
And give my poor pains but such gracious birth
As may sustain me in my desert age
With some power to my will, I still will wage
War with that false peace that exileth you;
And in my pray'd-for freedom ever vow,
Tears in these shades for your tears, till mine eyes
Pour out my soul in better sacrifice.
   Peace. Nor doubt, good friend, but God, to whom
      I see
Your friendless life converted, still will be
A rich supply for friends; and still be you
Sure convertite to him.   This, this way row
All to their country.   Think how he hath show'd
You ways and byways; what to be pursued
And what avoided.   Still in his hands be,
If you desire to live or safe or free.
No longer days take; Nature doth exact
This resolution of thee and this fact,
The Foe hails on thy head, and in thy face,
Insults and trenches; leaves thee no world's grace;
The walls in which thou art besieged, shake.
Have done; resist no more; but if you take

Firm notice of our speech, and what you see,
And will add pains to write all, let it be
Divulged too. Perhaps, of all, some one
May find some good. But might it touch upon
Your gracious Prince's liking, he might do
Good to himself and all his kingdoms too;
So virtuous a great example is:
And that hath thank'd as small a thing as this,
Here being stuff and form for all true peace
And so of all men's perfect happiness,
To which if he shall lend his princely ear,
And give commandment, from yourself to hear
My state; tell him you know me, and that I,
That am the crown of principality
(Though thus cast off by princes) ever vow
Attendance at his foot, till I may grow
Up to his bosom; which, being dew'd in time
With these my tears, may to my comforts climb;
Which when all pleasures into palsies turn,
And sunlike pomp in his own clouds shall mourn,
Will be acceptive. Mean-space I will pray
That he may turn some toward thought this way,
While the round whirlwinds of the Earth's de-
        lights
Dust betwixt him and me, and blind the sights
Of all men ravish'd with them; whose increase
You well may tell him, fashions not true peace.
The peace that they inform learns but to squat,
While the sly legal foe that levels at
War through those false lights, suddenly runs by
Betwixt you and your strength; and while you lie,
Couching your ears, and flatting every limb,

So close to earth that you would seem to him
The earth itself; yet he knows who you are,
And in that vantage pours on ready war.

CONCLUSIO.

THUS by the way to human loves interring
These marginal and secret tears referring
To my disposure, having all this hour
Of our unworldly conference given power
To her late fainting issue to arise,
She raised herself and them, the progenies
Of that so civil desert rising all;
Who fell with her; and to the funeral—
She bearing still the coffin—all went on.
And now gives Time her state's description.
Before her flew Affliction, girt in storms,
Gash'd all with gushing wounds, and all the forms
Of bane and misery frowning in her face;
Whom Tyranny and Injustice had in chase;
Grim Persecution, Poverty, and Shame;
Detraction, Envy, foul Mishap and lame;
Scruple of Conscience; Fear, Deceit, Despair;
Slander and Clamour, that rent all the air;
Hate, War, and Massacre; uncrowned Toil;
And Sickness, t' all the rest the base and foil,
Crept after; and his deadly weight, trod down
Wealth, Beauty, and the glory of a Crown.
These usher'd her far off; as figures given
To show these Crosses borne, make peace with
       heaven.
But now, made free from them, next her before;

Peaceful and young, Herculean Silence bore
His craggy club; which up aloft, he hild;
With which, and his fore-finger's charm he still'd
All sounds in air; and left so free mine ears,
That I might hear the music of the spheres,
And all the angels singing out of heaven;
Whose tunes were solemn, as to passion given;
For now, that Justice was the happiness there
For all the wrongs to Right inflicted here,
Such was the passion that Peace now put on;
And on all went; when suddenly was gone
All light of heaven before us; from a wood,
Whose light foreseen, now lost, amazed we stood,
The sun still gracing us; when now, the air
Inflamed with meteors, we discover'd fair,
The skipping goat; the horse's flaming mane;
Bearded and trained comets; stars in wane;
The burning sword, the firebrand-flying snake;
The lance; the torch; the licking fire; the drake;
And all else meteors that did ill abode;
The thunder chid; the lightning leap'd abroad;
And yet when Peace came in all heaven was clear,
And then did all the horrid wood appear,
Where mortal dangers more than leaves did grow;
In which we could not one free step bestow,
For treading on some murther'd passenger
Who thither was, by witchcraft, forced to err:
Whose face the bird hid that loves humans best;
That hath the bugle eyes and rosy breast,
And is the yellow Autumn's nightingale.
Peace made us enter here secure of all;
Where, in a cave that through a rock did eat,

The monster Murther held his impious seat;
A heap of panting harts supported him,
On which he sat gnawing a reeking limb
Of some man newly murther'd. As he ate,
His grave-digg'd brows, like stormy eaves did
    sweat;
Which, like incensed fens, with mists did smoke;
His hide was rugged as an aged oak
With heathy leprosies; that still he fed
With hot, raw limbs, of men late murthered.
His face was like a meteor, flashing blood;
His head all bristled, like a thorny wood;
His neck cast wrinkles, like a sea enraged;
And in his vast arms was the world engaged
Bathing his hands in every cruel deed:
Whose palms were hell-deep lakes of boiling lead;
His thighs were mines of poison, torment, grief;
In which digg'd fraud, and treachery for relief;
Religion's botcher, policy; and pride,
Oppression, slavery, flattery glorified,
Atheism, and tyranny, and gain unjust,
Frantic ambition, envy, shag-hair'd lust,
Both sorts of ignorance, and knowledge swell'd;
And over these, the old wolf avarice held
A golden scourge that dropt with blood and vapour,
With which he whipped them to their endless la-
    bour.
From under heaps cast from his fruitful thighs—
As ground, to all their damn'd impieties—
The mournful goddess drew dead Human Love;
Nor could they let her entry, though they strove
And furnaced on her all their venomous breath;

For though all outrage breaks the peace of death,
She coffin'd him; and forth to funeral
All help'd to bear him. But to sound it all,
My trumpet fails, and all my forces shrink.
Who can enact to life, what kills to think?
Nor can the soul's beams beat through blood and
  flesh,
Forms of such woe and height as now, afresh
Flow'd from these objects; to see Poesy
Prepared to do the special obsequy
And sing the Funeral Oration.
How it did show, to see her tread upon
The breast of Death, and on a Fury lean;
How to her fist, as rites of service then,
A cast of ravens flew; on her shoulders, how
The fowls that to the Muses' queen we vow—
The owl and heronshaw—sat; how, for her hair,
A hapless comet hurl'd about the air
Her curled beams, whence sparks, like falling stars,
Vanish'd about her, and with winds adverse
Were still blown back; to which the phœnix flew,
And, burning on her head, would not renew.
How her divine Oration did move
For th' unredeemed loss of Human Love;
Object man's future state to reason's eye;
The soul's infusion, immortality;
And prove her forms firm, that are here impress'd,
How her admired strains wrought on every
  breast;—
And made the woods cast their immanity
Up to the air; that did to cities fly
In fuel for them; and, in clouds of smoke,

Ever hang over them; cannot be spoke;
Nor how to Human Love, to Earth now given,
A lightning stoop'd and ravish'd him to heaven,
And with him Peace with all her heavenly seed:
Whose outward Rapture made me inward bleed;
Nor can I therefore my intention keep,
Since Tears want words and words want tears to
      weep.

COROLLARIUM AD PRINCIPEM.

THUS shook I this abortive from my brain,
Which, with it, lay in this unworthy pain.
Yet since your Homer had his worthy hand
In venturing this delay of your command
To end his Iliads; deign, great Prince of men,
To hold before it your great shield; and then
It may do service worthy this delay,
To your more worthy pleasure; and I may
Re-gather the spersed fragments of my spirits,
And march with Homer through his deathless
      merits
To your undying graces. Nor did he
Vanish with this slight vision, but brought me
Home to my cabin, and did all the way
Assure me of your Grace's constant stay
To his soul's being, wholly naturalized
And made your Highness' subject; which he prized
Past all his honours held in other lands;
And that, because a Prince's main state stands
In his own knowledge, and his power within,
These works that had chief virtue to begin

Those informations you would hold most dear,
Since false joys have their seasons to appear
Just as they are; but these delights were ever
Perfect and needful, and would irk you never.
    I praying for this happy work of heaven
In your sweet disposition, the calm even
Took me to rest; and he with wings of fire,
To soft Air's supreme region did aspire.

By the ever most humbly and truly dedicated to
your most Princely graces,

GEO. CHAPMAN.

PUBLICATIONS AND PAPERS

OF

The Shakespeare Society of New York

••••••••••••••••••••••••••••••••••••

THE SHAKESPEARE PRESS of New York City

Printers to the New York Shakespeare Society

Westfield, Union County, New Jersey